T E S T I M O N Y

Young African-Americans
on Self-Discovery and
Black Identity

TESTIMONY

Edited by
Natasha Tarpley

Beacon Press
Boston

Beacon Press
25 Beacon Street
Boston, Massachusetts 02108-2892

Beacon Press books
are published under the auspices of
the Unitarian Universalist Association of Congregations.

99 98 97 96 95   8 7 6 5 4 3 2 1

Text design by John Kane
Typesetting by Wilsted & Taylor

LIBRARY OF CONGRESS CATALOGING-IN-PUBLICATION DATA

Testimony: Young African-Americans on self-discovery and Black
  identity / edited by Natasha Tarpley.
      p.   cm.
    ISBN 0-8070-0928-8. — ISBN 0-8070-0929-6 (pbk.)
      1. Afro-American families. 2. Afro-American students. 3. Afro-
American youth. 4. Afro-Americans—Social conditions—1975–
5. Afro-Americans—Poetry. I. Tarpley, Natasha.
  E185.86.T38 1994
  305.896'073—dc20
                                                    94-14362
                                                       CIP

For
Marlene L. Tarpley,
mom   life-friend
sustenance
For
my sisters, Nicole and Elizabeth Tarpley
my "Big" brother, Omar Tarpley
For
Anna Mae Dudley (Nana) and Gladys Tarpley (Granny)
For
Herman Tarpley, Jr., daddy
(ever near)

You are
the space where there is no space a warm shelter
of love, hope, laughter, and acceptance in the midst of trouble;
the place where these dreams are born and grow strong,
where I lay my heart down, rest my feet and know that I am
home.
Love Always . . .

*The linking of those gone, ourselves here, those coming;
our continuation, our flowing not along any meretricious
channel but along our livng way, the way: it is that
remembrance that calls us. The eyes of seers should range
far into purposes. The ears of hearers should listen far
toward origins. The utterers' voice should make
knowledge of the way, of heard sounds and visions seen,
the voice of the utterers should make this knowledge
inevitable, impossible to lose.*

—Ayi Kwei Armah,
Two Thousand Seasons

Contents

Acknowledgments

MANY THANKS TO DEB CHASMAN, MY EDITOR, FOR walking this road with me.

Special thanks to Dr. Henry Louis Gates, Jr., and LuAnn Walther for helping me to begin the beginning; to Dr. Molefi Asante, Rita Dove, Sonia Sanchez, and all of the many other professors and writers who gave me encouragement and supported this project by spreading the word to their students and friends; to Ruth Forman, my "West Coast Connection"; and to all of the contributors: This wouldn't have been possible without you.

For being there, love to my aunts, Gwendolyn Hilary and Marilyn Lyle, and Aaron Reed.

This book was made possible in part by grants from Harvard-Radcliffe Education 4 Action, Harvard University Office for the Arts, Radcliffe Presidential Discretionary Fund, and Harvard University Department of Afro-American Studies.

A Note to the Reader

GWENDOLYN BROOKS, WHEN ASKED WHY SHE spelled the word Black with a capital "B," answered, "I capitalize my name." For some of us, capitalizing the word Black is indeed a way to pronounce, announce, and claim one's Blackness, in all of its various meanings and manifestations. For others of us, the word black, spelled with a lower case "b," is treated like any other word within the body of the work. However, this does not necessarily speak to the writer's political views on or identification with blackness. Suffice it to say, the use of a capital "B" or a lower case "b" in the spelling of the word Black can be, and often is, an indicator or signifying mark of the author's views on any number of political and cultural issues within the wide and expansive context of Blackness. In recognition of our diverse backgrounds, experiences, and the variety of political/cultural/aesthetic views which impact our work, the variations in spelling have been preserved in the essays that follow.

Natasha Tarpley

Introduction

On Giving Testimony,
or the Processes of Becoming

IN THE SPRING OF MY SOPHOMORE YEAR AT HARVARD University, I was almost arrested in my own dormitory for attempting to take my computer to my nearby home. My younger brother had come in with me to help me carry it, and on our way out the door, the security guard stopped us. He told us not to move, that we weren't going anywhere. My brother was able to motion for my mother and younger sister, who were waiting in the car, to come in. My mother tried to talk to the guard, but to no avail. He called for back-up. At least four squad cars arrived on the scene immediately. At that point, it didn't matter that we were a family, that I was a Harvard student, that my mother— herself a Harvard graduate—was a parent dressed in a sophisticated business suit, that my sister was only in seventh grade or that my brother was a sophomore in high school. None of this made a difference. All that mattered was that we were Black.

I relay this incident because I learned from it a painful lesson, one that many Black students on campuses across the country are also learning: that my education, my family, my person, my life even, do not carry the same weight or have the same value as other students', white students', on this campus. That day, I lost part of myself; the part that had held some faint hope—albeit naive—that the words of acceptance and belonging, spoken behind toothy grins during freshmen orientation or student group meetings, were true; that I, as a student of this "grand and prestigious" institution, could move about as I chose and could claim the same rights and privileges as seemed to be bestowed upon others of my classmates.

At some point, the guard began stopping people who were walking in and out of the lobby, asking them if they could identify me, to prove that I actually lived in the building. I thought about those Black folks who had come before me, whose lives had had to be accounted for by others; whose destinies had been placed in the hands of strangers. It infuriated me that all of our protests and reasoning, and all of our identification "papers" laid out on the table, did not hold the same weight as the slight nod of a white person's head; an X marked by a white hand; a word spoken from a white mouth. That day, tears flowed where words had escaped me. But in many ways, this marked not only the breakdown of my old vocabulary, but also signified the beginning of new words and sounds, to describe and encompass both where I had been and the new direction in which I was heading.

Certainly the incident I have recounted is one that is not unfamiliar to many of us—Black students, parents, and families alike. This type of thing occurs daily on college campuses, neighborhood and city streets. James Baldwin writes, "while the tale of how we suffer and how we are delighted, and how we may triumph is never new, it must always be heard." Thus, while the stories we tell are important, it is the act of telling and of hearing them told that sets us free. And it is at this most vulnerable moment, at the meeting place of pain, joy, desire, and renewed hope, where we gather up the pieces of the stories that have been waiting to be told, and where our voices—although changing—are clear and strong enough for the telling, that this book begins. Indeed this book is about the processes that we, young Black students and writers, go through in order to reach the point where we are able to open ourselves and release that which we held inside. And further, how this process of "coming into self" is connected to that of learning about, accepting, and loving one's Blackness.

Hence the title, *Testimony*, from the verb to testify: to bear witness, to bring forth, to claim and proclaim oneself as an intrinsic part of the world. The act of testifying or giving testimony has deep roots in African American history, reaching back to slavery (and before), to the places our ancestors created—behind somebody's wood cabin doubling as a makeshift church or meetinghouse, or in a nearby clearing—where they opened themselves up to one another, showed their scars, spoke of their day-to-day life, their hopes and dreams, prayed to their God, and tried to remember everything they had lost.

Testifying, although it has strong religious connotations, has also performed the important secular function of providing a means by which the slave could make herself visible, in a society which had rendered her invisible; by which he could explore the sound of his own voice when he had been rendered silent. Henry Louis Gates writes in his introduction to *Bearing Witness*, an anthology of Black autobiography: "If the individual black self could not exist before the law, it could and would be forged in language, as a testimony at once to the supposed integrity of the black self and against the social and political evils that delimited individual and group equality for all African Americans" (p. 4).

In this sense, testifying is not only a way to commune with one's Creator, but is also a way to define and redefine one's humanity; to ground oneself in community; to revel in the touch of hands and bodies familiar with the testifier's pain or joy, in voices that know how to reach her when she is far away and bring her back, making a bridge from this world to the next. And it is these simple gestures— touching and being touched, raising up one's voice—that helped to fill in the frame of the body, that gave it weight enough to anchor itself to the earth, instead of floating, a thin and airy shadow, above it.

Black people still live in a society in which we are often rendered invisible. The sun rises and sets to the deep gurgle, like a moan caught somewhere between the head and the feet, of a river of Black blood filling and overflowing. Black bodies, Black lives still hold little value, even to ourselves. This is evidenced by such national outrages as the Rodney King incident, as well as by those daily offenses to our personhood which somehow don't make national or local headlines: the subtle and blatant humiliation and discrimination that Black people experience on the job, at school, in their neighborhoods; Black children dying and killing one another, crimes punished only by the taking of another Black life.

In the classroom, Black students often find themselves fighting battles similar to those being waged against Black people on the streets. The same forces that work to silence and render invisible Black people outside of the classroom are also present in our educational systems. In interviews that I conducted with Black students on various college and university campuses, many students, particularly those at predominantly white institutions, spoke of discrepancies in grading and in the way they were treated. They talked as well about the pressure they felt to "speak for the race," as they were often one of a few or the only Black student in a class, their individual opinions and ideas pushed aside. But regardless of who they were supposedly speaking for, many Black students felt that their contributions were not valued or sufficiently recognized by the professor or other students.

James Baldwin writes that "to become educated . . . is to become inaccessibly independent, it is to acquire a dangerous way of assessing danger, and it is to hold in one's hands a means of changing reality." For many Black students, including the writers whose work appears in this anthology, the process of defining and redefining ourselves begins and ends with education. As a generation, we are among the first to taste the fruits of our parents' and grandparents' labors during the antisegregation and Civil Rights movements of the 1950s and 1960s, and are, as a result, able to make choices in terms of education and careers unimaginable forty or thirty, even twenty, years ago.

Although education takes many forms, oftentimes this journey to self begins with the choice to go to college. Armed with our parents' hopes, our own desires and interests, and perhaps, to some extent, expectations of achieving the mythical "American dream," we step foot on our respective campuses, reveling in our newfound independence and the thrill of possibility spread out before us. And it is here that the real work begins; where we start to question ourselves, explore various options, and make choices about our identities.

One's arsenal of knowledge and one's education strongly influence how one sees oneself in relation to the rest of the world. We live our lives according to a cultural narrative, a story woven from the tales and lessons from the past which we perpetuate. For the most part, this narrative is Eurocentric, meaning that it has at its core a celebration and promulgation of European, or more accurately, white American value systems, achievements, and history. We understand that this framework could not and would not exist without Black people, for in addition to having helped create it, Black people also function as the "other" to which this "system" or narrative is diabolically opposed.

Thus, I envision the process of "becoming educated" much like that of climbing a staircase with missing steps. As Black students, we enter (and in many cases leave) institutions of "higher" learning with incomplete foundations. This is by no means meant to imply that Black students are not—at least—as smart, as capable, or as productive as students of other races. But it is meant to point out that most of us, for most of our lives, have been subject to educational systems—both public and private—which negate Blackness and Black contributions or achievements. Although American educational systems are becoming increasingly "multicultural," this is still problematic. Multiculturalism, insofar as I have seen, has not addressed the crucial issues of inclusion which it claims or, to be fair, sets out to achieve. Its rhetoric has not been accounted for in our lived and practical experiences.

In our climb up this incomplete staircase, we learn to skip over and avoid the wide and empty spaces of unknown Blackness. It is this rhetoric that we have bought into, which we use as a rope to pull us over these chasms, to get us from one step to the next. And if we have not bought the rhetoric, we have at least made the assumption that we have a right to express ourselves as individuals without being intruded upon, and to be treated with a certain degree of humanity. However, many of us reach a point where our expectations do not match our experience. The space between stairs becomes too wide to cross over, our rope will not reach, we lose our footing, or perhaps the entire foundation caves in.

But it is at this moment of destruction that we can begin to pick up the pieces and, with our own hands, put them in a new order, construct or reconstruct a new foundation. We begin the process of educating ourselves, "unlearning" and resynthesizing what we have learned in the past. Much of the work anthologized here is grounded in this moment of self-recognition. In her essay, "Coming into Myself," Riché Richardson, who attended Spelman College, writes about "becoming whole" through the synthesis of her identity as an African-American and as a woman, recognizing the inherent contradictions and limitations of male-centered concerns often prioritized in Black nationalist movements.

Similarly, Tiya Miles and Keiko Morris, Tracy Hopkins and Paitra Russell, all write about the often painful processes of acknowledging and accepting one's beauty and self-worth as Black women. This is a difficult task in the face of Eurocentric standards of beauty which prize light skin and straight hair, and by which Black people continue to judge and devalue one another, despite popular "Black pride" rhetoric, in which Black features are supposedly celebrated. They touch as well on the very hurtful experience of being rejected by Black men as suitable romantic partners, and on the exoticism and objectification inherent in "judging" or "ranking" women based on these standards.

For others, like Omar Tyree and Touré, the process of rebuilding begins with the stark realization that we do not fit in where we thought we did or where we wanted to belong; that the places where we sought comfort can no longer—or never did—offer any solace. In his essay, "From White to Black Campus," Omar Tyree talks about his increasing animosity toward whites and the alienation he began to feel, both in and outside of the classroom, after taking a cultural anthropology class which detailed the devastation Western societies have wrought on communities of color. He eventually transferred to Howard University, a historically Black institution where, although it is not without its own set of problems, he found the support and encouragement he lacked at the University of Pittsburgh, a predominantly white institution.

In addition to alienation in the classroom, many Black students feel isolated socially from both Black and white peer groups. In his essay, Touré describes his deliberate choice not to socialize with other Black students during his freshman year. He writes, "more used to being the only Black than one of many, I chose what I knew. . . . I did not wince at the irony of wanting to be in a white world, but unwilling to be as invisible as they hoped. I wasn't bothered by constantly explaining myself, my race." It was only after reading *The Autobiography of Malcolm X* that Touré began to question and re-evaluate his choices, realizing that he had not been honest with himself, and sought out other Black students. However, he found many who rejected him in that community as well, as a result of the choices he had made in the past.

Other writers, such as Kevin Young and Ta-Nehisi Coates, begin their journeys not with their individual selves per se, but with a reconstruction of the history of African-Americans. By turning inward and reaching back, beyond themselves, to the collective heart, these writers are able to reclaim a history and to retell stories that have been manipulated and twisted out of shape, or which have not been heard at all. In "The Preserving," Kevin Young, by centering his poem on the routines of a family—their daily and monthly cycles of preserving food, preparing and eating what was stored—allows us a glimpse of the lives of Black folks behind the rituals, or better perhaps, the rituals of living life, of loving, preserving, and sustaining one another.

In "The Ones Who Stole the Night," Ta-Nehisi Coates not only looks back at the history of slavery but also blurs the lines or borders between the past and the present—which we often construct in order not to look back, to keep a safe distance from the past—providing a necessary sounding board through which he can release his own anger about the past, as well as his frustrations with the present condition of Black people in this country. And further, Coates issues a challenge to his readers, urging them to make connections between the past, the present, and the future, to acknowledge the elements of history—the remnants of slavery—that are still with us today, and to take destiny into our own hands, preventing the repetition of another vicious cycle.

The familiar structure of family also provides a foundation, a vehicle for gathering information about and exploring ourselves and our place in the world. Sabrina Shange McDaniel, in her essay, "Questions I Have Not Asked My Mother," asks difficult questions about her own conception—the result of her mother's choice to sleep with a married man, the sort of questions that penetrate the silences that exist in all families. Other writers, such as minkah makalani, Jawanza Ali Keita, and Tracie Hall, attempt to pierce and break open the silences surrounding the loss of friends and family members, stressing in their poetry the importance of remembrance and memory. Writers such as Corey Olds, Deborah Turner, and Lichelli Lazar-Lea, focus on the evolution of their relationships with parents and siblings, exploring the various roads we travel which take us far away from our families and which also bring us closer. And further, the impact that a racial and racist society has on this evolution.

I have highlighted here only a few works, but within them appear several crucial themes and issues which recur throughout the book, and which, I believe, are important in defining, or at least highlighting, the major struggles and concerns of this generation. Foremost of these is the need to recognize and create links—social and political—between the past and the present. Many of the contributors, both explicitly and implicitly, make connections between their own lives and experiences and those of their parents and grandparents, or other Black folks who have come before them. The title of Houston Baker's book, *Long Black Song*, is appropriate here for it acknowledges a continuum, one long note passed from one generation to the next, the perpetual cycles of love and struggle, movement and rest, that Black people in America continue to travel. And it is from these similarities that we draw strength, finding comfort in the knowledge that we are not alone, as well as learning how to keep moving forward.

However, as the song passes from mouth to mouth, the words and the tune begin to change. Each generation contributes its own verse, borrowing from the one preceding it, reshaping and adding on to the past in ways indicative of its own needs and struggles. It seems that this generation of young Black writers and scholars is humming a familiar melody, trying out different words and phrases, but we have not quite claimed the song as our own. We are still trying to define our rhythm, our beat, our struggle.

I believe part of the reason for this is that we are caught in between the past and the future. We are among the first to take advantage of the advances made during the 1950s and 1960s; to live in a racially integrated society in which most of us have never confronted the legal and social segregation that our parents experienced and fought against. But we are also left to answer questions like, what does it mean to live in an integrated society? Is it—or was it ever—an appropriate solution, and what are its implications for the future? These remain questions for us, for they are issues with which our parents are still grappling. Although we are aware that racism exists, we make the dangerous assumption that we will be accorded, at the least, some common courtesy and respect. However, we learn our lessons the hard way and are thoroughly unprepared for the attacks which attempt to strip us of even these most basic elements of humanity.

As several contributors have pointed out, many of us begin to wake from the dream of integration and confront its realities during our college careers. Although these are crude characterizations, there are several common responses to this. At one extreme, there are Black students who continue to try and fit into mainstream society at any cost, ignoring or tolerating racism, averting their eyes from other Black students, seeking friendship and partnership from those who are unlike themselves.

At the other extreme, some Black students, in response to the alienation and discrimination of which they have become increasingly aware, embrace essentialist notions of what it means to be Black. This can be equally as painful as the complete rejection of one's Blackness, for it imposes limitations, causing us to curb those interests which may not be perceived as "black enough" and to reject those who do not readily fit into this model or construct.

Others try to walk a tenuous middle ground between the two extremes, which often turns into a minefield, threatening to explode with every step. In most cases, these responses lead to further alienation and fragmentation; to hurtful and exclusive actions and situations which defeat the purpose of our newfound consciousness, and which serve to isolate a generation of people who have the potential to change the world.

In addition to confronting the issues raised by integration and the legacy left to us by our parents and ancestors, we are also grappling with our youth, the vast possibilities placed in our hands, and the responsibility of shaping those possibilities, of making something of ourselves. In many ways, this is our own struggle against invisibility and obsolescence. Perhaps, more than in any other area, the refusal to be rendered invisible is expressed most vividly in our art. Especially in the collage of Hip Hop, which, out of borrowed notes and fragments, creates a rhythm that matches the beating of our own hearts; and in rap, which refuses to allow the lives of Black youth to be confined and compressed into small urban spaces.

Increasingly, we are using our education to design structures for the future as well. Our poetry and other writings reflect the urgent need for change, to "MOVE," as Jennifer Smith writes. More and more Black students are choosing African and African-American or related studies as majors during college. Scholars such as Cecil Gray, whose essay "African Based/African Centered Females and Males" is included here, are putting their knowledge to work in tangible ways, creating alternatives to Western based scholarship and lifestyles.

In all genres and mediums, in all ways, this generation is involved in finding its voice, creating new traditions, laying a new foundation. At times we get distracted and confused. But part of the reason for this is that we are trying to define who and what we are in a society that requires its members to make binary choices, to choose sides—Black or white—with neither choice being more definitive or logical than the other. If we are to ask what it means to be integrated, for example, then we must also ask what it truly means to be Black, a question too big for one generation, and one which, perhaps, does not or should not have an answer.

However, Touré provides a way to begin to think about these issues, which is that "blackness is neither a religion or a choice. It is a race, culture, and nation we are born into and spend every waking moment constructing." Blackness is a living process of building and rebuilding; of rendering ourselves invisible so that we might see ourselves and each other more clearly; of learning to accept and love those parts of ourselves which society has deemed unacceptable; of gathering up the pieces of the past, unfolding and reshaping them into recognizable and workable forms for the future.

We all begin this process or journey at different times, in different places, along different paths. I want to create here a space, where space has so often been denied. A safe place, some small amen corner, where we, young Black students and writers, can begin again at the beginning, by telling our stories that need to be told, sharing the pieces of ourselves that we sometimes keep hidden from view, and, most important, listening to, supporting, and learning from one another.

My hope for this book is that it will be a medium for the exchange and formation of ideas and experiences (for young and old), both inside and outside of the classroom. And further, that it will be a resting place, at a point where all roads converge into one. I say resting place, for I hope it is only one stop of many, where we take account of and recount our experiences, and from which we gather up the strength to continue along the various roads we travel on this long lifetime journey.

Part 1

A Spell of Finding

Beginning the Journey

Tomorrow brings a hard and heavy load . . .
My life, my joy, my fear, my anger
My love, my dreams, my struggle for change
All of these I take with me
I'm on my way to tomorrow . . .

—"On the Road to Tomorrow,"
Sweet Honey in the Rock

A Spell of Finding

Trasi Johnson

I AM BROKEN. LITTLE PIECES OF ME LAY ALONG A stone path in a dark winter wood and I am afraid to run back for them. Afraid that all I'll find is glass—clear, cheap glass glittering for years at my back like stars or deep sea jewels.

I've come to a clearing crowded with snow. Black on white in the blue of midnight. No bird songs or cricket strokes. My feet, all that remain of what I was, are bare and cold. I peek from behind a tree, afraid to approach the center. The light place. The snow is a smooth disc. It has only fallen here where the thick trees stand aside. Nothing alive has touched this secret place.

I look back at the swirling miles and watch the little glass star pieces of me fade. I can't recover them. I can't go back for just a couple of jewels. Something to pay my way. I moved too slow. Hesitated too long. Now I must approach that empty, snowy place at the center of the wood, at the center of the universe, all broken and half-awake. With dull wits and cold feet, I must leave my mark on that smooth freshness or face the angry trees. Trees that are tired of my face. Trees too old for sympathy. I must go alone, in fear, and begin to gather new pieces. Make myself presentable again. I am lucky I was able to save my feet.

The Ones Who Stole the Night

Ta-Nehisi Coates

Do you know who stole the night?

They came disguised in pale bandannas
that fit like a body glove
and said they aimed
to carry the white man's burden like a bullwhip
searching for Black hides to caress
Heard tell they were passing for civilized folk
hiding paganism and savagery
behind white lies of civilization and a more perfect union
Do you know who stole the night?

Victims unlucky enough to be alive
say they were ripped from loving wombs
dragged from their homes,
chained and gagged,
stacked like sardines,
and shipped like day-old tomatoes
to somewhere approximately 400 years south of heaven.

Now tradition convulses violently in a pale corner
dying of MDS
or manifest destiny syndrome,
and righteousness drifts silently into oblivion
like ashes to ashes and dust being swept up
Do you know who stole the night?

Eyewitnesses said they came pouring rivers of blood
polluting the land with false gods,

thieving Zulu spears,
and making off with the golden stool
And while culture fades from Black,
and Ibo masks lay ratta-tat-tattered
pieces everywhere scattered,
Ghanian Gold does a dance of death
while bleeding exploitation from a million gunshot wounds
Do you know who stole the night?

Can you remember the amnesia they forced you into,
can you see the men dying in pools of blood and human waste,
hear the slave ship screams
that escaped from ghost vessels on one-way voyages,
can you recall that which the mind aches to forgive
but the spirit can never forget,

As the victim list gets longer but the victims just get dumber,
And the blood pools get wider as the days become numbered,
And the babies are still crying as the Atlantic keeps bleeding,
And the night is still screaming cause the thieves are still thieving,
Do you know who stole the night?

I'm issuing an APB to all real Afrikans
Suspect was last seen raping the world,
dressed in sins he can never shed,
has your momma's blood dripping from his jaws,
and a nasty habit of pillaging and plundering
I want the ones who stole the night.

Cause if impersonating God
and kidnapping nature is the crime
then the mandatory sentence is death by lethal knowledge

5 million days may pass,
4 thousand suns may set,
3 hundred stars may shine,
and 20 moons may dance
but the night will never return as long as thieves
prowl the darkness . . .

Malik's Brother Died in 1963
—A Direct Ramification of Segregation

Myronn Hardy

The road was Georgia red clay—
gray stones on both sides.
He walked at night—stars guided
him away from the hollow
phone—a shell—that rang
at 10:23 P.M.
Dad was in a den corner black hands

fused—head pressed
against them sobbing.
January 21, 1963, was the day
sirens rang and red lights spun
in our hammered heads.
Snapping turtles bit his toes—
he was numb, cold—last season's

blackberry bush. The steep ditch
was filled with tall weeds,
blue snakes, and brown spotted frogs.
One jump or slip his neck breaks,
lids close—eyes flip back blinded by
a pure light.
His brother is dead. Two cars smashed

like beets. The orange van came
in time, it only took the white one.

They left him there!
The other van came too late.
They took the black one away
but the chariots came and
left him empty.

The Fire This Time

Michael Datcher

WHEN I WAS ELEVEN, A POLICEMAN YANKED HIS GUN from his holster and pointed it directly at the bridge of my nose. He yelled, "Freeze!" I was shaking so violently that he yelled, "Freeze!" again.

My four preteen friends and I had found an abandoned newspaper machine that someone had forced their way into. There were a few more coins in the machine. We were trying to shake them out, and someone called the police. Three police cars rolled up, sirens off for the surprise attack. Out of the police car sliding to a stop closest to me, a white policeman jumped, his arms fully extended, both hands squeezed around his pistol's handle (just like on TV). He had to squat down to line up the bridge of my nose.

I have heard it said that when a person is extremely afraid, or near death, his whole life flashes before him. This is true. My eleven years rushed by as if being chased by time itself. I was eleven. I was eleven, and he had his gun ten inches from my head—he called me a nigger. I am from L.A.

I have known, lived next to, played with, admired, feared, and seen Crips kill two Bloods, at a party in Melody's Dance Studio. I lived in Crip hood. "Wassup cuz" was the greeting of choice, and necessity. It showed, at the very least, tangential allegiance to the gang that controlled our neighborhood, whose members commanded more respect than the peace officers, who routinely stopped black males and beat them. Beat us. This is why, I'm sure, my mother, like most mothers raising their black sons in the ghetto, taught me, at an early age, how to deal with policemen. How to call them "Sir" and feign respect for the badge that has, historically, given them license to beat on people who I grew up playing marbles with, my friends. Just as the white skin of their ancestral fathers served as a license to illegally, and inhumanely, hang black men from the limbs of Georgia peach trees, like sticky rotten fruit whose nectar, no longer sweet to the taste, was discarded.

Randy Newman is also from L.A. We, however, do not share the same reality. His point of reference emanates from a different experience, the product of a soul treated differently. He is not from my L.A. When he sings his song "I Love L.A.," he is really singing, "I Love My L.A." (I didn't see any people I knew in his video.) It is Mr. Newman's choice to sing what he wants to sing. However, a problem arises when a person, or people, begin to sing, or discourse, or report on places and people and cultures of which they are unfamiliar. Unfamiliarity with one's subject leads to a superficial understanding of the subject, which, in turn, results in the misrepresentation of the subject. An especially heinous, and dangerous, act when the subject is a complex race of people.

During the rebellion, some people came up to me to express their "outrage" at the not-guilty verdicts given to the officers who beat Rodney King. Each seemed surprised by the ensuing violence. None thought violence an appropriate response to violence. All were white. They do not know L.A. My L.A. The L.A. not seen on *L.A. Law.* They do not know, intimately, the long history of police brutality inflicted on our community. They have not seen a white policeman pull a black teenager from his car, in front of his girlfriend, and force his head to the curb with a pistol, seemingly made just for this purpose, and these people.

They do not know who Ron Settles was. Do not know he was a bright student and star tailback at Long Beach State, who was stopped by Signal Hill police because he was driving through their city, in a nice car, and it was dark, and he was dark. And at a time when, I, eleven, needed a role model, he was found hanged, suspiciously, in the Signal Hill jail. There was an investigation because there had been incidents before. No police went to prison. The city simply shut down the jail. Lights snuffed out. Just like Ron Settles's life. It was not a fair exchange. Ask his mother. Ask me. She lost her son, I lost a role model.

Mrs. Settles knows L.A. My L.A. She knew, and experienced, the hope created by finally capturing, on video, for the whole world to see, that which had become a daily part of our lives. A video that would give insight into why some black men are so angry. A video, we anticipated, would elicit not pity, but justice and understanding. What man does not want to be understood? Appreciated? His perspective proven valid? We really believed justice would be roused from her somnolence, loosing the chains of its pathetic antecedent, and rush from the great depths to gather us, like the mighty hand of God, close to her bosom.

Not guilty.
Not guilty.
Not guilty.
Not guilty.

I got the same sinking feeling I got when [Dr.] King got shot. I went to work. Left. Couldn't be in the same company with white people. I went to a bar. It was on the news already. I felt nothing for that white truck driver. When that cat came back and snatched his wallet, I said, "Right on."

— Norman, forty-nine, former history major in college, currently manager in large automotive chain

All of the guys I know round my age don't have nothin' to do with white people. Been round too long. Seen too much. Been lied to too many times. Don't trust 'em. Can't trust 'em.

— Frank, fifty-two, retired truck driver

What did those white people who walked up to me expect us to do? Analyze the situation? "Now what went wrong here?" "How can we constructively respond to this amazing injustice, again?" "Where can we possibly find another cheek to turn?" Black people are tired of being treated with heathenish moral imprudence, and then expected to respond like Jesus. Historically, this expectation has not been loaded on the shoulders of any other people, for none other could, or should, bolster such a pledge. This unfair burden of passivity was only exacerbated by the rebellion's television news coverage.

The visual image, especially when buttressed by sound and constant commentary, is unmatched as an agent of influence. This is corroborated by the oft-noted parasitic relationship Americans have with their televisions. By and far, the people making decisions about what images are transmitted through this powerful medium are not black people. Nor are they people who have significant insight into the black culture, or the condition of black people in this country. Nor, based upon their track record, have they shown a meaningful desire to learn about our culture or condition, so as to present a more accurate and complete picture of our people.

This shirking of responsibility was made manifest, ultimately, in the media presentation of the Los Angeles rebellion from the mind, soul, and experience of a person who is not from our L.A. A debaucherous voyeur, sensually aroused to passionate masturbation by large burning fires, and hot pistols, and long rifles; by screams for mercy and low, painful moans emanating deep from within tight abdomens, rising through parched throats, calling "sweet Jesus."

This display dominated the television coverage in the first twenty-four hours of the uprising. These first hours being so critical because they defined the timbre of the coverage to follow; more significantly, they left a lasting first impression, an indelible brand, on the minds and souls of white Americans. White Americans with a previously established, superficial knowledge of black culture. White Americans in a position to hire, and arrest, and jail, and fire, and judge, a great multitude of my people and our progeny.

In the crucial first hours, no news team talked to black boys, the next generation of would-be angry black men, and asked them, "How did you feel when you saw all those police beat on that one black man? Why do you think they beat him? Have you ever seen the police beat a black man? Do you believe the police are there to protect you? Do you think, one day, the police will beat you? Does that make you afraid? Does that make you angry? Why were those officers not guilty? Does that make you angry? Do you think the fact that Rodney King was black, like you, influenced the jury? Does that make you angry?" By failing to ask these insight-evoking questions, the media contributed to an already troubled relationship, embedded deep within the densely tangled forest of frustration, distrust, and fear.

. . .

Black children represent the black future. At an early age, they are acutely aware of the breach in the American moral contract that supposedly governs human relations. On June 12, forty-four days after the rebellion, I visited the 99th Street Elementary School in Watts. I wasn't sure if the school was in Crip hood or Blood hood, so I dressed in the most neutral browns and tans I could find. I left my sister's West Hollywood apartment, walked up to Sunset and Crescent Heights, five minutes from Beverly Hills, and hopped on the No. 2 RTD, heading southeast. Two hours later, I exited the bus in front of a large dark power plant and walked next door to the school.

The trip provided me with ample time to confront my fears of returning to an environment that I hadn't dealt with in six years—an environment I felt fortunate to survive the first time through. On the evening of the day that I received my acceptance letter for graduate school at U.C.L.A., I had a haunting nightmare that upon returning to Los Angeles, my first night, I was murdered.

As the bus rambled east, then south. I was struck by the gradual change in skin complexion of those riding the bus. By the time we passed the first burned, soot-covered remains of a former business, the only white face I saw was on a campaign poster next to the decimated building, ironically urging South Central to "Vote Lyndon LaRouche."

Upon arrival, I walked through the school visiting classes with the principal, Ms. Althea Woods. I was quickly convinced that she was yet another strong black woman, in the tradition of the African queens preceding her, who have been the very marrow of the black community. I met with six young black boys for a closed-session roundtable discussion. They ranged in age from Alexis, eight, to Donte, twelve. I asked the group, "Why do you think those policemen beat up Rodney King?" Derrick, the biggest and most aggressive of the group, talking fast with a slight stutter, jumped in with the following:

"Because he was black, and maybe they thought he was high cause he was driving fast. They [police] don't like to see blacks driving fast. They stopped him. Beat him because he was black. One time, this man was walking down by the power plant. A policeman rolled up on him, and said, "What are you doin'?' Then two more police cars pulled up. The first policeman pushed his [the black man's] head against the car for nothin'. Then one of the other policemen came up and started hitting him with his baton."

I asked the boys, "How many of you have personally witnessed a policeman beating a black man?" Five of the six raised their hands. I asked, "Are you afraid of the police?" Nine-year-old Gregg, chubby, with dimples and wearing a Jheri curl, looking a midget Ice Cube, raised his hand and slowly said, "I'm afraid of them."

I asked, "What would you have done if you were older, and the police beat someone in your family, or in your community, like they beat Rodney King?" Eleven-year-old Steve, startlingly intense for his young age, responded matter of factly: "I'd take the police off." His frankness, and the seriousness of his tone, revealed that the seeds of rage had begun to sprout. He was one of the five who had witnessed a police beating of a black man.

There was one dissenting voice throughout the discussion: Donte, a thin, soft-spoken, but very confident twelve-year-old. He confronted the others' opinions with an agenda of peace. His view, his voice, like that of one calling from deep within the tangled forest, calmly but firmly, spoke of patience, hope, and love. I raised the question, "What would you have done if you were old enough, and the police beat someone, like they beat Rodney King?" Donte replied with the following:

"I would have been mad, but I wouldn't have done a Rambo like you [talking to Steve]. I would have made sure my family was okay. Then went and passed out food [if stores were closed after looting] to people without cars, because my family has a car. Ain't no need for all that killin'. Ain't gon change nothin' anyway."

As Donte presented his nonviolent agenda, for a moment I felt ashamed of the anger and rage that had become so much a part of my being. Ashamed because I felt as if I had given up hope that the racial hatred I had been exposed to could be overcome by love. My Judeo-Christian background will never allow me to be comfortable with relinquishing my belief in the power of love as the agent of change.

I want to believe. My mom believed. She was born and raised just outside of Birmingham, Alabama: the heart of Dixie. She has intimately known racism; deep hatred has been her companion, but she raised us to treat everyone equally, regardless of race. To love. She taught by example. She still believes. I don't know how she does it. However, I, too, want to believe, because I know the anger that breathes just beneath my skin, like a beast, cornered and desperate, turning inward on me, a masochist, is destroying us.

When I was an undergraduate at Cal, I applied for a job as a police aide, trying to directly confront my hatred for the police. An opportunity to know them as human beings, as opposed to what I had experienced them to be. I told the oral board that interviewed me, honestly, why I was applying. They hired me. I was there thirteen months; it was like therapy. Although many of the officers I encountered were insensitive, simple-minded motherfuckers, there were a few who were genuinely wonderful people, thoughtful and sincerely concerned with the citizenry they were protecting. The experience affected me deeply. A new seed of understanding began to flower, and fragile petals of hope emerged where fallow soil had been before.

The Rodney King beating, like the harsh realities of Midwestern winter, destroyed my garden. The ensuing verdict roused my weary beast. I was in a café when the verdict was first announced. I stumbled, literally, in a state of shock, out of the café, then walked directly to a computer center on campus and wrote the following letter to a colleague in New York:

April 29, 1992
Dear Kevin,

It's 3:56 P.M. on Wednesday, thirteen minutes after the white judge read the four not-guilty verdicts handed to him by the white bailiff, who carried it from the white foreman, leader of the all-white jury that just set free four white police officers who beat up yet another brother (on film) and I'm surprised at myself for being so surprised. Something has fallen off the shelf inside of me to disturb the calm that I was allowing myself to enjoy these last few weeks before I leave for graduate school. I really don't know what to do, man. I am so hurt. I am so disappointed. I feel betrayed.

I know there will be riots in the streets of L.A. tonight. I know that people will die tonight. I want them to be white people, Kevin. I want white people to die. I want innocent white people to die, and experience injustice. To experience the land of equality like we experience it. To experience America the Beautiful like we experience it. To experience the melting pot when the heat is up and they ain't the ones stirrin'. I'm sick of this shit, man.

I can only imagine what I must have looked like as I walked down that crowded sidewalk, my facial expression. I needed any white person to bump into me, or just stare at me for too long, so I could unleash my beast outward, for Rodney King, and Dr. King, and Medgar, and Ron, and slavery. I just wanted to scream. I wrote instead, and I write now, every day, because it keeps me sane. Tames the beast. Mine, however, is only one of many beasts living in a people, in a city, that feeds the beast a steady diet of bloody, stillborn hope covered with the afterbirth of despair—ignorning all the signs that say, "DANGER: Please don't feed the animals."

Livin' Just Enough for the City

Jelani Cobb, Jr.

GLIDING THROUGH THE DETERIORATING URBAN landscape, a cobalt and onyx Mercedes cruises to a stop. The sleek vehicle stands in stark contrast to the surroundings, which comprise a vacant lot, a small Korean-owned grocery store, and an imposing trio of low-income apartment buildings. A bass-heavy rumble emanates from deep within the machine's designer interior. The charcoal-tinted window slides down, momentarily releasing an explosion of rhyming words laced skillfully over a resurrected James Brown drumtrack. A solitary coffee-complexioned young male is revealed as he sits slouched fashionably in the driver's seat. He is one of the most easily recognizable icons in urban America—the Black male drug dealer.

Although Black males constitute only a fraction of the drug dealers in America, it is their image that is most likely to be conjured up by the term. The unemployment crisis in the inner cities, as well as the explosion of crack during the 1980s, created circumstances that were conducive to the growth of the drug trade in many Black communities. A complex web of power relations has evolved as a result of the trade. This web can be best described as the new urban economics. The following article draws upon interviews with counselors, researchers, and some who are actually involved in the trade. Each person, for their own reasons, expressed a desire to see an end to this underground economy that has claimed the lives of so many Black boys and native sons.

La Shonda is a pretty honey-colored woman of about twenty-two. It is somewhat hard to believe that for five years she was involved in a cocaine operation that included some of New York's most powerful drug dealers. Beginning in 1984, she performed various tasks for what she calls a "family business," which included bagging marijuana, making deliveries, and cooking crack. "The first time I remember being exposed to drugs was when I was eleven," she recalls. "My stepfather used to grow weed under his house in California." She believes that she had probably seen illegal drugs even before that but "didn't really understand what they were."

After leaving home at thirteen because of her abusive stepfather, La Shonda moved in with her boyfriend. By the time she was fourteen she was pregnant and she, her sixteen-year-old boyfriend, and her three older brothers moved into an apartment in Brooklyn. They made money for the rent and the baby's expenses by selling marijuana out of the apartment. They soon moved to working as lookouts and making deliveries. She says, "I might deliver a package and pick up $500. Out of that $500, you might get to keep $50—now you want to get more involved because you see how much the dealer is making."

Within two years, the group graduated to dealing crack. "We would usually rent a hotel room in Queens to cook the crack," she says. She never used drugs "because of all the stuff we put in it. We would put the coke over the fire, add glue, roach spray, or any household products with formaldehyde because it gave it that extra kick." The mixture of chemicals congealed into the "rocks" that would then be broken down into smaller portions and put into vials. The group was making in her estimation five or six thousand dollars a week, and they took regular vacations to Jamaica and New Orleans. During one of the cooking sessions, the hotel was raided and she was arrested.

She managed to beat the charges, but the constant threat of prison and death was beginning to take its toll. She no longer wanted to be involved with the trade. In addition to death and prison, there was always the prospect of becoming addicted to the "product." One associate who never used any drugs became addicted to the fumes generated when he cooked the crack. If all these factors motivated her to leave, there was at least one impetus to stay—the idea of raising a two-year-old daughter on a sixteen-year-old's wages was less than appealing. Over the course of the next year, the operation began to unravel. First, her oldest brother was killed and her boyfriend was convicted of possession. Her other brother was charged with possession but managed to get bail set at $5000. Shortly after she bailed him out, he disappeared, and she has not seen him since. All this encouraged her departure from the business. Four years later, La Shonda works as a counselor and teacher in Harlem.

A three-ounce bag of crack is poised precariously in the left hand of the President of the United States as he sits stern-faced in the Oval Office. Words tumble from his lips declaring that America is in the midst of a national crisis. The crisis he speaks of is the explosion of drug abuse. The small cocaine pebbles he holds were purchased in Lafayette Park (directly across the street from the White House). The date is September 5, 1989, and George Bush is about to initiate his "war on drugs."

The crack was purchased hours earlier by Drug Enforcement Agency officials from Keith Jackson, an eighteen-year-old Black male. What the President fails to mention is that Jackson had been given handwritten instructions by DEA officials to find the park. In the end, he had been driven to the park by a DEA informant. Jackson was acquitted of the charges brought against him due to his obvious entrapment, but Bush had already shrewdly manipulated public fears and stereotypes of Black males. In the words of Clarence Lusane, author of *Pipe Dream Blues: Racism and the War on Drugs*, "just as the Bush team had used Willie Horton to fan the flames of racism and law-and-order during the presidential campaign, Keith Jackson would become the Willie Horton of the drug war." *Pipe Dream Blues* is one of the studies that examines the economic and social factors in the inner-city drug culture and the impact of racism on the war on drugs.

Lusane is a slender soft-spoken man who looks more like a college student than someone who has spent years traveling and researching drugs on three continents. According to Lusane, "racism influences the drug war primarily in who gets targeted. It is clear that 80% or more of the people who use drugs in this country are white, the people who principally get arrested for drugs, close to 50% are African-Americans." Racism also influences the availability of treatment, to which "the African-American community has less access."

In addition to being more likely to be arrested on drug charges, Blacks spend more time behind bars than do whites for similar offenses. In some cases pregnant women who use drugs are being sentenced to prison terms for child abuse. Lusane points out in his book that although the rate of drug use for Black women and white women is virtually the same, "physicians turn in the Black women who test pos-

itive for the drugs at a rate of nearly ten times that of white women."
He also notes that "of the forty-seven cases identified by the ACLU in
which pregnant mothers were imprisoned for drug use, 80% of them are
Black." The statistics are reminiscent of the scene from "The Godfather" in which the heads of New York's five families sit gathered at a
round table discussing the merits and disadvantages of the drug trade.
After some debate it is decided that it is allowable as long as it is "kept
among the colored people." They are animals anyway, so let them lose
their souls.

Social commentary looped over subjacent drum-
tracks has long been a trademark of Hip Hop. Pioneers like Grandmas-
ter Flash and the Furious Five translated life in America's urban con-
tainment quarters onto a reel-to-reel with songs like "The Message" and
"White lines." More recently, the tales of brothas caught on the cutting
edge of hardcore economic reality and the predator-prey relations of underground entrepreneurships have come from Public Enemy, Boogie
Down Productions, and Ice Cube. PE's "Night of the Living Baseheads"
is a lyrical polemic against the sale of drugs to Blacks by Blacks. In his
Hip Hop narrative "Love is Gonna Getcha," KRS-One unchained a lyrical monologue that did more to explain the mindset and motivations of
many drug dealers than a hundred Heritage Foundation studies. After
becoming involved in the trade the character in the song states "I do it
once, I do it twice / Now there's steak with the beans and rice." Lastly,
Ice Cube's most profound commentary lies in the question asked in his
"Bird in the Hand," which begins, "I gotta serve food that might give
you cancer / Cause my son don't take no for an answer / Now I pay taxes
that you never give me back / What about diapers, bottles, and Simi-
lac? / Do I have to sell me a whole lot of Crack / For decent shelter and
clothes on my back? / Or should I just wait for help from Bush / Or Jesse
Jackson and Operation Push?"

On the flip side of the lyrical assaults on the dealing
and the conditions that produce dealers, Hip Hop artists have been used
to endorse a number of legal drugs such as the St. Ides Malt Liquor
advertisements that have attracted such artists as EPMD, Ice Cube, and
Rakim. Others have openly endorsed illicit drugs, particularly Cypress
Hill's "Feel the Effects of the High," GangStarr's "Take Two and Pass,"
and Redman's "How to Roll a Blunt." In all three cases, the artists ad-
vocate the use/legalization of marijuana. According to April Silver,

President of Cultural Initiative, and the organizer of that group's third annual Hip Hop conference, "Hip Hop is a realistic reflection of what goes on in our community—we relate to the music through how we live."

So what is to be done? News reports nationwide bear the same grim statistics of destruction, despair, and death in Black communities. Superficial sloganeering will not help. Many of the brothas arrested for selling do not believe in "the system" as an option to put food on the table. Given the fact that the "trade" offers immediate rewards—and a highly visible icon of advancement draped in designer clothes—in many places where hope got exported to Mexico along with jobs and resources, the Black community is facing an uphill battle. Another problem lies in the fact that many now see "slinging rocks" as an ultimate objective, whereas many in the past saw the trade as a means to an end. The "Godfather" trilogy depicts the struggle of a mob family to "go legitimate." The fortunes of many of this country's wealthiest and most respected families had their origins in illegal businesses.

When asked why the current anti-drug efforts have been unsuccessful, Clarence Lusane pauses pensively. He begins, "they start with false assumptions. They assume that the people use drugs because they are morally decrepit . . . if you attack the problem with moralism and 'Just Say No' sloganeering and think that you persuade people not to use drugs, that's false. . . . The use of drugs has little to do with morality. It has to do with the people that are produced in a society where there is inequality." He sees the need for improvement in "housing, employment, and education" as necessary to divert those who might become involved with the trade.

The bass still emanates from the Mercedes, advertising to the deferred dreamers and future cocaine capitalists. Poised coolly in the neighborhood, slinger living life on fast forward. Today, tomorrow, or maybe a year from now, a gun will erupt, a bullet will tear through his brown frame and he will be gone. The sad part is that there are a dozen brothers lined up to replace him.

In Remembrance Of

Taigi Smith

KHARY AND KOFI. Both found shot, execution style, in a San Francisco schoolyard. The murderer was never captured. *Peter Lee.* The victim of a drug-related drive-by shooting. *Anthony.* He lived a dangerous life and eventually died last week at the young age of twenty-two. *Dexter.* He died in a car accident. The newspapers said something about alcohol. *Kareem.* Also accosted by a drive-by assassin. He was only nineteen years old.

This is not an obituary, but a short list of men whom I witnessed fall prey to inner-city violence. These are the men who fought to survive in the deadly streets of San Francisco and lost. These are my friends. These are my brothers. These are my acquaintances. They are all dead now, but in a better place, I hope. None of them deserved hell, for they already lived it in this life. On the exterior, San Francisco has lush neighborhoods, wealthy inhabitants, a beautiful landscape, but on the inside, it is a dangerous place for low-income African-Americans. Each day I ask myself, "Who will be next?"

I experienced the city not only as a woman, but as a Black woman. My experience is not a rare one, but a way of life for most young, Black women in the United States. I grew up in a cramped, three-room studio in San Francisco's Mission District. It is here that I spent sixteen years of my life learning the skills that are necessary to survive in the city. I grew up poor, but it was not until I was about fifteen years old that I realized other people considered my neighborhood a "ghetto." Yes, there was crime. Yes, there was litter on my street. Yes, people were robbed, or beaten, or mugged on a weekly basis, but in my eyes my neighborhood was not a "ghetto," but the place I called home.

I never questioned why I lived in the place that I did, I only accepted it. I accepted it because I knew no other life. I accepted it because society conditioned me to believe that People of Color deserved no better, and, greatest of all, I accepted it because my mother shielded me from the reality of our situation. She forced me to go to dance lessons, violin classes, and white schools. I was not allowed to eat candy, watch television, or hang out on my street corner with the other local kids. I was not allowed. I was forbidden to come home past dark, and the only stop I could make on the way home from school was the local library. It is now that I realize my mother felt that she could protect me from the ills of urban society by shielding me from its dangers, but it was then that I felt she was wrong.

My mother's methods of deterrence only made me hungrier for street life. By the time I entered high school, the fast life of the streets seemed even more attractive. I had convinced her to send me to a school designed to prepare inner-city teenagers for the challenges of college life. Although she wanted to send me to a conservative preparatory school (I assume on scholarship), she sent me to the school of my choice instead. Philip and Sala Burton Academic High School was located in historical Hunter's Point. Hunter's Point is now and was then a mecca for both Black culture and Black violence. It is a haven for drug lords, and a home for the poor. The streets of Hunter's Point drink the blood of Black people every day. Located on the farthest outskirts of San Francisco, it is a place that a San Franciscan could live a lifetime without ever seeing. Surrounded by warehouses, shipyards, and abandoned factories, Hunter's Point houses a great number of San Francisco's poorest inhabitants. Embedded deep within the neighborhood lay hundreds of housing projects and miles and miles of substandard housing facilities. It is both a home and an urban jungle, but most important, Hunter's Point is where I learned the psychology of the inner city.

Poor people in urban ghettos inevitably yearn for that which is virtually unattainable, a psychology that is fed by the constant flow of media images telling America's poor that they are meaningless in this society without certain material objects. The messages sent to the impoverished via the media cause them to want that which they cannot have, and it is these messages that cause America's economically disadvantaged young people to do almost anything for material gain. I was one of those young people.

While attending high school in Hunter's Point, I quickly learned that wit, humor, intelligence, and beauty could get me almost anything that I wanted. At the age of sixteen, petty objects were all that I desired. I wanted the leather coats, jewelry, and expensive clothing that earned females clout among their friends and peer groups. I wanted to drive the fast cars that belonged to boys who stood on the corner of Third Street all night long. I wanted to go to the beautyshop every week and own Gucci handbags; but I was poor. My mother cleaned houses for a living and I lived on Shotwell Street. These things could never be mine . . . or so I thought.

By the time I was a sophomore in high school I had all these objects and more by exercising my femininity. A pretty face and a sense of humor enabled me to become close friends with many local drug dealers. I became involved with a clique that chose fast money and fancy clothes over minimum wage and hand-me-downs. They liked me because of my innocence, intelligence, and the virginity they could never have. I loved them for their fast cars, fast money, and fast life. Most of all, I loved them because they exposed me to those parts of the urban jungle that my mother fought so hard to keep me away from. It is today that I understand my mother.

"I have a 3.8 GPA" are the words I shouted the day I packed my bags to leave my mother's home at the young age of seventeen. "A 3.8 GPA won't save your ass from a flying bullet while you're hangin' in the streets with those drug dealers," is the reply I received the day my mother evicted me from her home. My mom knew that my $5.00 per hour job at Nordstrom's was not buying the gold rings, fancy clothes, and Gucci handbags I now possessed. She released me to the streets hoping that I would not die in the hands of street violence and praying for my life. She was tired of hearing me say "I have a 3.8 GPA" in order to justify my open defiance of her rules, so she let me go. My mother always secretly hoped I would return home, but I never did.

Somehow I survived the streets, graduated from high school, and entered college at the age of eighteen. The fact that I survived on my own for a year with little more than a $5.00 an hour job, street sense, and my mother's prayers is nothing short of a miracle. I am not proud of my past, and I would not wish the life I was forced to lead on any woman, but I survived life in San Francisco's urban jungle.

The story that I have told is not only my story, it is a way of life for many young Black women growing up in The City. The stories of African-American boys growing up in urban areas have been exploited and sensationalized. I do not wish the same for young Black women. Yet I believe it is important that we document our own struggles to survive and that these stories be recognized, not ignored.

Memoirs after Surviving Well

Melanie L. Mims

THE TREES SWAY GENTLY IN ATLANTA ON WINDY days. I've never thought of myself as a nature lover, but the sight of wind blowing through trees and foliage and around buildings and bodies could keep me engrossed for minutes at a time. Sometimes I would sit there in that dark office, looking out of the window at the blowing objects as one of the women would talk about her experiences. Clearing my mind and focusing on green and wind were my specialties in the beginning because it took too much effort to try to relate to the words they spoke. How do you tell distressed people, women who have as much right to feel as dirty and as used up as you do, that you feel that you are even dirtier than they think they are?

We were supposed to discuss how we survived daily. Some of the women talked about everything—who they loved, who they used, who they let use them over and over and over. I watched. I studied their expressions while my mind wound itself in and out of the discussions, alternately reading contortions and smiles against my own painful musings.

The trees sway ever so gently when you're alone and seven years old with no one to tell you who to be afraid of or even who to run to.

It was my third meeting. I could tell they were getting tired of me because not only did I refuse to open my mouth, but I wouldn't conceal the fact that I was judging them, and this was no place for private evaluations. Just like the other women, I was here because I had a problem with myself, or rather because my life was currently shaped by my problems. Sitting was torture. Every space and object in the office seemed to invoke my memory. That's why my attention was turned to the window.

When you're blessed in central Texas during summer the wind will blow gently and diffuse the heat. From infancy I was mesmerized by monotony of any sort, and even at the ripe age of seven the sight of wind blowing through trees, over buildings, and around bodies could keep me quiet and still for long periods. But like most children of our time, the TV could keep me mesmerized even longer, and the rare blessing of a cool wind in the midday of a Texas summer didn't lure me outside most days.

It's painful to tell your own story, but we love pain. That's the other thing that I would be thinking while the women's voices weaved in and out of my notice. Why else were we here, except to embrace our pain and acknowledge that the experience itself was vital to who we were at that moment? Wasn't our pain special, didn't the very specialness of our pain invite our presence into the denomination of agony, and the gospel of victimization?

My brain attempted to run its own commentary while others spoke. A sort of call and response "me too" to each evocation of affliction and misunderstanding. That was the hardest part of being there, to admit that something horrible enough had happened to me to justify my presence there. Not just being an audience member, but a circus performer. That I was distorted too.

That day was no different. I opted for the hum of the air-conditioning unit in the back room that was just softer than the hum of the TV. Often I've tried to understand the possibility of power in a single day, hour, or moment, to be able to locate the pivot in a minute, to know just when my life would turn from nebulousness and jelly to permanency and concrete. I'm sure if my mother had known where the pivot of a minute was she would have never sent me to visit my grandmother that summer. Or she would have warned my grandmother to let me stay with any one of my great-aunts, who weren't working while my grandmother worked daytime hours. Who knows where the pivots are? Mother didn't know then and for many years to come that the pivot is not only elusive, but criminal.

I really didn't know until that specific day, my third meeting day, that to be able to tell your own story to someone else you have to tell yourself first. You have to trust that your story is real and worth telling, you have to give it some coherence. My brain had been trying to tell me my own story for a while but you have to be ready. Ready to rehearse your own trauma.

". . . and my mother was looking at me just like what's your name again, yeah I forget your name cause you haven't been here that long. Anyway, when I told my mother about Daddy she looked at me just like you're looking at me now—." I had just caught the fact that someone was referring to me.

"How am I looking at you?" My first words since introducing myself to the group. Raspy, low-throat words that made me seem slightly condescending, slightly terrified.

"Like my mother. Like you have something else much more important on your mind, but since I am talking to you, you're gonna try to figure me out, and see if you have time to care whether I'm lying or not."

"I'm paying attention to you, and I don't think you're lying." I wasn't trying to think anything. I hated that the comfort of my trees was being replaced by this attack of words.

"Sometimes you don't even seem like you're here, let alone paying attention. Looking out that window as if what we have to say don't even matter. You haven't even told us yet why you're here."

"I told Dr. Lindo—"

"But Dr. Lindo isn't us. And she doesn't have to sit, look at you, and not know you. We have to decide whether we feel comfortable talking with you listening, especially since you seem to think we just have to accept you."

My story. MY story, I was thinking to myself. My words, my secret. My timing. My story to tell, if and when I chose. I made up my mind that I had two choices, either to get up and leave, or to share. My brain had been preparing all this time to share with somebody, anybody who cared. The women had to care. It had happened to them too.

For a very long time I didn't remember that I had existed that summer. I didn't notice the hole in my memory; I knew many people who couldn't remember whole sections of their childhoods. Even when they were teenagers. So I never really thought about not having lived the summer after I turned seven years old. I never tried to think about that time. The memory came out once when I was fourteen, but it was so unbearable that I put it back in again and didn't remember until three years later when I was seventeen and the memory came silently and heavily. With enough centrifugal force to make me think that my mind was disintegrating or that I was going crazy. I don't know why the memory chose to come completely then. Sometimes I think it was because I was just realizing that sex was real, and that if it was real then it could happen to me. Sometimes I think that when my mind made the connection between sex and me the glitch in its memory came out full force. Out of my mind's necessity to survive whole.

To tell your own pain, your own disgrace, in your own words. Not to look to others who experienced it, not to turn on "Oprah" and see the woman crying and say, "Yeah, I know." Not to be silent and hope that the memory will go away again when you know that it's out for good for all time. Not to hope that you can think about it without caring or hurting. Not to condescend and think you're handling things just fine unlike others, because you're strong and don't have to think about those moments in your life. Not to be alone trying to heal private wounds, but to incorporate suffering. I opened my mouth and gave way to memory.

The worst part was that I didn't know how to believe myself. And when you lose trust in your own memory, your own ability to retain thoughts, you lose the ability to trust the minutest things in your power. I wondered how I was able to walk, if I could trust the integrity of my speech, if the people who housed, fed, and clothed me were truly my own parents. If I could still be called a virgin. Most of all I wondered about all that I had learned up to that point about sex and desire. I learned that children weren't sexy, and that sex was not something that happened to you, but something you wanted and anticipated. I thought that sex involved a man and a woman. I thought that when it finally came to me I would be ready for it.

"It was summer. I was visiting my grandmother. My babysitter, who was my cousin, made me do things to her, and did things to me. I was seven years old." Four sentences that took me twelve years to utter. At that point I couldn't embellish, I couldn't rehearse the pain in elaborate terms, describe what parts of my present life were wrecked. All I could do was give this sparse commentary on my personal tragedy.

I think when something this deep happens to you even the people closest to you (because either they won't or they can't) don't give you the time and space you need. To remember. To be emotional. To express your anger visibly and audibly. To embrace your own pain.

Untitled

Jawanza Ali Keita

for Pop

Spring Break, 1991

I heard how th cancer burns
through yr back lk lye.
But today I see firsthand how
radiation turns a man's skin to ash
and you into some brutha
I don't recognize.

At a time lk this, when
we're supposed to say it,
we hold th silence
that keeps our tongues still.

As usual, we shake, grippin
each other up lk boyz
as if it's been said. A man is born
wit th number of days
in his hands.

visitations

minkah makalani

for evelyn mathews & narvis penn,

my mama & (gran)mama, & all those who've traveled

this death road

I

steel breathes 3 weeks in my chest
already i know the fire of fists
how men cry when opened like fish
how sunlight falls cold through a web of bars.

this morning i count the bars that shadow my face
till i realize there is one for each day of america.
readied in greys pressed sharp as ice
i retrace snow-faded footprints

to the visiting room.
here, the thunder of closing cells
rings low under the weight of voices.
i have come to an ocean's wet sands

but there is no tide washing away footprints here
no waves splash against rocks like music
no birds call across the foam in harmony
with the slow whisper of wind,

only the salt-bitter taste of blue tears
running down a face gives resonance to this cave.
smiling through a cloud of helplessness
is a mother i once knew.

her arms carried me through venomous winters
and no dinners. now she offers them like bread

holding me with hands that embrace calm as silk.
like a woman still dripping birth

she counts my fingers
reads my pupil's red lines for sickness
runs a steady finger down the scar
sliced on my forehead by a stubborn wall.

she veils her fear in the promises of god
but her questions have given in to myth:
you eatin well? they treatin you good?
you need cigarettes? thad said you'd need cigarettes!

a quiet moment stills our trembling voices,
words, like black feathers of a hawk,
slice the air swelled silent around us.
polite smiles fill the speechless void.

mama slides a crystal tear slow down her cheek,
the smooth dew thinning to a shallow pond
that shows laughter dance on plates
holding our reflections

boys diving in leaves piled up like pyramids
the football games she spent cold in the stands
loud as the cheerleader whose arms
she said were too skinny.

junnie's baby can sit up   she says
i got a new t.v.   she says
i'd die to get you out   she says
mama, it ain't like the movies   i say

II
(visits are over)

the words fall like an ax.
mama's voice fades slow,
beating against the cave that, like a black-hole,
sucks me into a permanent night.

here, i search my mind for her words
locked in that room's mysterious haze
they are more important than breath
than the smell of women rubbed against my flesh

here, under the burlap blanket of night
i hold close the memory of her tear-stained cheeks
the sunlit smile of a woman who has taken me
in and out of this labyrinth of time.

i want to pin the smell of her hands to mind walls
curl in fetal form and fall in her arms
release the tears in my eyes as rain into her streams.
a swift image weaves

through a maze of starlight and shadow.
maybe it is steam rising slow from steel
or breath from the soil reaching through years.
in my eyes it is the strong hand of a woman

stretched across an ocean and ten lives,
soft nights lost in a lover's palms,
fingers spread wide as the sky
grasping for the crest of my brow

touching my lips, telling me
tomorrow will sing the names of the dead
move the clouds quicker than wind
dance and shake different the stale air

of so many prisons across the world
and kiss me human once again.

Part 2

The Preserving

Family and Friends

Mississippi Midwife

Myronn Hardy

After the baby was born,
she pressed her hands on
the father's head.
White cotton rag held
close to wet eyes—
his nails were skin
thick—hands black
wax. Torn sheets
rinsed in blood—he
can hear his son's soft cries.

Her hair was greased back with
pomade—glasses at the tip of her
flat nose—her heavily starched dress
smelled of bleach. Her hands were
first to touch thousands of children playing
on swings or flying airplanes. Her
goatskin bag contained alcohol, salt,
aloe vera, scissors—all giving her a
quiet strength. Eyes in a circle of lines—
Mouth—a pressed smile—
sparrows in a cold room.

The Preserving

Kevin Young

Summer meant peeling: peaches,
pears, July, all carved up. August
was a tomato dropped
in boiling water, my skin coming
right off. And peas, Lord,
after shelling all summer, if I never
saw those green fingers again
it would be too soon. We'd also
make wine, gather up those peach
scraps, put them in jars & let them
turn. Trick was enough air.

Eating something boiled each meal,
my hair in coils by June first, Mama
could barely reel me in from the red
clay long enough to wrap my hair
with string. So tight
I couldn't think. But that was far
easier to take care of, lasted all
summer like ashy knees.
One Thanksgiving, while saying grace
we heard what sounded like a gunshot
ran to the back porch to see
peach glass everywhere. Someone
didn't give the jar enough room

to breathe. Only good thing
bout them saving days was knowing

they'd be over, that by Christmas
afternoons turned to cakes: coconut
yesterday, fruitcake today, fresh
cushaw pie to start tomorrow.
On Jesus' Day we'd go house
to house tasting each family's peach
brandy. You know you could stand
only so much, a taste. Time we weaved
back, it had grown cold as war.
Huddling home, clutching each
other in our handed down hand-
me-downs, we felt we was dying
like a late fire; we prayed
those homemade spirits
would warm most way home.

Tracie Hall

oh . . .
but on a tuesday
a small day
an inconsequential day of the week
saying nothing about the hope for new beginnings
nor the weariness of endings all the same
i will think of you
just as i think of you now—
sitting grinning on the porch
rubbing the gritty edge of a shiny quarter
between your index finger and your thumb
i will think of all the cherry soda
drank in your company at your expense
the gleam in your eye anticipating
my belched appreciation
the way you never turned your head disapprovingly to the side
when in my eagerness i answered the door
dressed in grandma's slip with hair uncombed
and the way you always said yes yes yes
when i offered you what in another life
would pass for something edible
and when everyone else made it known that my childhood
                    opinions
were not welcome in a living room full of grown-up problems
you would run your hand quickly over my head as i quietly
                    exited
and before you left the house each time

you'd call me to the screen door and say in a voice that sounded
                    sincere
that you'd be looking forward to the next visit
and i remember waiting in the back of your station wagon
while bessie handed out her medi-cal stickers
in exchange for another painless week
and me interrupting you reading the paper
to ask if you could change the radio station whenever a song i didn't
                    like came on
doing it so much i could see you was getting tired
and you saying it wasn't any bother at all
and i remember you taking an extra long time to sit and talk with the
                    children
on holidays when we were consigned to the kitchen table
while the adults ate in the dining room
and even in those days when i really didn't have anything important
                    to say
(at least i don't think i did)
i remember feelin that though i was yet young i was important to you
and it made me feel good
when you asked about my school work or my thoughts about the
                    weather
and patiently listened through my rambling and exhaustive accounts
                    of fifth grade life
—and you know
it is hard to believe that this is how it ends
it is hard to think that after everything, this is the way it ends
that your kindness did not render you immortal
but on another day
a small day
a day which exists in between the days that create the years
i will remember you
i will remember youth
and i will remember always to remember

To Set upon a Shelf

Corey Olds

WHEN I WAS YOUNGER, AT LEAST TEN YEARS younger, I had a copy of George Orwell's *1984* on my dark brown, simulated wood TV stand that was my bookshelf. One day, a rather unusual thought popped into my head: *Put your books into some sort of library-like order.* I obeyed this dictum from deep down in me. I cleared the items on the TV stand and then placed my three dozen or so books in vertical columns atop of it. My TV stand had never actually served as a stand for my TV, but instead only held an assortment of paperback books, textbooks from school, loose, random papers and several three-ring binders, all of which were spread flatly across the stand's two shelves. I arranged these books vertically, first placing the taller books at the left-hand side of the stand, in a kind of descending order of height.

Most of these were books given to me by my father; books with titles like *The Destruction of Black Civilization, Stolen Legacy, Message to the Black Man in America, How to Eat to Live, Sex and Race* (volumes 1 & 2), *The Finding of the Third Eye, Dick Gregory's Cooking with Mother Nature: For Folks Who Eat, Back to Eden, The Master Within, Sugar Blues, Secrets of the Great Pyramid*, and others. The books that my father presented to me as gifts could invariably be subsumed under the categories of black history, diet/vegetarianism, astrology, occult, spiritual and mental awareness. Growing up (from about the age of eight onwards), I had a concrete and steel impression that any book that did not address the above subjects was not really worth reading; was, in fact, not really a book at all, but some ill-suited impostor. I also thought for many years that all books were therefore true, since, according to my father, all REAL books were TRUE. My father's urgent and well-oiled rhetoric, full of street aphorisms and simplistic quotations, domineered and ground me into believing that I should only read the species of books that he bought for me.

FATHER: *The truth shall set you free.* I was also cowed into accepting that all of black people's pitch-black ignorance would be magically flooded with light and their elephantine problems made to lightly disappear if only they commenced to read and study such books as my father promoted. My father's pedagogy crudely boiled down to the belief that if black people knew who they were (descendants of the former rulers of the world) and where they came from (Africa), then they could again rightfully assume their roles as the true kings and queens, true supermen and superwomen that they once were.

I myself actually believed in the power of these books. Consequently, when I became President of the Afro-Latino-American Society at Phillips Academy in my lower and upper years (tenth and eleventh grades), I knew that I could stir and resurrect the dead, dry bones of our members if I (a bearer of my father's TRUTH) could persuade them to read what I myself had been browbeaten into reading. FATHER: *Once you come into the light, you can't go back into darkness.* So, at our weekly meetings, I preached and lectured and pontificated about what they needed to know. I told them stories about black people's mind-blowing achievements, feverish and possessed myself because I thought that I was administering abracadabra, alchemical secrets that would transmute them. I can still see the blank, brown faces of Monifa Brown, Malieka Bundy, and Naomi Cromwell, sitting as close as three grapes on a vine at the weekly meetings. What I had trusted to be as a sparkling, wizard's wand turned out to be a charred and ashy twig. The faces and eyes of the trio from Double Brick dormitory, as well as the faces and eyes of everyone else, remained as dimly lit and cobwebbed as a sealed attic room with no windows. Even after leaving Andover, I would make this same observation about other, new faces many, many more times.

Because my father never bought me nor encouraged me to read books other than the ones he invariably gave me, I gradually began to regard such *other* books as taboo, much like girls or television or a pair of expensive sneakers. My father poured hot, molten dogma from his mouth whenever he lectured me about how the books that we read in school and works of fiction in general should be avoided outside of the context of school itself. While not in school or preparing school-work, I was supposed to read only the REAL and TRUE books that he gave me. I, as might be expected, developed the habit of hiding these books that I bought for myself. I did everything but stash the books I purchased at the bottom of some drawer. I worked hard to keep all such books out of my father's sight, in much the same way as I often hid the expensive sneakers that my grandmother bought me under my bed, or in the way that I turned off the television, picked up one of those REAL books, and pretended to read whenever I heard my father coming up the stairs. I lived with my maternal grandmother and not with my father, so I successfully managed to keep my father slightly in the dark about these and other things that I knew and feared he would never have tolerated if I had lived in his house.

There was one book that I, for reasons unbeknownst, did not attempt to hide. This was *1984* by George Orwell. Its grass-green bordered, paperback cover, with a white background and GEORGE ORWELL in big, block letters and 1984 in carrot-orange letters of the same stood on my TV stand/bookshelf in a neat vertical column with other of my books. As I recall, *1984* first came to my attention while I was at the Canton Country Day School, which means that I first learnt of it somewhere between fourth and seventh grades. I purchased this copy at Walden's Bookstore at the Belden Village Mall, where I had before purchased certain paperback works of fiction. I, no doubt, bought *1984* because I had heard an English teacher of mine talk about it. Or perhaps I bought it for the same reason that I, some four to six years later, went out and obtained a copy of Ralph Ellison's *Invisible Man*; that is to say out of sheer curiosity. All that I had really known about Ellison's *chef d'oeuvre* was that the upper (eleventh-grade) English classes were reading it and that the drawing on the book's cover showed the cocoa-brown, elongated face of a black man. The first and well-known fact that the book narrated the life of a black man and the second and *less* well-known fact that the upper English classes at Phillips Academy were reading it were enough to send me to the Andover Bookstore.

The appeal of the first fact is simple enough: I was a very young black man in an all-white setting that offered no meaningful affirmation of my blackness, academic or otherwise, and so I gravitated to what I took to be an accessible symbol of my identity. The appeal of the second fact seems more illogical and complex: as a lower (tenth-grader), the reading list of the more advanced upper class intrigued me. Maybe I thought that by reading a book they read I could somehow be a rung higher in the academic and social hierarchy of the school, or perhaps I found the reading for my own English class less exciting and I therefore sought a new and unfamiliar realm.

When my father discovered *1984* on my shelf, he did not react as I had imagined he would. I remember him picking the book up with some interest in his hands and eyes, as if he were trying to assay its contents by merely touching and eyeballing its cover. I did not at first believe my father's response, for it seemed too extraordinary. It made me feel the way I imagine one would feel upon witnessing a supernatural event, like a black moon in a white sky, or snow that felt hot, or raindrops that were dry. This bit of supernaturalism exhibited by my father allowed me—if only temporarily—to find favor with him. During that very brief moment in which I detected that he was not going to scold or sermon me for owning a copy of *1984*, that perhaps he would even support my interest in reading such a book, I lowered my impenetrable wall of self-defense that was made up of a contracted stomach and throat and pursed lips.

I awaited a certain approval from my father, as a child anticipates Christmas or birthday presents. However, my father scrimped and scamped, held back like a close-fisted Scrooge when it came to encouraging or even inquiring about any of my ideas and interests that he himself had not *suggested* or *impressed* upon me. Anything that I discovered for myself or that other people led me to discover he met coldly, as if he were holding ice cubes with his naked hands.

With weak-willed words that faltered and stumbled, my father told me that *1984* was *all right, a good book*, to paraphrase him. I do not know how he could make such literary judgments, for to my knowledge he had never himself read the book. Obviously, somewhere in his travels he had come upon the title and some favorable opinions of it. I suspect that my father approved *1984* because he saw it as providing yet another example of the WHITE MAN's *wickedly wise* and *scientifically devilish* means of ruling the world and, in particular, black people. FATHER: *If he* [THE WHITE MAN] *will do that to his own, what do you think he'll do to a nigga?* My father, of course, did not favor the book because of any literary merit it might possess; after all, he had not read it. Even if my father had read it, he unquestionably would have trivialized any of the book's aesthetic qualities, for my father had the crude and offensive habit of reducing all of life to a conspiracy on the part of the WHITE MAN to keep black people down. I am not here denying that such unconscionably cold and malignant designs do not sometimes or even all the time

occur. Rather, I only mean to point out that my father's relentless, paranoid preoccupation with the crimes and evils of the WHITE MAN angered
and sickened me, angered and sickened me because I felt that my father
was stifling me with his talk of plots and persecution the way he said
that the WHITE MAN had stifled him.

My father, nevertheless, could recommend the book
because he said that he himself had already discerned certain nascent
forms of totalitarian control and surveillance of the public in the United
States. I can still hear him saying, "How do we know that instead of
watching the television that the television isn't watching us?!?" At the
time, the year 1984 had not yet arrived, and so Orwell's depiction of
totalitarian regimes represented some kind of divine proof of the evil
nature of the WHITE MAN for my father.

During those four to six years that intervened before
my upper year at Andover, I read all of the first couple of pages of *1984*,
and my father never said another word for or against the book. After I
finally did read *1984*, I realized that part of the reason that I could never
get beyond the book's opening pages was because the beginning went
slow (as they say), especially in comparison with the fluent flow of the
rest of the book. *1984* was one of the many books that I read (or rather,
was *supposed* to have read) for Mr. Thorn's English class on satire. Unlike
many of the other books, I read *1984* in its entirety and found myself
fascinated and enthralled by the grimness of such Orwellian creations
as the thought police, Big Brother, wordspeak (newspeak), the ubiquitous and ever-vigilant monitor screen, and the pithy equations: "War Is
Peace," "Hate Is Love," "Truth Is Falsehood." I had never before read
any book like it and I, along with my friends, Soji and Chuck, quoted
and paraphrased its contents as a priest or devout churchgoer does holy
scripture. *1984* was wondrously thrilling and mind-stirring for me and
my mates because it told of guarded secrets, clandestine plots, and clas-
sified information and of the suspicion of betrayal and the fear of cap-
ture. For us, the book's narrative of secrecy and concealment served as
a metaphor for the discovery of self that we all were experiencing to
varying degrees. Mostly, however, we discovered our hormones and
those of the girls. We, nonetheless, also managed to find out a little about
the mind's remarkable fertility and powers of absorption at such an age.

I cannot be certain, but I rather suspect that my fa-
ther would not fully or even partially have appreciated the fact that Orwell's book opened up portals for me. Whatever Orwell himself might

have accurately depicted or predicted about the white man's nature or human nature in general grabbed me far less than the manner in which his words and images led me out onto the womb of a calm and indigo-dark sea. There, afloat on imagination's warm waters, I pondered the yeasty sensation of trying to conceal things from the omniscient Big Brother and his omnipresent electronic spies, like trysting with my lover in a small room above an old, dusty bookstore, or else I closed my eyes and tried to see the woman, with the red sash tied about her waist, nude, imagining how she would actually look and feel naked.

The portals unlocked for me were those of the imagination. Through reading such books as *1984*, I was permitted a temporary leave of absence from my immediate surroundings and allowed to enter worlds seemingly far removed from my own. Though I had to eventually return to my own world, the treasure of jeweled sights, feelings, and sounds that I brought back with me made my return all the more bearable, but all the more distressing as well. The trips I made to sea bolstered my self-confidence, because they showed me that other people felt and thought some of the same things that I had, but which I suppressed out of shame, fear, or guilt. While on these trips, I discovered the silver-tongued articulation of matters that had remained speechless in me.

In my quest I set sail for such ports as those of *The Catcher in the Rye*, *The Death of Socrates*, *1984*, *Equus*, *Manchild in the Promised Land*, *The Importance of Being Earnest*, *Animal Farm*, *Franny and Zooey*, *Paul's Case*, *The Best of Simple*, *Big Boy Leaves Home*, *Inferno*, *Flying Home*, *The Fall*, and *Invisible Man*. I do not make any pretensions to having then understood these works, for I have since come to suspect that I did not. Nevertheless, they did kindle the embers of my imagination, as well as show me parts of myself in others.

As I grew older and began to read authors other than Salinger and Orwell, Wright and Camus, I longed not just to read, but also to write. The nonfiction of James Baldwin and Ralph Ellison impregnated me with the desire to put my own words on paper. I wanted to get drunk on and seduced by *my* pen's offspring the way I had been by the offspring of others. To do this, of course, meant that my pen would have to give birth to voluptuous, bright-eyed expressions of my own thoughts and feelings. I thought that if I could achieve such a thing, then I might somehow be able to more permanently dwell in a world that could accommodate my dreams and visions of myself.

My first attempts at writing, though, sought to discharge the pain of failure, alienation, and rage that I felt while at an all-white, prestigious boarding school, which I had found to be full to the tiles with mealy-mouthed, Janus-faced students, teachers, and administrators. I came to resist, through the ink of my pen, the notion of my own inferiority or badness because I refused to conform and submit to the deluded, self-aggrandizement of that institution. I called it as I saw it, and what I saw was the oily-faced insincerity of white students and teachers, unwilling to admit their racism, and the bowed-down, shuffling servility and ass-kissing of black students, who themselves believed that white people could confer a patent of humanity upon them. At nearly every twist and turn, I resisted such deadly, dishonest notions. The price I paid for such resistance was made in disbursements of a distracting, destructive rage that seeped through the pores of my mind, and that eventually forced me to attempt a self-rescue through bleeding my pain on paper.

But whether I needed to let out anger or pain, or the fever of infatuation for pretty-faced girls, reading literature had shown me that the act of writing gave me access to quiet, *wine-dark* seas, where I could resist and rebel, laugh and cry, accept my queerness, even make myself mythic, epic, grand.

Inasmuch as my father never encouraged me nor showed any excitement about my reading these *other* types of books, I came to regard him as a grand inquisitor, seeking to stamp out my fancy to myth-make or tell stories *to* and *about* myself.

My father's books had to be read, were compulsory and sacred. All other books had the fate of ending up on what I took to be my father's *index librorum prohibitorum* (list of prohibited books). Strangely enough, the books of which my father disapproved and those like *1984* which he commended, but which he still deemed of secondary importance, proved to be the very books that taught me the most about myself, others, and the world. They did so because they were not mere silly fiction, as my father referred to them; mere fiction could never have suggested to me that I might discover something hidden or silent of my own self if I too began to write, like quirks and assumptions, attitudes, motives, and tastes.

I thus dipped my oars into darkened waters, in search of the sleeping, buried meaning of my life, during my freshman year at college. At the time, I was taking a course called "Advanced English Composition." For class, we used an anthology of essays written by celebrated American writers. James Baldwin numbered among these and so I had my first delicious taste of crisp Baldwinian prose. I found myself instantly smitten because Baldwin articulated things that I felt and intuited as a young, black man, but which I could never articulate. Upon reading "Notes of a Native Son" or "Fifth Avenue, Uptown: A Letter from Harlem," I read and reread certain passages, trying to commit whole sentences to memory, in order that I might never again be wordless when it came to voicing who and what I was and the world's reaction thereto. I thought, therefore, that I had discovered a sort of Bible for my own personal experience, albeit a profane counterpart to my father's sacred books of TRUTH.

When it came time to practice my own prose, I chose Baldwin as a model. I mimicked his style, as well as his subject matter (issues of race, being black in America, etc.). The required and optional writing that I did for class allowed me (for the first time) to make myths or stories about myself and to have someone (i.e. my professor) think that such self-illumination through writing was important. While the class lasted, I received the necessary and desired encouragement to continue writing. I had enough momentum of support to even continue writing after the course ended. What is more, I had become addicted to the high that came with arranging certain words on paper. I thought and still think that certain arrangements of words produce magic the way heat applied to sulfur produces a blue flame. The magic emitted from the friction of words and sounds *is* magic (I believe) because it contains crystal and quartz and the rarefied essence of seeing more clearly.

Although I eventually abandoned my dreams of being a writer in college because I found that good writing entailed more than arranging pretty words on paper, that it, in fact, entailed fastidious practice and patience, I have of late retrieved my once orphaned dreams of writing. I rescued my dreams from the darkness of neglect not out of sentimentality or nostalgia, but because I suffered a feverish, foggy confusion for nearly five years on account of denying that the itch in my hand and the hot swell of things in my head signaled that I must start to write again and forever.

This summer I have learned that writing still (in part) consists of pretty words on pages, but that those pretty words emerge out of a crucible of pain; pain of fear and loneliness and rejection;

pain of being excessive, wrong, foolish, inadequate; or simply pain of having been hurt one too many times by others.

Ten years or more have vanished since that day when I first placed George Orwell's *1984* on my dark brown, simulated wood TV stand that was my bookshelf. I have changed very little since that time. By this I mean that I still like those books, which my father *prohibited* because he considered them mere silly make-believe, for some of the same reasons. Holden Caulfield's New York made me loathe the rusticity of Canton, Ohio, forever, and I still envy and long to experience the adventures of both Holden and the Invisible Man. Despite the fact that guilt and doubt (etched into my conscience by my father) or my father himself often heckled me whenever I inclined to embrace and sup at the milk-swollen breasts of reading and writing stories, I never became so disheartened so as to attempt to annihilate my impulse to suckle myself through myths, whether my own or those of others. Who knows? Maybe such an impulse cannot be destroyed without totally destroying the individual in whom it resides, just as a pearl cannot be extracted from its shell without gutting the shell in which it is lodged.

But here I am now writing, weaving yet another story, as I have done all summer long. Such weaving is symbolic because it means that I have at last stripped naked and opened wide my senses to all the itching and swellings inside of me. The sourness of guilt and doubt that flowed from my father's prohibition now ceases to flow. It ceases to flow not necessarily because I am now older, a grown man, or because I presently live on the other side of the country in California. Rather, its flow has ceased because I now know that I need never again feel uneasy about who and what I am.

I think the first bookshelf that I buy will be dark brown and of wood, but hopefully of natural wood and not simulated. Upon it, I'll place one book before the rest. It will be my ten-year-old copy of *1984*.

Questions I Have Not Asked My Mother

Sabrina Shange McDaniel

I HESITATE TO ASK MY MOTHER WHY SHE SLEPT WITH Mark, my father. He was a married man with three children. She was eighteen years old. She did not just fall prey to a slick dog or a sophisticated stranger. She knew him well. As a friend of my grandmother's he had been to her house on frequent occasions. She knew he was married, knew he had children, she had even met his wife. Yet she slept with him. More than once I do not know, at least once I am proof of.

My grandmother does not provide all the answers I want, and I am reluctant to ask my mother. I asked Gma about five weeks ago, "Why did you send my mother to the United States only three months after I was born?" She replied, "You do not want to know the answer to that." I assured her I did. But she still hesitated and I did not want to ask my mother, so I coaxed, "Did you think they were in love?" "Him but not her," she alleges. She says nothing else. I do not want to question her further because I sense that my probing may uncover distortions she has protectively wrapped around her consciousness for many years. For her the questions of secret passions and requited desires that swam beneath her nose, that flowed without her detection would not be welcomed. How can I ask my grandmother about the sexual act that took place in her own house?

I really should ask my mother; these are questions only she can answer. Even if Gma knew, I doubt she would admit if Mom liked Mark for a long time. And I know she wouldn't know if he lit fires in her virginal body, ripe with adolescent maturity, smothered behind the barricade of protection Gma erected around her constantly sick body and surely prying teenage mind.

Was he the first man to mystify you? Did he mystify you, or believing in the hype your friends spoke of as he caressed and kissed you inside and out, did you start to feel loved? Or did you just have one time with this man who is my father? Mother, was I conceived in passion or in pain?

When I pushed your truth into the light as I demanded more room in your uterus, what did you feel, Mother? How much did you want me, a little, a lot, or none at all? When did that change, the night I fell out of the bed because you forgot a two-month-old baby can roll even if it can't crawl, or was it six years later when you called Gma from New York and said you wanted me to come visit? Had you stayed away from me because I reminded you of him and his broken promises or dreams? Or did I remind you of what could have been if Gma hadn't stepped in? Did you stay away from me, or was Gma shielding me from the child she was angry and disappointed with? Only you know, Mother, if I was Gma's penance or yours. But twenty-four years later I am still afraid to ask.

Yearning

Natasha Tarpley

AFTER SEVERAL TRIPS AROUND THIS HUGE CEME-
tery, my mom and I have finally found the quaint lane that leads to my
father's grave. We don't often visit this place. Maybe this sounds callous.
But for us, as is the case in many African traditions of remembering
those who have gone on, the memory doesn't stop (or start) with a cold
marble stone on a grassy plot of land. Thoughts of Daddy are with us
every day, are a constant presence in both our waking and dreaming
hours.

However, along with these memories, we carry an
aching space, a yearning inside of us, reminding us of his absence; driving us to seek some small but tangible comfort in running our fingers
over the letters of his name, carved out of stone; sitting beside the earth
where the physical evidence of his being rests.

Mom and I don't speak as we drive down the narrow
road lined with stately mausoleums, fresh-cut grass and flowers. It is
just the two of us today. My younger sisters and brother had made themselves scarce, the thought of visiting the cemetery just too heavy for such
a bright and sunny day. I missed their voices, the chatter that would
have at least covered up the silence that now filled our car.

Things were different, we could feel it. We were
coming back to this place after two years with new lives, new ideas, new
dreams. But for all that had changed, we still felt the same pain, the
same loss. Grief surfaces and submerges in waves, sometimes a faint
ripple, other times a tidal wave crashing against the walls of your in-
sides, but constant. It never completely disappears.

I could feel a tidal wave coming on as we pulled up
and got out next to the tree that shades my father's grave. Warm tears

swelled in my eyes, and I pinched myself to keep them from falling. After a few perfunctory remarks on how well the caretakers were keeping up the land, and after we had laid out our offering of brightly colored flowers, Mom and I sat beneath the tree, drifting into our own thoughts and memories.

I will always remember pacing the green carpet on Nana's living room floor waiting to find out whether my father would live or die; whether he would come back to my arms or fly away to a place where I could no longer reach him, touch him, talk to him; laugh again at the stories he told, or at those funny dances he did, popping his fingers to Al Green or Marvin Gaye.

I will remember the night before he died, how he listened at the other end of the phone from his hospital bed while I talked incessantly about Michael Jackson and Barbie dolls. Then Mama, who never left his side, getting on the line mumbling about medicine and doctors. I reluctantly gave my father over to the people I hoped would make him well. She said, "Say goodbye to your father," and I did. I don't know if either of us knew it then, but it would be the last time I spoke to him.

The next morning there was trouble. Nana spoke in whispers to Mama who was still at the hospital. I demanded to know what was going on, but Nana just told me to be still. And as I wore out that green rug, walking back and forth past the telephone, I realized that I had not told Daddy that I loved him. But it was too late. The phone rang. He was gone. I thought about angels; about the story I'd once heard that whenever a bell or a phone rings an angel gets his wings. Maybe this was a sign that my father was on his way to a new life, but for me it signalled the end of the only life I had ever known.

My father's death, for me at age twelve, was a wave I couldn't swim through; one that went over my head and choked me. For two days after that I was bedridden. I would not eat. I was given to nightmares and spells of delirium. Mama was the anchor in this tumultuous sea, a steady place for me and my two sisters and brother to hold onto, take refuge. But where was her steady place? The foundation she'd thought would be lasting had crumbled. We were all frail then, in our own way. We learned the hard lesson that life has no guarantees, no debt owed to anyone.

At age twenty-two, I have to ask, why it is that some people seem to pay a higher price than others? We often talk about the effects of the lack of male figures on the lives of young Black men. But what about us, the ones who are left behind? The aunts and mothers and grandmothers whose husbands are gone, through death or other means; the daughters, who grow up without the benefit of a father's wisdom or support.

This day, as I sit before Daddy's grave, I am grieving for more than the loss of my father, I am also grieving for what I have not found: a strong and lasting relationship with a man, someone with whom I can share my whole self. I am being selfish, I know. But for me, these aspects of my life are intricately connected. The men in our family are disappearing. With each holiday gathering the number of men present gets smaller. Both of my grandfathers have passed. Uncles and boyfriends and cousins are scattered branches on this tree of women.

I have learned from the women in my house that life does not revolve around a man. All of us have done fine, have played the hand we were dealt and made successful lives for ourselves. But, as my mother says, you never get away from the loneliness. It's as if you're walking around with a piece missing. Even if it's only a small piece, there's still an empty space inside and you can feel it.

At times I surrender to this ache of loneliness and doubt. I scrutinize myself, ask the inevitable question: Is there something wrong with me? These are the moments I need my father most. Bebe Moore Campbell wrote in *Sweet Summer*, "I tried, but I couldn't crowd [in] . . . enough of my father to dilute completely the Wonder Woman potency of my female world. I was a girl and my mother and Nana figured that their love . . . [was] enough." My mother will always be my anchor, but I need my father to be the deep voice at the other end of the phone, telling me that I'm beautiful; whose arms are a place where faith and hope are restored, when I feel like closing myself up tight as a fist, shutting down, giving up.

Many times, I have been furious, have wanted to strike out against this emptiness, against my father, with every ounce of the pain I felt was inflicted upon me in his absence. I try to recall his face or his voice and I can't quite fix them in my mind. I am still the twelve-year-old girl looking towards the sky, hoping for a sign from Daddy. I chase after memories of him like wish seeds, the soft spindly bits of white fluff riding the summer air, which never did fall into my hands, only kept me running after hope. There is a yearning growing inside me; questions unravelling like weak cloth, answers scarce as memory.

I turn to look at my mother and she looks back at me. She knows my thoughts well, because they are very similar to her own. She has been thinking about the dreams I sometimes hear her dreaming, when she calls out my father's name in the night. She has been thinking about the years she's spent by herself, about her own aching empty spaces.

I let my hands fall helpless from my lap to the ground, wishing I could shape this earth into something that would soothe our hurting places. My mother takes my hands into her own. Her eyes tell me, as she, my aunts, and grandmothers have so often told me before, "Be patient. You're young yet." This I know. But with youth comes impatience and fear. What if I am alone forever? What if every time I open myself, my trust is shattered, my love taken for granted? For now though, Mama's touch calms these waves of anxiety raging inside me.

We return to our car, another visit ended. Again, silence surrounds us. But this time it is a comfortable silence, of gathering together again all of our pieces into a workable (and working) whole. I lean back into my seat, giving thanks for being blessed with a family whose love is a bridge across these rough waters; especially for the women and the places of sustenance and support we've created for one another. Although they cannot replace Daddy, or fill the gaps made by the other men who are too soon gone from our lives.

The women have been rocks, mountains even, on which our family could lean and depend. But we are not made of stone; we break, falter, feel lonely. There is a space in our hearts carved out for all the baritones, as Campbell writes, whose deep notes still flow through us, whose song we remember every day. In their memory and in hope, we keep holding on.

the trio

Tracie Hall

summertime heat sticks like oil
people outside screamin at each other just for livin
its the kinda day in Watts make you wanna do somethin.
theo comes by, she a girl wid a boy's name
she older than me—high school
like a big sister, but she my second cousin
(grandmother's youngest brother's daughter)
asks bessie if she can take me to uncle little twin's house
make me tuna and pickle sandwiches
way i like 'em
she smile at me, my nose pressed to the screen door
she don't come in cuz she know bessie ain't the warm type
like to stare at people rather than talk to 'em
bessie look down at me
my eyes wide wid "can i?"
tells theo she gotta have me back at 3
so i can help her snap the peas she picked from her garden
i run to find my sandals
bessie gives me a quarter and a dime
tells me to behave
and watches me and theo
descend the high porch
i look back at her when i close the gate
she shakin her head like she know somethin

theo holds my hand
as we walk the block

i see the kids lookin, specially the older boys
i feel good cuz theo pretty
her hair short and curled tight
wearin a close fittin cotton t-shirt
and shorts to match
she walk fast wid her long brown legs
i do doubletime to keep up
we get to the store near her house and go in
theo buys the mayonnaise for the tuna salad
i buy a 50/50 ice cream bar like always
orange on the outside, creamy vanilla ice milk inside
we wait by the counter til he comes:
the boy in the jacket
he theo's boyfriend but she say don't tell nobody
his name is todd, or chris, or somethin else i can never remember
(i never did like short names, they don't stay in your mind good)
he wearin a jacket and its summertime
but he not even sweatin
he calls me 'lil bit' and 'short stack' and other stuff he thinks
                    is cute
and reaches out for theo,
we walk out into the street like that
holdin hands
theo in the middle

mike, or bob, or whatever his name is
whispers somethin low to her
and after while we change directions
(normally we go to the park where i swing and tease the other kids
                    wid my ice cream
and theo and the boy in the jacket sit on the benches and get real
                    close)
after we been walkin for 5 minutes i ask theo where we goin
she don't answer
but when we come to one of those underground tunnels
that the city workers use when they tryin get the streetlights to work
                    right
we walk right down the stairs
i tell theo that we ain't supposed to be down there

she just giggles and tells me to stay by the entrance and finish my
                    50/50 bar
she say that if i don't bother her and the boy, she gone buy me
                    another one when we leave
it sounds like a deal to me and i go sit on the stairs where the
                    sunlight is
theo and the boy move further into the shadows until i can't even see
                    them no more

i pass time tryin to convince a ladybug clinging to blade of yellow
                    grass near the stairs
to climb onto my sticky palm
i can't hear theo and the boy talkin no more
but she makin other sounds like she cryin or somethin
i get real scared, so scared feel like i'm gonna pee
what if the boy in the jacket beatin on her and hurtin her
like little darren's daddy hurts his mama sometime
so bad, you can still see the prints of his knuckles for days after
i yell out theo's name
but she don't say nuthin
i can hear her moanin gettin louder
she must be gettin beat real bad
i stand up on the steps and yell out theo's name again
she whispers somethin i can't hear good
then after a few minutes she comes out from the darkness

she still adjustin her clothes when she makes it to where i am
her face looks different and it shinin like she been doin some kinda
                    hard work
her neatly pressed hair has started to turn back round the edges
she smiles at me and asks if i'm hungry
i tell her i want to go home
"but what about the ice cream?" she asks, surprised
i say maybe next time
the boy in the jacket finally emerges from the shadows
he ain't wearin the jacket now
and as he fastens the belt on his trousers he looks up at me
                    and grins
"what was you hollerin bout, lil bit?"

"i don't want you hurtin my cousin," i answer back
"i wasn't hurtin you, now wuz i, theo?" he asks, smiling at her
                    smugly
she stares him straight in the eye and then turns to me
"he wuzn't hurtin me"
i don't like their tone or the way they lookin at each other

"i'm goin home" i say, and start to walk up the stairs
the full brightness of the sun appears fluorescent making me squint
"you can't walk home by yourself" theo says as she catches up to me
pulling one of my flying braids
"well then you better come with me"
"you don't want no tuna?"
"no"
"what about make-up?" theo says, pulling her trump card
"i wuz gonna make yo face up today. i got blue eyeshadow and
                    everything"
the eyeshadow does sound temptin
"no i wanna go home"
"you mad?" theo asks suddenly
i don't respond
"you still my play lil sister?" she puts her long thin arm around my
                    shoulders
"i don't like that boy" i say finally, "he funny"
"you jus don't know him good. he real nice," with that she smiles
a smile that make me feel bad inside
i don't wanna share theo wid nobody
i wanna have her all to myself like i did before what's his name came
                    'round

it's the last block
i free myself from theo's embrace
and run as hard as i can towards bessie's
"what you runnin for?" theo yells
even her long legs can't keep up wid my angry trot
i close the heavy iron gate in front of her just as she reaches the yard
i wait for a minute
hopin she'll say she's sorry and that she'll make up my face tomorrow
and that we don't have to meet that boy again

instead, she reaches over the gate and digs her long fingernails into
                                    my arm
turning the skin
"don't you tell nobody!" she sneers, her eyes narrow
i slap at her hand until she removes it
and examine the spot, now a deep and wounded burgundy
tears well inside my eyes but i dare them to fall
"did you hear me?" she asks
i study her thin face wondering what beauty i ever saw there
"give me the money for the ice cream," i mumble
theo looks at me quizzically and then feels inside the pocket of her
                                    shorts
she hands me two quarters
i reach for them and then study her face now contorted with urgency
"you still my lil sister?" she asks softly
this time it's more of a statement than a question
i clutch the quarters tightly in my palm
and nod my head faintly,
up and down

Letters to My Sister

Deborah Turner

Ann Arbor, MI

10 April 1993

Dear Jessica,

I'm sitting on my sky-blue blanket. I raised my bed to the level of my window so I can look outside even when I'm lying down. I stripped the wood paneling off my walls which I've painted opaque white to maximize the light that's reflected into my space. People warned me about Michigan winters, especially for us California transplants, so I've created a peaceful shelter here in my room. I'm sending you some of that peace now.

I've got some final term projects that are due soon. I don't know if you understand this. It just means that I don't have time to write much. It doesn't mean I don't care about you or what you're going through. Here are some thoughts that keep passing through my head in no particular order:

—I know it's hard for you to face your daily medication when it's been prescribed to you by the same system that drove you to your nervous breakdown.

—I'm very grateful to you for having cared for me through years of abuse & incest when we were young, then later in high school & college . . . and know that you have to take care of yourself now,

—I love and miss you a great deal, but know that all my loving & missing can't provide the professional help you need right now.

I can't be your doctor, but I'll always be your sister. Hang in there, Jes, nobobdy told us the road would be easy.

Love & big hug,

—Deb.

Hi Jessica,

I spoke with a dean outside of my department today. I told him about that incident with my professor. I think I told you about it. I was answering a question he had put to the class when he interrupted me. Attempting to test my newly acquired middle-class and professional skills, I continued, "As I was saying . . . ," then, "If you would just let me finish." But the man was determined not to let me finish.

People keep telling me that I should forget the whole incident. The idea is foreign to me. Generations of people not forgetting got me here. Who am I to stop such a necessary chain of events to reduce inequality? Even if it means making an "inconvenient" appointment with a dean during the busiest month of the term.

Academicians pay such lip service to multiculturalism. I should have showed my professor some of *my* culture from the get go, "Look man, shut da fuck up & let me finish!"

How are you getting along with Dr. Sully? What are sessions with her like? Is there anyone else in the ward you can talk to? Any people of color? Any Black folk? College grads? I know it's hard, but you need to talk to your doctor. Though it's hard to listen, I do hear you. And, I believe that you think people are watching you. But Jes, Dr. Sully's the one who's trained in providing the type of help you need at this moment in your life. She can help you learn to deal with the mania and the depression, but you've got to take the first step and trust again. Tell her what's going through your mind if and when you can. And, I know you can.

It's so different to work within a system (me with a dean & you, a psychiatrist) especially when such systems ignored us for umpteen years. I'll always wonder why our teachers, coaches, and church members ignored the scars and even the tears on some days. But those days are over, Jes. Yes, you're in a foreign place right now, but you're safe there. Our stepbrothers won't enter your room at night, our stepmother won't yell at you for next to nothing all day. Your health means a lot to me even if it doesn't to you right now. You're not another patient in the system, you're a woman in my heart.

Off to study . . .

Love,

—Deb.

Ann Arbor, MI
21 April 1993

Hi Jes,

Did you get the care package I sent? Hope I'm not ruining the surprise. I'm sorry if I upset you by writing to your doctor. I don't want to make your doctor into a family therapist either, but I didn't want to send anything that wasn't allowed in the ward. I hope you like the dried apples. I figured they'd be a healthy snack and I know you're worried about gaining back all the weight you lost in the past few months. It took a while to find that book on indoor exercises. I hope you find it useful.

Mom told me you can't go outside. She said you can't even open any windows there. It's hard to think of you not getting any fresh air. They must think that by giving your body less room to wander, your mind will conform to their limits. Something tells me that you are only briefly aware of the padded cells and the straitjackets . . . of the drugs and their side effects . . . and even, of me. I think of you in your own reality, a battleground perhaps. I see you fighting to be an assertive, intelligent, dark-skinned Black woman in a society that praises quiet, white beauty. You're fighting past battles on a present-day battleground. And, I'm here waiting for you, or at least your spirit, to arise from the wreckage. I know you'll always be essentially the one I grew up with, but I don't want you to change as we grow older, not too drastically anyway. Maybe I'm just being selfish. It's not like I don't have a life of my own with the career I'm building.

Well, I just finished one of my research projects. It was supposed to be a group project. My "partner" is a single, Black woman with a teenage son. Knowing that little bit about her makes it hard to call her irresponsible, even though she didn't contribute to the project all term. I'm worried about my grade in the class because of her "irresponsibility." I learned a lot about research methods. I have dreams of unobtrusively measuring the sociological effects of the information glut that's going on today. People claim it's stressful to have so much info coming at us not just from libraries like in times past, but from newspapers and TVs and radios, advertising, faxes, portable phones, answering machines, computers and the Internet and practically everywhere. I conjure up visions of scientifically measuring the increased stress our generation deals with just to stay informed. But, my grades don't show how the class has inspired me. It's too bad such inspiration can't somehow be factored into our grades. I've been so out of it that dreaming and envisioning anything except the end of the term is a big effort. I only worry about grades because they affect how departmental money is dealt—you know how it is.

Hang in there, Jes, you've been sounding a deep blue lately. Remember you're not a failure. I'm a master's degree candidate at University of Michigan and a product of your efforts. Quit using society's definitions to define your beautiful self. They weren't written with us in mind. Love you much.

Love,
—Deb.

Washington, DC
25 April 1993

Hey Jes!

I'm at the March!* It's so amazing to see the minority in the majority. All these homo couples "Out & About" (I saw that on a t-shirt). I'll probably fail all my finals, but hey, I was counted! I'm wearing that funky pink and black jumper you got in Seattle. I'll probably be wearing your hand-me-downs till I'm eighty. It makes me feel like a part of you is here.

My decision to caravan out here was pretty last-minute. I was lucky to get my shift covered at the reference desk on the weekend before final exams. Do what you gotta, right? It's so absurd! I have access to so much information in one of the largest library systems in the nation, yet I'm not able to help you. I've settled for low-paying student jobs to gain experience in librarianship when I could be making more money somewhere else—one way that I actually could help. Here, I feel like I'm with other people who've been marginalized and are demanding to *be* in the minds of our national leaders. It feels more tangible than studying for another exam for another degree.

The people here are beyond beautiful. All colors, all ages, all shapes and sizes . . . the full range of political activists, conservatives, liberals, radicals all checking each other out. It's empowering . . . inner beauty radiates when we speak out for ourselves en masse. I can't help but compare this to what the '60s March for Civil Rights must have been like.

Even though being out here won't make our lives any easier, I couldn't take all my anger, pain, confusion, and mixed blessings

* *The 1993 March on Washington for Gay, Lesbian, and Bisexual Rights*

lying down anymore. It's true I have made it all the way to grad school and have little to complain about compared to you. But, inside I'm still battling the same abusive patterns that afflict you. Earning a master's degree doesn't make me *feel* like I'm doing enough. I don't want super-human powers to heal, I just want to break the cycles of abuse . . . I want to make the pain go away.

I love you more than you know right now. Take your time & heal up right, Jes. The world and all the hard questions will still be here to explore when you get out. Love you loads, I'll let you know how the term ends if I ever get my butt back to Michigan.

Love,
—Deb.

Ann Arbor, MI
20 May 1993

Hi Jes,

It's summer and I'm still waiting to feel a sense of ac-complishment. I managed to get through the term without any incom-pletes—thank god. My grades reflect my turmoil, but I've got too much hanging over my head to let the term drag on any longer. As a matter of fact, I'm on academic probation. What do ya know? The powers-that-be finally did notice me.

Looking back, I see that my first year in grad school was difficult, especially adjusting to the Midwest. At times, I wished I had stayed in-state, but I was sure that the economy would have affected my education. Still it's hard to be away from you, John, and Mom. I'm away from you right now and too tired and broke to really keep in touch the way I'd like to. Some day I'd like to get y'all a computer and hook ya to electronic mail. I'm not sure that I'll even have an e-mail account after I leave academia, but it's so convenient and it's nice to dream.

To be here at UM, I examine and try to understand my world every day. I constantly try to figure out why being here doesn't feel right. Then, I rely on my usual intellectual rebuttal to re-mind me that I, too, belong here, no matter how different & out of place I feel. I keep this debate going inside my head. It helps me to always be aware of all the different dynamics going on around me. It helps to keep my self-esteem from going away completely. After Berkeley, I shouldn't be surprised at how the details of my efforts mean nothing in the wake of my GPA. It's all about them grades—what you produce, what you publish. I'm sure I can get off probation. I'm just not sure if I'll adhere to the mindframe to want to.

Mom said you're being transferred out of the hospital soon. Are you ready? She says you'll be moved to a residential care facility. You'll even have some freedom to go in and out each day depending on your condition. I haven't heard from you, but assume your pending transfer is good news. Send me your new address when you get it.

Well, it sounds like your body's getting used to the medications and you're dealing with the side effects alright. Mom said you complained about sleeping a lot, moving slowly, and eating too much. These are all side effects too, Jes. It doesn't sound like you're overeating. You described what sounded like well-balanced meals to me. Forget the dieting for now, Jes. Your body needs nutrients and rest while you're healing and recovering. I'm sure you'll look great when I see you.

Yep, I'm coming home. Finally! I figured out a vacation time that agrees with both of my job schedules. So, I'll be there sometime next month. I'll call you as soon as I get some dates set.

Just keep taking your meds and getting rest.

Love,
—Deb.

For My Sister

Lichelli Lazar-Lea

I DROVE MY JEEP SIXTY MILES AN HOUR ALONG THE winding Vallejo street, running two stop signs. My foot ground the accelerator into the carpet, third gear roared past its maximum speed. A million thoughts raced through my mind, competing with my urgent need to cry, something I had not allowed myself to do for some time.

I replayed the events of the evening at my parents' house: how I sat down to talk with my younger sister to discuss a letter she had written to me, a last-ditch attempt to recapture our relationship before we went irreconcilably our separate ways. It was my turn to talk and air my views, but as always my point of view went hurtling past her, crashing into the wall behind. Likewise hers went skimming past my ears and out of the window. Tempers flared; hurtful things were said; I left.

As I drove in my hysteria, thoughts of suicide raced through my mind. Sweet revenge, a way to make her hurt as much as I was hurting at that moment. However, as I thought about why my death would cause her so much pain, I knew it was because she loved me so much, a love so strong, no one but my mother could touch it.

I remembered our childhood and the bond we had, two "high yellow" black children together in England's harsh racist world. I remembered watching her ant-like body competing in gymnastics at seven years of age. Defending her at high school when she was challenged to a gymnastics duel by her local competition, the other black child in town—I would not let my sister risk injury to show up a stupid schoolgirl. My sister was going all the way to the top, and now, at twenty years of age, she was well on her way, having outgrown gymnastics and moved into track and field. It was ironic that a back injury held her career in jeopardy.

I thought back to the time she and I were boxing on the living-room floor at nine and eleven years of age. Our mother's second mistake en route to my stepfather came home, pulled me off her and slapped my face. I remembered lashing out at him hysterically, missing him with every stroke. Then my little sister came to my rescue by jumping on his back and biting his neck, yelling, "You hurt my sister! You hurt my sister!" The fact I had been choking her in the first place meant nothing. We were sisters, strong, black, proud, and he was the outsider. The poor man did not stand a chance against us.

Then what happened? At what point did we lose this fighting force? As I tore down the street I grew angry. Why should it be over? How could I be so foolish as to let an argument stand in the way of perhaps the only true friend I would ever have, my sister. So I put my foot on the brakes and turned the car around.

Back at my parents' house we sat down at the dining table. My mother and stepfather acted as mediators as we both took it in turn to express our feelings. Knights of the oval table, my sister and I sat opposite each other, like veterans nursing wounds from an unknown attacker.

My sister went first. As she recounted incidents in our childhood that had caused her pain, I marvelled at what an eloquent speaker she had become. As a child she had been extremely introverted and had had a great deal of difficulty expressing herself orally. In verbal arguments she would sometimes resort to hitting me with furniture, such as chairs, in her frustration at not being able to speak. As I was to realize later, my white extended family bought the racist stereotype that blacks are less intelligent than whites, and thus they took it for granted that my sister was slow to learn. She was treated differently as a result, by the adults as well as the children. Our mother, fully aware of this dynamic, and intent on countering any insinuation that my sister was less intelligent, became overprotective of my sister while trying to bolster her self-esteem. She showed my sister what I as a child interpreted as favoritism, thus fostering in me a strong resentment of both my mother and my sister collectively. When I was with either of them alone, we got on well. However when all three of us were together, a kind of friction grew that none of us could understand. As my sister grew older, her choice of activities—gymnastics, then track—needed the kind of attention from my mother that my art and writing did not, and to me as a child that clearly meant my mother loved my sister more than she did me.

My sister talked for a while about different incidents she remembered as being painful. Yet she kept being drawn back to the times we found ourselves playing with our cousins. As she remembered it, whenever the six of us got together, she was always excluded and "picked on." She remembered me being the ringleader in these games, and this hurt her even more, as she had looked up to me and loved me so much.

When it was my turn, I too went back to the times we were together with the cousins at our grandmother's house, usually on the holidays. There, in her four-hundred-year-old house deep in the English countryside, we would make elaborate sets in the dining room, where we would perform for the adults. A happy place for me, my grandmother's house represented a sanctuary for me as a child, a safe place away from the racism I was forced to live with every day. There I was in my element. There people saw me as talented. There people laughed with me, not at me, and it was they who cried with my drama, not me from their persecution. At my grandmother's house I, Lichelli, was in charge.

As I probed deeper into my memory I took off my rose-colored spectacles and saw myself clearly for the first time. I saw a black child whose need to belong to the group among whom she found herself most of the time—her white extended family—had motivated her to use her great presence and dominating personality to render her ethnicity invisible, to divorce herself from her African ethnic group of origin. I saw a child admired by her cousins, who would never have dreamed of categorizing her with the rest of the black population, for that would have meant that all the familiar stereotypes which validated their privileged lifestyles were not true. I saw a child performing for a white audience, desperate for its approval as if her success in entertaining them would distract them from her blackness. Thus I as a child practiced the truly British pastime of dividing and ruling; a pastime practiced expertly in the United States today. I separated myself from my sister, and dominated her, to make sure I stayed on top, at least within the family.

I looked back at the games I played with my cousins. My cousins looked like mischievous devils sitting on my shoulders. It was as if they had whispered into my ears, "You're the one we like, we don't need her, she's stupid." I looked to where they might have pointed and saw my sister sitting alone in the corner, tears streaming down her face, an invisible force preventing her from speaking.

Then it suddenly occurred to me what had been happening at these gatherings. I was being used. Just as I performed for the family as a whole, I was also performing for the cousins. Themselves unaware, my white cousins found great joy in seeing two black children turn on each other. They instigated our arguments, driven by that powerful ideology known as racism that had been handed down to them by their white society that claimed not to be racist. Furthermore, the only reason they gravitated towards me was because I was an extremely dynamic character, and thus was entertaining. Had my sister been born with a loud mouth, then she would have been the popular one.

Similarly, at our high school in England, my sister's aforementioned rival at gymnastics, a black girl, was encouraged by her white friends to compete against my sister. She knew full well that she could risk injury by doing so, but her need for approval was so great she did not care. She needed that power over my sister just as I did, in a society that degraded her and made her feel her worth was dependent upon the approval of white people.

I cursed the fact that, despite my mother's struggle to give us a black consciousness, I had not been able to engage in higher order thinking when I was nine, and I sat back in my chair feeling guilty and hurt. I had been used, and deep down I had grown up knowing this. It was evident in my need to belittle people. Quick wit and sarcasm are separated by a fine line, and I had frequently crossed it. I had validated my "sense of humor" by saying that it was "very English." Sarcasm *is* very English, but it is also one of the more destructive ways in which people have been socially controlled within the English culture. Sarcasm has a way of making you question your own worth, of destroying your self-esteem, thus reducing you to a pathetic pawn quite easily manipulated by those in power. Here in the United States of America, word games have had a similar, if not more lethal, effect: the self-hatred of black people has been taken to heightened forms as we "play the dozens" and "cap" on each other. Here we rip each other to shreds, and then laugh it off without even questioning why we need to degrade each other.

The fact of the matter was that I was not to blame for my actions as a child. I was not simply "mean" to my sister because I was born that way. We are all born with certain character traits and potential abilities; in my case aggression and creativity predominated. Racism makes us use our gifts, with no regard for our people, so that we can be accepted by the whites who have taught us that we are inferior. I, as a child, used my abilities to gain popularity with my white cousins, and to therefore divorce myself from my sister who represented that from which I sought to remove myself: the unacceptable, the dreaded Black Other.

Racism, as we all know, is the powerful force that is dividing the black community today, visible in many different forms. Thus we see light complexioned people against dark, and dark against light, in reaction. We see rich black people turn their backs on their poor brothers and sisters, partly out of fear of losing what they have, but also out of hatred for their people, and themselves. Racist ideology, in the form of images of worthless black peoples, affects us all. Meanwhile the white ruling class stands by, is entertained, and literally profits from our ignorance. All across the globe we as black people are being used by racism. This unfortunately does not end by our looking into ourselves and our childhood, as we still have to live in a system that is built on exploiting all of its people in racist, sexist, and classist ways.

I was not to blame for my actions as a child, but I was and am today responsible for them. If we do not take responsibility for our actions we cannot possibly change the direction of our future dealings with people. Likewise my cousins will remain racists if they are not made aware of the reasons they behaved as they did to my sister and me. Without being aware of why we behave as we do, we are not able to make conscious choices about our lives and the people we love. Now, as young adults, my sister and I are able to embark on a true friendship; as both of us have our eyes open to the world around us, aware of how it affects us individually, we are able now to truly see each other.

To my sister, Tanya Lazar-Lea, may we struggle on forever.

the wind still breezes your name

minkah makalani

for Oscar Bills, Jr., 1969–1991

I

as kids me and Junnie pissed murals upside buildings
and marveled at how fast the summer sun
dried our gold paint as colorless as the grey walls.
little girls skipped over ropes
spinning faster than tornadoes
as their feet barely touched bottom
before they'd lift 'em in a split second arc
kicking dirt on their sockless ankles.
babies paraded half nude
in side street diaper shows
as the older boys got pick-up games
going; the goal was netless,
but they made they own *swiisssh*
sounds and pretended the breeze
was fans screaming their names.

II

at night dirt would settle back
on the double-dutch spot
where those young smiles
and rhythmic tennessee chants
rose into the dust-filled air,
flies buzzed around the smell

of our forgotten murals
and we swore the wind
was still yelling Willie's name
for that j he got off in Big D's face

    swiisssh
we sounded, flicking our wrists
fading back on our beds
like paratroopers falling out planes.

    swiisssh
the sound had a milk chocolate taste,
and we could feel the breeze cheering us on
as we called out
                skunks niggaaaaazzzzzzz!

we dreamed about
kicking our legs through the air
doing 360 reverse jams,
and how we'd jog backward down court
smacking palms, mumbling
we jist warmin up!
Junnie said
           we'll call ourselves
           the fab-u-luss five
           & own the final four!
we drowned in wet dreams
of girls jockin us
after showin magic
we could pull them passes
out our mama's panties;
we was gon be the shit!

and the only thing that could stop us
was physics!

III

words?
our fab-u-luss five died

before we bounced
our first ball outta high school.
but i still say
swiisssh
on the netless goal
bent up like a cowboy hat,
and the breeze still yells our names.

IV

now i'm a poet
slicing air with words.
but all we wanted to be
was poets and painters.
we was gonna metaphor
a darryl dawkins shatter slam
through the heart of traditional games
and paint brush a dr. j. jordan gravity breaker
over men glued to parquet floors.

but now i'm a poet
slicing air with words
painting lives college and cosby
said to forget.
but what would you be
had you weaved through that
asteroid belt of 9mm slugs?

would you be that ghetto bastard
shredding the college educated cape
i once hid under?
the flyboy in the buttermilk
saying chinga su madre to the world
and writing in your own groove?
would you have been the fighters calling in sick
and pulling dollars outta timeclock pockets?
or the rebellers who rub blistered kisses
on oiled necks at night
and roll pelvics in the jazz cinders

of another blunted rhythm
swirling around silk hoodies?
would your stomach coil in knots
as Robin Harris tongued poverty into Bebe's kids?

me thinks you wouldda played pick-up
by dim-flickers of broken street lights,
caught sparkles off a rusty netless rim,
shook 20 shadows
& with night pasted to your face
pulled up
faded back
flicked wrist   &

    swiisssh

listen,
i can still hear the wind
breeze your name.

Part **3**

In Love and Trouble

we sit on the stairs sometimes

Yona C. Harvey

we sit on the stairs sometimes
with our plum-painted lips
with our heads brightly wrapped
and our laughter emerging like womanhood
despite our empty pockets

we sit on the stairs sometimes
and the heat numbs our skin
and we wipe our brows
and shake our heads at the men
who walk by and wink at us

we sit on the stairs sometimes
and drink water from jars
and get up and dance
with the setting sun as our spotlight
and the radio playing our song

we sit on the stairs sometimes
and Emma throws her hands up in disgust
at another twisted newspaper story
and i smile because
she's funny when she's mad

we sit on the stairs sometimes
and i'm convinced there's a girl in Africa
with a bracelet on her ankle
and a fire in her heart
who looks just like Emma

we sit on the stairs sometimes
and the moon befriends the sky
the stars stand at attention
and Emma and i are at ease

we sit on the stairs sometimes
and trade dreams and secrets
and listen to folks at their windows
and watch the last of the shadows walk by

when we've had all that we can take
when we need to speak our minds
to keep from giving in and up
we sit on the stairs sometimes

Obsessive Love

Tracy E. Hopkins

I REALIZED THAT I HAD A PROBLEM ABOUT FOUR years ago. It was my best friend's eighteenth birthday party, which was thrown at her uncle's scenic suburban home. There, on a picture perfect day, I sat surrounded by friends, barbecue, and a swimming pool, with a detached expression on my face. Although I wore sunglasses, it was obvious that I was unhappy. The weird thing is that I wanted to be unhappy. I meant for my building anger to be visible, in hopes that the target of my look of death would notice. But he didn't notice, or he simply didn't care. In a moment of frenzy I had even called my mother and asked her to come and rescue me. "I have to leave because he's here. . . . And he's ignoring me," I told her.

You see what had once disguised itself as harmless infatuation unmasked itself on that day. I was obsessed with pursuing a relationship with Marcus, a young man who could care less about me; a young man who was having a good time at my best friend's birthday party despite the cloud that hung over my head because of him. My friend had later asked what was wrong, and when I told her she bluntly but compassionately said, "Oh forget him. I don't know why you go through changes over that loser." But if only it were that cut and dried I would have let him go, and I would not have continued to become involved in dead-end relationships.

Over the course of our torrid relationship, Marcus had mainly called when he wanted sex or money (which I never had to give), or to brag about how many other women were in love with him. Once, he even told me to jump out of a window if I was so depressed all the time, but yet and still I literally clung to him. My eyes widened when he walked into a room. I was happy if he even looked my way, and was thrilled one night at a party when he took the time to blow marijuana smoke in my face. "I know you really love me, but you just don't know how to show it," I told him frequently. For the most part, it wasn't even the sex that I craved, because that only left me with a temporary sense of satisfaction. It was the attention I craved, and in my best "Fatal Attraction" imitation I remember once telling Marcus, "I'm not going to be ignored."

But after two years, when the closest Marcus had come to the confession that I sought was, "Yeah, I love your dumb ass," I gradually lost interest in our sadistic love affair. And while I would like to say that I emerged from that relationship with a new attitude, I can't lie. Instead of taking a much needed break from men for self-evaluation, after Marcus I delved heart-first into a number of unfulfilling relationships with guys who either had girlfriends or were content to play the field.

Despite the torment I had put myself through in the past; the uncertainty of not knowing where "my man" was, what he was doing, and with whom; and the disappointment I felt when his excuses didn't ring true (but I bought them anyway), I was determined to pursue men who could offer me nothing but, as my girlfriend would say, hard times and bubblegum. And there were many times when I could have used a stick of Juicy Fruit. While I'd like to believe that these guys were just idiots, I can't avoid shouldering some responsibility for staying in relationships long after I knew they were destined to fail. I tend to get so caught up in the notion that being with a man I am attracted to is better than being without one, no matter what hell I put myself through. A man who, no matter how disrespectful, callous, or blatantly self-absorbed with his own misery or delusions of grandeur, I hold onto for dear life.

At times, the only thing that boosted my ego high enough and kept my head above water long enough for me to avoid hitting emotional rock bottom, was dating men who liked me more than I liked them. But abusing them for the actions of others didn't satisfy me for long. It seemed I wouldn't be happy until my heart ached again, with the intensity it once had for Marcus.

That's when I met Gerald—one month before I graduated from college. Since, at twenty-two, he was married but separated from a wife and a two-year-old daughter, I was cautious at first, but Gerald knew how to break down the protective wall around my heart. Although he was just as manipulative, his method was different from Marcus's. Not brash or disrespectful, Gerald was romantic and seemed sincere. He fixed me dinner the night before my graduation ceremony, came to commencement to support me and to meet my parents, and he called the next day to tell me how much he missed me and to wish my mother a happy Mother's Day.

Besides being charming, witty, and very funny, Gerald was gorgeous, and I had always had a weakness for pretty boys. Who would have thought that I'd be content in such shallowness, but one gaze into those dreamy brown eyes and I was through. Gerald had a smile that was like Wonder Woman's lasso of truth. It just wrapped around me and made me empty my soul, while he remained guarded and secretive. Never mind that we rarely had any insightful conversations and didn't go out much. He gave me the drama I craved and unknowingly unleashed the obsessive bug that had laid dormant in me for at least a year. He told me everything I wanted to hear, and I believed him. I needed to believe.

Even after our two-month commitment was transformed from a "I can't live without you" love connection, to a "Did I say that we would be together forever?" disappearing act, I pursued him. He had told me to my face that he had simply lost interest in me, but somehow the rejection didn't register. In fact, that's the biggest part of my problem. I don't let go, even when I see the relationship is doomed, or even after the man has let go of me. It wasn't until I moved home after college and lost contact with Gerald that I decided that no matter how thrilling the chase seems, it's not worth sacrificing my dignity. I became tired of waiting for the phone to ring and getting angry and depressed when it didn't. I became tired of feeling envious of other girls that I had no reason to dislike, other than that Gerald had dated them; of feeling insecure and not attractive enough for him. Love is supposed to elate you, not make you doubt yourself.

Although I recognized my problem, I didn't know why I became obsessive in relationships. Such behavior signaled that I believed that I didn't deserve better. But through individual and group counseling, and by busying myself with new friends and my writing, I became less tempted to obsess over smooth operators like Marcus and Gerald, or over any man, period. My mother always tells me that I can do bad by myself, and I'm learning that I can do good that way too. I may be a spoiled brat who's used to getting her way, but some things and some people are just not worth having. I do deserve better, and the next time I open my heart to a man, I'm going to be treated with respect or keep on walking.

Mirror, Mirror on the Wall

Tiya Miles

THE BLACK COMEDIENNE "MOMS" MABLEY ONCE
told this story: "There lived a little girl. . . . You'all call her Cinderella. . . . She had long black hair, pretty brown eyes, pretty brown skin.
Well, let's face it—she was colored. Cindy-Ella turns to the mirror and
says, 'Mirror, mirror on the wall, who's the fairest of them all?' The
mirror replies, 'Snow White—and don't you forget it'" (Porter, 26).

Walt Disney released *The Little Mermaid*, a new version of the fairy tale about a mermaid princess who rebels against her
father's wishes and falls in love with a human. When I saw the film I
was pleasantly surprised that the heroine did not have blond hair. I was
impressed that she was thinking independently of her father. I took notice when the little mermaid argued during a discussion with her father
that he should not prejudge all non-mer-people/humans negatively because they are different. After noticing these details, I had hopes that
the film would revise past stereotypes and the exclusion of people of
color, as well as the portrayal of traditional gender roles, in many of
Disney's other films.

As I watched more of the movie, however, my expectations fell. Although the little mermaid does not have the typical
fairy tale blond hair, she is white. The man she falls in love with is
white. Every random mer-person and human in the film is white. The
only characters who are of color are animals. The little mermaid's guard-
ian is a crab who speaks with a Caribbean accent. A "black fish" in the
film sings briefly in what sounds like a black woman's voice.

In addition to these black characters being sea creatures rather than humans or mer-people, they are stereotypically por-
trayed. The crab's lips are exaggerated in size. Like the black cops in the

ubiquitous white-black duo action adventures, he is subservient to the white king and is at the center of comic moments. When the "black fish" is allowed her three seconds of attention, she sings gospel music.

Although the little mermaid is able to think independently of her father, she contemplates the same old, tired thing that all fairy tale princesses contemplate—marrying the prince. The little mermaid falls in love with the prince after seeing him only once. In a familiar portrayal of catty, jealous women, she and the evil female octopus fight to gain the prince's affections. The octopus steals the mermaid's voice, and, once again, a princess must be saved by a prince's kiss. The little mermaid will regain her voice only if the prince kisses her within three days. The prince's character is also defined by gender stereotypes. Like the typical prince of fairy tales, he quickly falls in love with a woman because he is attracted to one of her physical attributes. In this case, it is the little mermaid's voice. The prince is so focused on this single characteristic that his common sense fails him. He spends three fun-filled days with the little mermaid while she has lost her voice. Despite the fact that he has a wonderful time with her, he is holding out for the woman with the beautiful voice that he once heard. When the evil octopus disguises herself and sings to the prince with the little mermaid's stolen voice, the prince immediately falls for her.

The Little Mermaid was a big hit among little girls. I'm sure that many Black, Hispanic, Asian, and Native American girls saw the film and loved it. Unfortunately, when these girls left the theater, the love that they had for the film may have chipped away at the love that they had for themselves.

Even before a child reaches five years of age, she notices the variety in people's appearances (Porter, 13). Once a child can separate people into groups based on these differences in appearance, she learns to assign meaning to the differences according to the attitudes her family members, peers, and the media express (Porter, 13). In this way a child begins to distinguish between racial and gender categories and to determine which groups are considered superior and inferior in society. Children then fold what they learn into their developing identities: "Group membership is one aspect of the self-concept of young children. The child will value himself as he values the group to which he belongs" (Trager and Yarrow, 115, 117). In American society, this development process is likely to lead to a lack of self-worth in children who are neither white nor male. Many children's fairy tales, which are now cultural icons, contribute to the creation and reinforcement of these notions.

Last summer I worked with a group of little girls and saw my own theories and these psychological findings come to life. The group consisted of eight- and nine-year-old Puerto Rican and Haitian girls who lived in a Cambridge housing development. One of our projects was to identify and break down stereotypical ideas of race and gender.

The girls had all seen and loved several Disney fairy tales, so we worked with what they already knew. We began with a general discussion about fairy tales. I asked them to name as many as they could—*Cinderella, Little Red Riding Hood, Rapunzel, The Little Mermaid, Snow White*, and *Sleeping Beauty* were what they listed. I then asked them to think about things that those fairy tales had in common. The princess is always beautiful and blond, said Alisa. The princess is always white with long hair, said Jahyra. The princess always falls in love with a handsome prince, said Mary. The princess always kisses the prince, said Mimi. The princess always gets married and there is a happy ending, said Jahyra.

The next step in our project was to watch or read one of the fairy tales on the list and try to identify the characteristics that they had listed. We began by watching Disney's *Cinderella*. In this film we found the things on our list and more—all white characters, instant love, the conflict between the beautiful and the unattractive woman, the evil, ugly older woman (in this case, the stepmother, in other cases, the witch, the bad fairy, the female octopus), and the idealization of daintiness (Cinderella's small feet that could fit into the slipper).

After pinpointing these characteristics, we planned to revise what we disliked about the fairy tales. The *Cinderella* assignment was to alter her appearance and have her do something in life besides marry the prince. It is important to note that all of the girls described and drew pictures of Cinderellas who looked like them. When the girls wrote about Cinderella doing something, they wrote about things that were within their frames of reference. In one story, Cinderella married the prince and worked in a store. In another, she ditched the prince altogether and went to college.

We revised several fairy tales in this manner. Throughout the ongoing project, though, I recognized to my dismay that the children resisted changing the stories. When they had the power, they made the heroines look like them, but they knew from storybooks, movies, and television that their descriptions and pictures were not "right." They believed that the white princess was the authentic princess, and they wanted to identify with her. At the same time, they knew that they were not pale and blond, that they were unlikely to move into a prince's castle. Negative feelings about themselves born of this conflict between the traditional stories and their realities became evident in our discussions.

We watched and read three versions of Cinderella: Disney's version, a cartoon about a Native American Cinderella, and a story about a Cinderella with brown hair who is happy when she completes a book report for school. When I asked the children which version they preferred and why, the majority chose Disney's *Cinderella*. Mimi, one of the Puerto Rican girls, said she liked Disney Cinderella's hair and wished that she also had blond hair. The Haitian girl, Paule, quickly responded that she thought Mimi's hair was prettier than her own.

As the end of the summer approached, we chose one of the revisions, "A Puerto Rican Cinderella," to perform as a play. When two older Black and Puerto Rican girls in the neighborhood heard of our plans, they asked me who would be Cinderella. They said that they hoped I would not choose Paule, the Haitian girl in the group. They wanted Cinderella to be played by Marybeth: "It just wouldn't be right to have Paule as Cinderella," they explained, "and Mary is so pretty." In the eyes of these adolescent girls with years of societal training about who is worthy of princess status, Marybeth was right for the part. Mary is a delightful, outgoing girl, but she was also the only girl in my group who most closely met traditional American beauty standards. One of the girls was Black; two were chubby; most had dark hair and eyes; the only child with blue eyes had already volunteered to be the director. Marybeth, on the other hand, has reddish-brown hair, hazel eyes, and a white, blond-haired mother.

When I asked the girls to choose the parts they wanted, Mary was the only one who volunteered to be Cinderella. Paule said she wanted to play the wicked stepmother. At only eight years old, they knew their roles well.

Perhaps this would change if those who create and perpetuate pervasive cultural narratives would write and legitimize new scripts.

Works Cited

Porter, Judith D. R., *Black Child, White Child*. Cambridge, MA: Harvard University Press, 1971.

Trager, Helen G., and Yarrow, Marian Radke. *They Learn What They Live*. New York: Harper and Brothers Publishers, 1952, pp. 118–84.

Why a Black Woman Could Never Be President

Paitra Russell

"GOOODDDD-DAMN! SHEEE-IIIT!! LOOK AT the ass on that BITCH!! Look at the titties!!" a man says to introduce the song. There is laughter in the background. An innocuous little melody, reminiscent of the "Gilligan's Island" theme, comes in, supported by a nice bass beat. They are marred only by a man's voice sampled into the background: "Hol' yo' legs up, ho!"

These are the first few seconds of 2 Live Crew's latest hit, *Pop That Pussy*. The radio version has been renamed, of course, and has fewer swear words, but the imagery is the same. It would be best to ignore the lyrics, so tasteless that to think of them makes my face burn. I try not to let these things depress me. I should be used to hearing myself referred to as ho, bitch, or hootchie, by now, especially in a rap song. But I can't help wondering if the men who penned the lyrics, or the men who listen to them, even give a second thought to the sisters, wives, girlfriends, mothers, and friends they are tearing down.

The first verse is so ridiculous that I have a hard time believing I am really hearing it. I stand rather stupidly staring at the stereo, frowning. I hear someone say something about freaky ho's with silicone breasts and oily chests. Whatever I have missed, the chorus clears up rather quickly: "Pop that puss-ay! Hey! Pop that puss-ay baby!"

Disclaimer Number One: This is not a diatribe regarding 2 Live Crew, nor a suggestion that all black men regard black women in the same derogatory manner. In fact, the song to which I refer

Long extracts from "Pop That Pussy" are omitted from this essay as it goes to press because Luke Records, 2 Live Crew's producer, has not yet granted permission to reprint the lyrics.

is a relatively small part of a much larger issue. I do not know what it is about particularly offensive and insensitive rap songs that reminds me how desperate the situation is between black men and black women, but here I am, having neglected to finish my paper, hoping to illustrate to someone, some black man, or anyone who has laughed, how frightened I am for all of us.

This is their experience, I have said to myself each time I have heard a song like this one. This is how they think. But I never extend that same excuse to whites who daily assault my existence, and I wonder why I allow black men this leeway. Why am I so willing to forget my own suffering in remembrance of theirs? I have always considered the destruction of the black man as much my problem as anyone's. I have always taken their pain personally. My "we" has always been inclusive. But increasingly I sense that a black man's "we," meant to include all black people, only *assumes* that what is good for them is also good for us.

I try to forget that two of my close friends have been raped, and that two of us have been sexually assaulted, by men on this campus. None of us has said anything to anyone except each other, supportive parents, or in a few cases, to our assailants. They were friends, boyfriends, acquaintances. Black men whom we wouldn't want to see dismissed from school, or sent to jail, or publicly humiliated, their futures ruined. I know I will never mention what has happened to me; writing a piece for a literary magazine is as close as I can come to a vindication of my self. But as dire as the situation is for black men, I cannot say that their pain is greater than ours, or that we should keep our mouths shut for the greater good. I am tired, oh so tired, of our being labeled "traitorous" when we try to be true to ourselves. Disclaimer Number Two: I am not a "raging-lesbo-feminist-man-hating-bitch." Nor am I on my period. I am your sister, your mother, your daughter, your lover. I am you: black, strong, and determined, but infinitely tired.

There are some days when it is worse than others. Today, things haven't been so good. A series of events, in fact, have led to this feeling inside of utter hopelessness. I was in a support group for a while. The twelve of us would get together each week and try to talk things out, about what it's like to be a black woman here. We were all quite different in our backgrounds and aspirations, but we were each able to grasp, inside somehow, to feel, to understand, to *know* the incessant tearing down of self that we experience, the slow, painful process of rebuilding the soul. Often we were quiet, too exhausted to even re-count the past week's insults and abuses. Many times, the daily assaults we endured from whites were not even an issue of discussion; they were expected and familiar. What was always more painful was the abuse from men. Our own men, to whom I had expected to be able to turn for support, advice, and perhaps peace. Instead, I have found my dinner conversations dominated by heated debates regarding a black woman's duty to her race. I have tried to make the point that one cannot separate one's femaleness from one's blackness. But the men just don't seem to understand my tentative allegiance to a struggle that has at best rele-gated women to the role of passive supporter, a struggle that leaves no space for hammering out problems *between* sisters and brothers.

"I'd have to leave the country if a black woman be-came president." That was the statement that began the downward spi-ral this time. A black man said it. A man who, for some reason, is not able to fathom a black woman commanding respect from other world leaders. It seems that before he can expect anyone else to respect black women, he would have to respect us himself. I doubt that he realizes that, essentially, he has sanctioned the words of 2 Live Crew. In his own, intellectually deficient way, my brother has called me a bitch/ho/hootchie. Sadly, I do not believe that this man is unique: I know a brother who routinely spits on his girlfriend, and quite a few others who believe the concerns of black men should be more important to black women than the concerns of black women should be to black men. Yes, we all know that black men are dying. But how many black men know that black women are dying, too? Black people can never succeed as *people* without the cooperation of the men *and* the women. We are daily confronted by those who cannot understand the erasure that operates against all of us. Why then, must we perpetuate the pain in each other?

Please, my brothers, you have to understand; when all the women are gone, when we have quietly collected the remnants of our selves, tucked our hearts away for safekeeping, withdrawn into collective imaginings of a peace we cannot find, who then will raise, sup-port, defend, and love you?

Shades of Grief:
The Plight of a Battered Woman

Michelle White

Tired

I am so tired of waiting
Aren't you.
For the world to become good
And beautiful and kind?
Let's take a knife
And cut the world in two
And see what worms are eating
At the rind.

—Langston Hughes

The poem "Tired" by Langston Hughes has become a resounding war cry for me when dealing with the perpetual injustices or demons that plague my consciousness. One demon in particular still rides my back in a roughshod manner, its grasping talons digging into my subconscious, where unforgettable nightmares and horrific dreams lurk below the surface. The demon raises its ugly head to unmask those dark nights, or was it near dawn, when I heard his hand make contact with her flesh. I remember her screams cutting through me while pulling me outside of myself and thinking if only I could scream louder maybe her tortured cries would quiet. The woman is my mother and she was a victim of domestic violence. Her beautiful honey-brown skin was constantly marred with purple bruises of battle. The man who dispensed this kind of punishment carried the pseudo-title of "father." My mother was just one of the four million women in the United States beaten by their husbands or partners (Telch & Linquist).

Domestic violence is a cancerous sore that eats a hole right through the heart of a family. The violence is acted out by the primary actors (mother and father), but the supporting cast (children) standing slightly offstage also get caught up in the sucking vortex of brutality. When the scene has been played out, the remnants consist of a battered wife whose self-esteem has been beaten down, confused children who may develop behavioral problems ranging from delinquency to withdrawal, and a dysfunctional family.

I have seen pictures of my mother when she was younger, and reflected there on those square documentations of captured time was a woman without worries; with straight, black hair hanging down to her butt; wearing sassy smiles with mischief in her eyes and unmarred, beautiful skin that drove the island men crazy. Those pictures became mocking testimonies of the woman who now had to face my father's left hook and his right fist.

It is very difficult to fight through the murky, uncertain waters of fear and confusion when someone (abuser) is constantly trying to pull the victim under. Looking back to my real-life nightmare, I remember a particular incident when my mother tried to get her head above water by showing signs of defiance. She was trying to find the view her "self" but he beat her until she relented. The day after she wore a pair of dark shades that seemed to hide more than the bruises around her eyes. The shades hid her shame and pain from outsiders.

After all of the abuse it might be shocking to learn that my mother stayed with my father, but in actuality a majority of battered women are still living with their abusive partners. The one difference is that Momma did not lie down and play victim for very long, because she decided to fight back with threats of boiling water and a butcher knife that could quarter a chicken or man. She was either going to make chicken soup or hurt my father very badly. That incident seems funny when I think about it now, but as a child I always wondered why mother could not escape her debacle of a marriage. You see, if she did not leave, then I could not leave, and I was being destroyed emotionally from having to witness my mother's suffering. Children then become victims themselves.

The trauma of watching my mother being abused has proved detrimental for me psychologically and emotionally in my relationships with men. The physical abuse is not one-dimensional but two-dimensional, affecting the child drastically and resulting in specific extreme behaviors like withdrawal into an imaginary world to escape the violent dynamics. This was my reaction to my mother's abuse. Other extreme behavioral consequences like difficult temperaments or violent displays are nurtured in the acidic belly of a hostile environment. In theory, the abuser may provide a violent role model for male children, while exposure to an abusive marital relationship may cause female children to view violence toward women as the norm. Young boys grow up to be future abusers while many young girls grow up to be victims like their mothers before them.

My mother is a survivor, and she fought back to reclaim the spirit that was lost in that haze of abuse. Layers of degradation and low self-esteem were shed to lighten the load of the conquering heroine.

When Words Contradict Actions

Askhari

SHE LOVED TANTRUM, AND HE SAID HE LOVED HER; she could not tell if he loved her, so she just hoped he did. He acted like he did most of the time, and for two years now, everything had been fine. Sometimes Tantrum cooked homemade pancakes for her in the mornings; he was faithful, and very gentle; he was beautiful, and Black; Tantrum was generous, and sexy, and, besides, he said he loved her.

She thought back to the very first time he verbalized his love for her—it was after their first fight. They were sitting on the couch in her living room, watching a basketball game. She was rooting for her favorite team, the Lakers, and Tantrum wanted Detroit to win. During half-time, Tantrum asked for a key to her apartment. She did not think it was such a good idea. When she tried to explain to him he could not just come over any time he pleased, and told him he should call first, he accused her of hiding something from him. When she told him she needed time to herself, so she could finish her novel, he accused her of seeing someone else, or having some clandestine affair. When she told him he was being insecure and ridiculous, he slapped her, hard.

Her heart fell to the floor with her favorite earring; she took four steps backwards and covered her face with her arm. Tantrum started toward her, his arms wide open; she took another step back and stared at him, trying not to blink, so the tears would not come. The tears did come, however, and something about her tears brought the words she wanted to hear, "Baby, I love you." Nobody said "Baby" like Tantrum. He put his arms around her, pulled her head close to his chest, and kissed her forehead with the beautiful lips that always reminded her of candy. Tantrum took his middle finger and wiped away one of her tears. He swore he wouldn't hit her again: "Baby, I'm sorry . . . I didn't mean to hit you." She pulled away from him. She wished that he would stop staring at her with those eyes that always said exactly what she needed to hear. She tried to ignore the way his eyelashes brushed his wonderfully high cheekbones when he closed his eyes momentarily to think. She stopped herself from gazing at his slender black fingers as they traced the tracks her tears made. She turned away when he opened his full lips to say something . . . anything. The words came again, "Baby, . . . I said, I love you."

She believed him because he was holding her like he would never let her go, because he kissed her forehead so tenderly. She believed him because the word "Baby" glided from Tantrum's throat like butter, taking her breath away temporarily, and because his scintillating voice could stop a summer storm. She believed him because he led her to the couch where they finished watching the game together. The Detroit Pistons won.

One morning, while Tantrum was fixing her wheat pancakes with blackberries and raisins for breakfast, he said he thought she needed to see other people, that she shouldn't "confine" herself to one man. "Baby, I love you and all, but I don't think you want a commitment right now. Don't you need some time to yourself to finish that book?"

"Do you want to see other women, Tantrum? Because if you do, you should just say so."

"You're the only person I want to be with, Baby, you know that, don't you? Don't you know that I love you?" He turned around, pulled her close, and rubbed her cheek with his lips.

She did not know if he loved her; she walked into the living room and sat on the couch. She fingered the silver bracelet Tantrum had given her to apologize for giving her a black eye. She remembered worrying about what to tell her mother, but that was before she became skilled at covering the bruises with make-up. She was thankful for make-up in shades that were compatible with the Black woman's skin tones. It was still difficult, however, to explain the tiny crescent-shaped scar that Tantrum's class ring had left on her cheek, especially to her mother, who also paid too much for just a little love.

Tantrum sauntered into the living room, "Baby, we can still work things out . . . it's just that you are not opening yourself up to me, you don't give yourself to me completely." And when she heard the word complete, why did she always think of him? She stood and walked upstairs to take a shower. She had expected this.

Being in love scared Tantrum because he was inexperienced at it. He did not know you simply cannot make love with the television on, or when you give someone you love a bath, you should wash their entire body, even their feet. Tantrum had doubts about her and her feelings; he thought when she brought him breakfast in bed, it was because she wanted money or something. He often wondered if she could really love him. He didn't think she could ever really love anyone who didn't write love poetry as easily as she did. Tantrum didn't tell her he had won the statewide poetry contest once.

She got out of the shower, wrapped a towel around her wet body, and began brushing her teeth. Tantrum was insecure, she knew that. In fact she was a little insecure too, she was scared of being alone, scared of becoming addicted to television and food again, of only being equal to the sum of her functions. She looked down at his bright, blue toothbrush; she liked having it there, and she liked not sleeping in the center of her bed, alone. She started to brush her hair; it was getting long, too long for her to manage with her red, black, and green pick, longer, in fact, than she wanted it. She had only let her fade grow out because Tantrum said he liked long hair, and if she had to have natural hair, at least it should be long.

She began going through the crevices of her mind, wondering what she could have done to make him leave her. Somewhere in her heart of hearts, down where she could not fool herself, deeper still, underneath all the fear, insecurity, and socialization, she knew it was not her. She realized it was not her hair, or the way she bathed his entire Black body at night, it was not her unfinished book, or her love handles; it was not her need to always be on time, or her choice of basketball teams. It was not her refusal to give up her quiet time—it was not her love. It was him . . . Tantrum was a thunderstorm, needing some sunshine.

What he really wanted was for her to put her arms around him and beg him to stay. And she wanted to open her arms wide and beg him to stay because when he was little all the kids had called him midnight and spooky; no one had ever told him he was beautiful in his blackness. She wanted to put her arms around him and beg him to stay because his father walked out on him and his ailing mother when he was nine years old, and never came back. He needed to be reassured of her love because when he was fifteen, his high school principal called him a no good nigger and he did not the get the job promotion he deserved just because he was Black. She wanted to pull his head close to her chest because "nobody understood him," and wanted to kiss his forehead tenderly because she was the first woman who had ever given him a flower. She wanted to say, "Baby, don't you know I love you" because no one ever had, and she wanted to say, "Baby, it's okay to be scared" because it was.

She strolled out of the bathroom and started to list the reasons why they were perfect for each other, but couldn't think of one, because loneliness doesn't count, so he looked into her beautiful, big, brown eyes when she emerged and she avoided his.

"Are you sure this is what you want?" She was giving him a graceful exit, if he wanted one.

"Yes." Tantrum was not a wordy man. He zipped up his faded blue jeans. "I'll come and get my stuff later on tonight. Is that okay?"

"Yes." If he wanted to go, she was going to let him. He was hurting her even if this was a game.

"Then again, I'm going to take my stuff now, okay?"

"Okay." He went into the bathroom to get his toothbrush. Her heart was in shock. He came out again, made up his side of the bed, opened "his" drawer and took out his socks and underwear. He didn't even look unhappy. She put her Billie Holiday tape in the stereo.

"I'll see you around." He put on his jacket, walked past her, and left the room. "Come lock the door behind me, Baby." She turned just in time to see the heel of his right tennis shoe turn the corner of the stairway. She could stop him. Maybe if she said, "Baby, pleeeez don't leave me" just one more time, he would come back and put his arms around her and tell her everything she needed to hear but didn't know how to say. She heard him walk down the stairs, open and then close the front door. She watched out the window as he walked to the bus stop. He always looked like he was running, even when he was walking. What was he running from?

She dashed to the bathroom to put on her robe—if she ran, she could catch him, she could grab his hand, and lead him back into the house, into her life, into her heart. She looked out the bathroom window as she reached for her robe, but he didn't even look back. She remembered a quotation from her creative writing class at Spelman College: "When words and behavior contradict each other, always go with behavior . . . always."

. . . So the most heroic thing Harriet did that year was stay in her bathroom, cut her hair, listen to Billie Holiday, and not cry.

A Liar in Love

Quinn Eli

WHEN A BLACK MAN SITS DOWN TO WRITE ABOUT black women and relationships, the reader is well advised to take cover. Because whenever a man writes about male-female relationships in the black community and, like some cross between Cupid and Rodney King, argues that "we should all just get along," chances are that writer has an agenda up his sleeve. And that agenda, concealed in some flowery language about "preserving our unity as a people," is almost always self-serving.

I should know. I'm a male writer who has spent the last couple of years in a graduate creative writing program, spinning tales about black folks in love. Most of my stories have had some pressing conflict at their center—certainly there are enough hateful forces in the world that conspire against black love—and so I would artfully depict the way my two protagonists, a black couple in Boston or Brooklyn or Philly, beat down the conflict that threatened to tear them apart, and, hand in hand, defeated the forces of racism, poverty, and joblessness that might've otherwise destroyed them and, by implication, the entire black community.

But as I look back now—from my new position as a Ph.D. candidate, a four-eyed student of literature—I can't help but think that my short stories in the past were a little too self-righteous, and too assured of their own political and artistic consequence. In other words, I'm thinking now that maybe my stories were full of shit. Which is not uncommon among young writers—we always think we have something terribly *deep* to say, and that we're the first people ever in the history of humanity to see the world as we do—and in fact it would have been a miracle if I hadn't shoveled at least a little manure onto every page

I ever printed out. But what's bothering me now is that I think the shit I was dishing out—and attempting to feed to a hungry, unsuspecting public—was manipulative and self-serving. When a black man writes about relationships, or at least when I wrote on that topic, I was almost always trying to preach to black women about the way they should treat us black men: a little less attitude, I would subtly suggest, a little less giving us lip, and black love would flourish and grow and eventually defeat the menace of racism.

Some nifty trick, wouldn't you say? Putting *all* the responsibility for black liberation from oppression and injustice onto the shoulders of black women? If y'all would simply get your act together, I hinted, and quit with the mood swings and humiliating back talk, maybe we could all finally come together as a people and overthrow the devil who keeps us in chains. In the short stories I wrote, all that stood between black folks and freedom was the black woman's refusal to emotionally support her man. And since life invariably mimics art, I believe I began to carry this point of view into my own romantic relationships. Before I'd even had time to consider the absurdity of my attitude, I found myself saying to the women I dated, "This is why the white man is able to keep us down—'cause we ain't unified. Every time I say one thing, you gotta say another. But you and me oughta be on the same side, baby."

In these discussions, of course, "the same side" that I was referring to was actually "my side." And so the gist of my message wasn't much different from anything my father had said to my mother, back in the fifties, when she thought she might like to go to college: "You figure if you get all that schoolin'," he reportedly told her, "you won't need me around?" Like him, I was afraid that if the woman in my life developed ideas and opinions that differed from my own, she would eventually come to think of me as a fool and have no choice but to leave me. But because I was a man of my times, a member of the first post-Civil Rights Era generation—well-educated, politically sensitive, and passionate about social causes—I was able to disguise my fear with a language that would have dazzled my father. I would simply suggest to my partner that by clinging so tightly to her own point of view, she was demonstrating "a slave mentality" and thus undermining our progress as a people.

And most of the time, it worked like a charm. Not because the women in my life lacked the intelligence or common sense to see through my ruse—more often than not, they were much more intelligent than I was, in every imaginable way—but because all it takes to push a lot of black folks' buttons is for one of our own to suggest that we ain't down wit da cause, that we done lost what it means to be black. It wasn't their identities as *women* I was challenging—on that subject they were thoroughly confident and would've stood for no instruction from a man about how to be a woman—but rather, their identities as *black folks*. I had come from a long line of black agitators—during the sixties, my brother accumulated a record with the F.B.I. as thick as a telephone book—and so I posed convincingly as someone who could speak on such matters, and who had only the best interests of the black community in mind.

In truth, of course, all I really had in mind was my own obsessive need to be always in control. I'm a diminutive man, book-ish and jittery, so I could never have gotten away with the macho posturing that some of my larger male friends had adopted. (I tried once, though, with a woman I met in the Bronx, who looked at me as if to say, "Nigga, you MUST be crazy," and then sat laughing at me for something like an hour.) So, instead, using the power of words in either a spoken or written form, I transformed my insecurity and crazy need to control into something that seemed to have political urgency, with our very survival as a community at stake.

It's only fair to point out, however, that controlling behavior in the black community, whether it's a woman's or a man's, is something that is difficult to escape. And while the behavior should never be condoned or encouraged—God knows it can have unhealthy ramifications and can drain a person both emotionally and mentally—it must at least be acknowledged and understood. Like a lot of folks, I grew up in a household where money was always tight, and opportunities for a better life were scarce; and because of liquor, depression, and feelings of personal worthlessness brought on by social restraints, the relationship between my parents always seemed to me like a time bomb, ticking loudly through our cramped apartment, likely to explode at any minute. It made for the kind of anxiety that is still with me from childhood, and which I detect in so many other black men and women. Is it any wonder, then, that when we grew into adults, we sought ways to keep that anxiety at bay, and to maintain a tight grip over our lives so that nothing would suddenly fly apart or spiral out of control?

When my need to control met head-to-head with a partner's need to control, the struggle that would ensue was better than anything you'd ever see on World Federation Wrestling. We'd fight like we were in the middle of Madison Square Garden, two dark adversaries circling the canvas of our apartment, both of us determined to pin back the other's shoulders, to drop our opponent to his or her knees. Most of all we wanted to leave the struggle without surrendering too much, and with our sense of personal dignity still intact. And as all black folks know, battles like these are loud, fierce, and never really end: some part of it comes up again in the next battle between you, or leaves emotional scars that never quite disappear. And in my struggles with women, I was a particularly cruel opponent—because whenever I thought I was in real danger, and might not survive the fight, I trotted out that ol' broken-record business about black unity. It was, I guess, my secret weapon—the suggestion that the disarray in the black community was due to exactly the kind of shit she was pulling right now, refusing to see things my way. And more often than not, it was this accusation that brought the fight between us to its bitter, and bloody, conclusion.

Other folks have their own secret weapons, of course, and the black unity song I sang like a canary was just one of many options available to a liar in love. If I'd wanted, I could have borrowed a line a friend of mine often uses when the women in his life assume points of view different from his, and thus threaten his sense of control. "Fine, baby," he says, "have things your way. But it seems to me you done worked too hard and too long pulling yourself outta da ghetto to go backslidin' now."

And, man, what a panicky response he gets from these women when he reminds them of their modest beginnings—the Section 8 housing and low-income projects that they fought tooth and nail to escape—and suggests that by refusing to follow his lead, they could end up back at square one. "All I'm tellin' you," I've heard him say, "is that what goes around comes around." My friend understands that for many black folks, words like these can conjure up all our worst fears about our accomplishments—maybe it's just an illusion, we think to ourselves, another handout intended to keep us from complaining or to pacify some white liberal's guilt. Our professional successes often seem founded on something only as sturdy as, say, a butterfly's wing, and pointing out how easily any of us could end up back in Bed Stuy or South Central doesn't necessarily make my friend a bad person. But pointing it out to keep a woman in line puts him in league with the master who warns his house slave that one false move will land him back in the fields. What I mean is, keeping somebody back in this particular way isn't something my friend invented; rather, it's a strategy as old as the hills, the one thing that oppressors have always done whenever they've feared the oppressed. And so it doesn't take a rocket scientist to figure out from whom my friend could have learned such behavior.

The only other secret weapon I've ever seen used was in fact used on me. A woman I knew had a way of convincing the men in her life that her unhappiness was somehow their fault—and that this inability to make her happy was related in some way to their masculinity. The suggestion was that a woman's spiritual fulfillment—like, I guess, her sexual fulfillment—was based on her man's performance; and so any man who couldn't get the first job done right, sure as hell wasn't cutting the mustard in every other regard. So in my fights with her for dominance and control, she was almost always the victor—because as soon as she felt threatened enough, she'd invariably call out, "You don't know shit about being a man." And like a balloon stabbed abruptly with the tip of a pin, I would burst and then sputter to the ground.

Despite my grim encounters with this woman, I get some comfort now when I think back on her behavior: it's nice to know I'm not the only black person who ever blamed somebody else for my own failings and insecurities, and for the hurt I experienced at the hands of an intolerant society. And lately I've seen lots of other folks doing the very same thing. Here in my West Philly neighborhood, for instance, we've got brothers standing on street corners, holding their dicks, still swearing to anybody who'll listen that it was WHITEY that kept 'em from going to college and getting ahead in life. Or else it was some woman—usually his mother, but it may be the old lady he's sharing his crib with now—who (figuratively) emasculated him and made it impossible for him to function as a man. Or check out some of the magazine articles and current fiction aimed at (and written by) black women: "You'd be having a happy life, a rich and fulfilling life, my sister"—they all seem to suggest—"if these brothers of ours would simply get their shit together."

It seems there's no shortage of places to assign blame for the emptiness and dissatisfaction so many of us experience in our lives. But, more often than not, we point our fingers in the wrong direction—we point them at one another. Because to look inside ourselves for ways to be happy in a racist society is, admittedly, a monumental task; and to take personal responsibility for our own individual failings is just too damn scary.

So we find somebody else to blame. Or, as in my case, we find some concept outside ourselves—for me it was black unity—and, pinning all our hopes for happiness on that concept, browbeat and bully those who appear to be rocking our boat. Confused by my own need to be in control, and fearful of taking any scenic excursions into my own heart, I believed the thing that would bring me happiness at last was a unified black community. But the unity I was working toward had a tyrant at its helm—namely, me—and like some Stalin of the ghetto, I thought I could determine happiness for *all* black folks according to my own terms. Which is why I would get so impatient with those women in my life who saw the world differently from me, and who had their own ideas about how to live a fulfilling life. Sometimes these ideas were as suspect as my own (I once dated a woman, beautiful and dark-skinned, who thought she'd be happy at last if she could just get herself a chemical peel); but this didn't mean they should let me determine the course of their lives. Looking back, I'm ashamed at the number of times that I tried to convince them otherwise.

But there was just so much at stake for me in those days. If I were to give up the concept of black unity—a concept that is, by the way, as flawed as Afrocentrism or any other concept that discusses black folks as though we were some monolithic entity—it meant I might have to look to myself for a way to be happy. And I damn sure wasn't going to do that. It was easier and much more convenient to assume that all that stood between me and my ideal were the women, the black women, who were undermining "the cause" by insisting on their own point of view. Like the street brothers who maintain that it's Whitey keeping them down, or like the sisters who swear black men are the ones making their lives so unhappy, I was content to point fingers and pass the buck about the pain I was in, without ever once stopping to wonder if I had brought any of it on myself.

I'd love to say that I suddenly had some dramatic experience that removed the blinders from my eyes and made me see what a fool I had been. But that kind of stuff only happens in fiction—or, at least, it happens an awful lot in the fiction I write. In reality, the only thing that caused me to change my way of thinking and start taking responsibility for my own life was the everyday, ordinary business of living. But I guess there were two incidents that you could say put me on a better path . . .

A while back I was standing on a crowded street corner—my mind wandering as usual—and without stopping to look both ways, I stepped out into a rush of traffic; of all the people who were standing beside me, only one reached out a hand and pulled me back to the curb. That person was a woman, the only other black person in the crowd, and if I owe my life to anyone, then certainly I owe it to her. More recently I was feeling pretty bleak about my life, wondering what the hell to do when I was finished with grad school, and in the meantime drinking my evenings away. But one night in a bar, a brother asked me what was wrong, and patiently listened to my entire sob story. Then he gave me the name of some people he knew who were hiring at a local school and, together with his wife, made it his personal business to cheer me out of my depression.

When I thought back to the kindness of this man—and then remembered the woman on the street corner—I realized I had spent too much damn time thinking it was necessary to mobilize entire armies against the devastating effects of racism, and no time considering how one person can help another person to heal from those effects. A chain, after all, is only as strong as its individual links; and it seemed to me suddenly that the way to help strengthen my community as a whole was to improve the quality of my relationships—romantic and otherwise—with the individual black folks that I met every day. To do this, of course, required tearing down all the walls I had built around myself, and taking a long, hard look inside; but what I discovered, much to my surprise, was that the view really wasn't all that bad.

So, recently, I finished a new short story—another romantic saga about a young black couple in love. But this time, neither of them is more responsible than the other for whether or not their love survives—and, by extension, whether or not the black community survives. They are, quite frankly, a lot more cynical than characters I've created in the past: they know the world is an awful place, and not likely to ever get much better. But they also know they've got a pretty good thing going—what Alice Walker would call "a council between equals"—and so they spend each day showering each other with kindness, and rescuing one another from the unfriendly climate of the world outside their door. And if there's a lesson to be gathered from these two characters of mine, I'm hoping I'll be the first one to learn it.

Slow Dance

Natasha Tarpley

It was the summer they dragged
Emmet Till's almost body out of the Tallahatchie,
and our friend Toby Brown got sliced in half on the railroad tracks;
The summer everybody's crops went bad
and the bills went unpaid I pressed my hair anyway,
sewed my dress, and danced
at Mickey's Saturday Nite Jams   That summer,
a boy held out his hand to me
on the last slow number   He said, Girl
bring your sweet blue love here
I took his hand and I knew
what it felt like when white girls let their eyes roll
to the backs of their skulls   when they fainted
to the arms of some whiteman hero   Except
I didn't swoon and couldn't faint,
cause me and that boy was holding each other up,
finding our rhythm in those blues

Part 4

The Eyes of Seers

Educating and Re-educating Ourselves

To Phillis Wheatley

Lisa Clayton

While an intrinsic ardor prompts to write,
The muses promise to assist my pen;
'Twas not long since I left my native shore
The land of errors, and Egyptian *gloom:*
Father of mercy, 'twas thy gracious hand
Brought me in safety from those dark abodes.

Students, to you 'tis giv'n to scan the heights
Above, to traverse the ethereal space,
And mark the systems of revolving worlds.
Still more, ye sons of science ye receive
The blissful news by messengers from heav'n,
How Jesus' *blood for your redemption flows.*
See him with hands out-stretcht upon the cross;
Immense compassion in his bosom glows;
He hears revilers, nor resents their scorn:
What matchless mercy in the Son of God!
When the whole human race by sin had fall'n,
He deign'd to die that they might rise again,
And share with him in the sublimest skies,
Life without death, and glory without end.

Improve your privileges while they stay,
Ye pupils, and each hour redeem, that bears
Or good or bad report of you to heav'n.
Let sin, that baneful evil to the foul,
By you be shunn'd, nor once remit your guard;
Suppress the deadly serpent in its egg.

Ye blooming plants of human race divine,
An Ethiop *tells you 'tis your greatest foe;*
Its transient sweetness turns to endless pain,
And in immense perdition sinks the soul.

—Phillis Wheatley, "To the
University of Cambridge,
in New-England"

In his introduction to *The Collected Works of Phillis Wheatley*, Henry Louis Gates, Jr., points out that when Wheatley published her first volume of poetry in 1773 she simultaneously founded the black woman's literary tradition and the black American literary tradition. Either of these would be an accomplishment to be proud of; the fact that they occurred together is truly amazing. As with so many women's accomplishments, it is also a fact that many people miss. I am considering spending my life as a scholar studying the black woman's literary tradition, however; I find these facts important.

Last spring, I heard the black writer Elizabeth Alexander reading some of her poetry at Harvard and Radcliffe. She is studying at the University of Pennsylvania right now, and one of the poems she chose was written for that school's two hundredth anniversary. It was about black women who had gone before Alexander at Penn, and about the ones who are there now; it was dedicated to Phillis Wheatley. In introducing the poem, Alexander spoke about the dedication. She explained that she had originally thought that for a black woman writer to dedicate a piece to Wheatley would be clichéd and corny; she said that she later understood that a black woman writer could not get by without doing it.

"To the University of Cambridge, in New-England" was included in the book of poetry that Wheatley published in 1773. The university that Wheatley speaks of is Harvard College. I am about to graduate with that college's class of 1992; I would like to think that her letter to the students there is somehow, by extension, a letter to me too. It is my turn to write her back.

I know two stories that come from the time when my family was in slavery. The idea that they are stories is important; I have no way of knowing how factual they are, how close the version that exists in my head may be to what actually happened. As African Americans, we cannot find ourselves in town registers or history books; if pressured, it might be difficult for us to prove we existed at all. Our family is a living example of the dangers of existing within an oral tradition; from the entire antebellum period of our American history, all that remains are these two stories.

The first is from my father's mother's family. The Macon men are known for their tall stature and broad chests. We can see this today in my great-uncles, in my father himself, in my two brothers. The story is about a Macon who was seven feet tall and an enormously powerful man; the story is that he once got into a fight with another slave and in the heat of his anger killed the man with his bare hands. This is not a story I can do much with. I do not think it is something to be particularly proud of, and I do not see any lessons in it for me to carry forward; I accept it as information, but I am unsure how it relates to me. I do not think this experience is unique. I think many of us believe that every detail of our pasts holds meaning for us, that the lives our ancestors led should give us clues about how to lead our own. I think these are the kinds of hints we all search for. But the details we find are often more like this one—clues whose meaning remains hidden.

The second story is more complex. Its length adds uncertainty, each unprovable detail casting new doubt, but I prefer to pretend I have no questions. This one comes from my father's father's family, the family that gave me my name. I have heard that the name Clayton comes from Clayton County, Georgia, where we were once slaves; I think that is where my unnamed grandfather is when this story begins. The time it begins is uncertain too, but my faraway grandfather was only a boy. He was playing ball with another boy—another slave—when they accidentally broke a window in the Big House. Because they were afraid of the consequences, they decided to run away; at twelve years old, my grandfather became a fugitive.

The two boys faced a crisis early on when they came to a body of water that was almost too difficult to cross; the other boy did not survive, but somehow my grandfather did—and somehow, all alone, he made it all the way to Virginia. He was able to keep himself alive and keep himself free until slavery was abolished. During his freedom, however, he always kept the pain of leaving his mother and his family behind, of knowing how impossible it would be to find them ever again.

His story ends much later in his life, when he was on his way to visit New York. The train service was segregated, and there were no porters for the black cars; as he was getting on, he saw a young black woman who clearly had more children and baggage than she could handle, and he helped her board the train. They sat together during the ride and exchanged details about their trips; the woman was on her way to New York to visit her dying mother. She mentioned that her mother was heartbroken because her entire life she had held out hope of having a last chance to see one of her sons, a child who had run away during slavery while he was still a boy. Through that detail, my grandfather discovered that the woman he had just helped was one of his own sisters. He was exceptional among those who endured slavery, because he found the family he assumed he had lost forever. He was able to see his mother again before she, as African Americans say, went home.

This is a story that gives me things to hold. There is my grandfather's incredible strength, incredible will, and the incredible grace that watched over him; the way that together they brought a twelve-year-old alone through hunger, swamps, animals, and slave-catchers from Georgia to Virginia. There is one concrete example of how the systematic destruction of families that was endemic to slavery made itself felt in one small piece of my own family. These stories, however small, are valuable. But I find that something important is missing.

In the essay "Coming in from the Cold," Alice Walker writes about hearing the spirits of her ancestors. One of them is a slave woman out working in the fields; she tells Walker that she is proud of what she is doing, that she must keep on making her voice heard. She says this in the decidedly down-to-earth tones of one black woman to another. This is really the kind of ancestor I want for myself. I can picture her in my mind: she has braided white hair, and deep brown eyes, and a ready smile. Her low voice has a Southern melody, and she sings spirituals to herself as she works. Her sturdy hands are always occupied—perhaps kneading dough, or piecing a quilt, or tending a garden. She talks to me while she works too, and when she has a point to make she stops and shakes her finger for emphasis. Her advice is always encouraging, always direct, and always right. The two stories that I do have are from my father's family, and they both revolve around men; I cannot help but wish I knew more about my grandmothers.

My mother's grandmother was a writer. She wrote throughout her life and published little volumes of her poems and plays.

She helped raise my mother, and my mother raised me, so I know her spirit is strongly felt in what I've become. But I wonder about the grandmothers long before her too. Their names are lost to me, and their voices and words are forever silent. I would like to know if there were more writers. And if any of them were writers, I would like to know what else was in their lives that the writing had to compete with.

I wonder if my grandmothers kept other people's houses, or other people's fields, or other people's children. I wonder if my grandmothers were married until old age, or if they had lovers sold away from them; I wonder how many of them had children who were sold away, or had more children who ran away, or had children they raised on their own. I can see in the mirror that I have a good deal of white blood; I would like to know if it was by choice. Most of all, I would like to know how living all of these lives felt. I would like to know how close they were to my own, and how much they differed. I wonder if I have a grandmother who would stop her work in the fields to say she was proud of me and that I should keep on doing what I do.

I have no reason to believe that Phillis Wheatley was actually one of my grandmothers; the chances that her family became entwined with mine are probably very small. But I share something with her that I could never share with a woman who spent her life on a plantation in Georgia: place. This may be even more important than blood. They say that when you eat from the soil of a place, you always hold that place inside you; this shared soil of Massachusetts is our bond of ancestry. The ties of place and race together are even stronger; finding an African American New England woman writer is too much to let go.

I would not ask Phillis Wheatley the same questions I would ask my nameless grandmothers. The details of her life are more closely reported, so I can find her facts for myself, and beyond facts, there are different things I would like to know about what she and I had shared. I would know more about which questions to ask her, because I know more about what her life could have been like—and because I suspect that in many ways it might have been like my own. This is what I might say.

How did you deal with being the only black face on the white streets you walked down, the only point of color in a pale world? I grew up in rural New England towns, and along the way I learned that feeling well. I still often find myself in situations where I am the only African American in the room. No one else ever calls attention to this fact, but I feel sure it is something we all must notice. I respond by being as self-assured as possible, but it is the unspoken comments that continue to frighten me. Were you conscious of the way people stared—in surprise as you walked in, or looking twice as you walked by, or when they thought you wouldn't see them? Did you ever get used to that feeling, or were you self-conscious your whole life? Did you always look away, or did you ever stare back?

Would you understand me if I said I feel ambivalence, sometimes guilt, about what it means to be "chosen"? You were well educated; you had influential friends; you travelled abroad; you met President Washington. Without knowing it, you too were in our "talented tenth." Did you wonder what separated you from the other nine?

I am often curious about why I have escaped overt racism as much as I have—if people suspect me less because I am light-skinned, because I am upper-middle-class, because I am educated, because I am quiet. I wonder how much more "black" I would need to be to be exposed to more. Sometimes I question my own friends. I am bothered more than my quiet protests show when they stereotype Catholics, or Italians, or when they joke about locking the car doors when we drive through certain neighborhoods. I know that they accept me as an individual, but I also know that if they tell me these prejudices they must have stereotypes of black as well, which they avoid mentioning in my presence. Did you ever look at all of these people who condoned slavery, who kept their own slaves, and wonder how they behaved so kindly to you?

Your masters educated you, encouraged your writing, presented your poems to publishers. You were reportedly given no more work than a daughter in the household; the letters and papers you left show you thought of one another as family. But did you ever hate them for having *bought* you?

I vividly remember riding through Harlem for the first time during a school trip and being frightened by all of the people I saw. It was not until much, much later that I realized the white society I live in has taught me to fear myself. Did you learn to respond that way when you saw other blacks—as if they were "other," and somehow you were special—and if so, how did you feel when you realized what you had done?

And were there times too when you felt even being "chosen" was not good enough? Did you ever think how much easier it might be to be white? I can remember having that idea often when I was small, during the time when my other grade-school friends began to find their first boyfriends. I was as excited as everyone else by the possibility of romance, but it did not take me long to realize that none of the boys in my class had any interest in me. My family had brought me up to believe that I was extremely special, but my experiences made me feel very unwanted. Did you ever stop, as I did, to imagine how your life would be different if you had blonde hair and blue eyes? If so, did the memory of that moment of self-negation later make you feel ashamed?

When I begin graduate work I plan to study literature by women writers, especially women of color; I am interested in the unique ways they use language to make their voices heard. As a writer and a scholar, did you have questions about language—did it worry you that you were reading and writing a voice that was not your own? I love Shakespeare and Eliot as you loved Milton and Pope. Sometimes I wonder about the irony of that attraction; did this ever occur to you? Did you think about the way your poetry followed a form and meter established by white men? As a black woman writer today, you would feel pressured to make your own voice heard; as a black woman writer then, were you pressured to assimilate? Did it bother you? Did you know you had a choice? Did you have a choice at all? Did you know ways of expressing yourself besides the ones you were taught in America? If not, were there ever things that had to be left unsaid?

Two hundred years after your death, Nikki Giovanni wondered in a poem if she were unhappy because "*i am black female and bright / in a white male mediocre world.*" This is not a kind sentiment, but I admit that I repeat it to myself sometimes. Do you think it might ever have helped you?

Most of all, were you as unsettled about your own grandmothers as I am? I feel as if I have lost mine because the bonds of memory and space have snapped, but you must have felt the same loss so much more—taken so far away from them all at the age of seven, never to look back, never to return. The only detail you were ever able to remember about your home in Africa was that every morning your mother poured a libation of water to the sun. My history tapers away as it stretches back; yours was severed completely, leaving you only yourself. I wonder if you looked for your ancestors as I do, and if you did, I wonder what you were able to find.

I also have a hope. I hope that because you could still see your children, you looked to the future too. I hope this for my real grandmothers as well; I hope that even though I cannot see them, they have found me, and that in me they see themselves. This is the remaining hope when history cannot look backwards—that there is still a place where the past looks ahead. You may have wondered about what life for African American women would ever become; when you see us now, I hope you are joyfully surprised. Poet Phillis, I look at the letter you wrote to the students at Harvard College and I smile to think that you were speaking only to white men. I hope you smile when you hear someone reading it and you look and see me; a black woman to whom " *'tis giv'n to scan the heights / Above.*" I hope all of you smile at all of us, all the ones who came after.

Southern University, 1962

Kevin Young

for my father

Let's see   first afros I saw   were on these girls from SNCC
                they had dark
berets with FREEDOM NOW on them   that barely covered their helmets
of hair   they sang of the struggle   of the nonviolent demonstration
                in town
that weekend   By Saturday it was raining like hell   me and Greene
we were home boys   from Opelousas High
                we were trying to pour in
the last of the blue and white buses this black man in town
                had let SNCC use
I had my arm in the door   trying to get on out of the rain
                and so split my
fiveninetyfive raincoat   right down the side   I tossed it on the ground
and me and Greene got on just before the bus pulled away
                When we got
outside campus   ten big beefy white guys
                with red faces and silent yellow
slickers to their knees   blocked the bus and began pounding and
                pounding
on the door with billy clubs   they tore the door off   and stormed on
dragging the driver off the bus   throwing him in the trunk
                they said there
wasn't gonna be no demonstration today   not here
                but once their lights
disappeared   under all that water   someone said let's go
                so me and Greene
and everyone else got off the anchored bus   and walked the four

miles to town   by our soaking selves   When we got to McKays
                the whites'
only five&dime   it was empty as a drum
                they knew we were coming
had locked up and gone home   the street was a sea   of umbrellas
and soon as the wind came   which of course it did
                my threeninetyfive
umbrella blew in on itself   so I left it on the walk   a broken black
bird   as we started to march towards the city council
                Greene's fiveninety
five cardboard shoes   began falling apart
                I could just see the top of the white
marble building   we had started to cross Main Street   when about
six cop cars   came wailing out of nowhere
                a dozen or so plainclothesmen
jumped out   holding these cans of tear gas   they said
                don't even try
crossing this street   go home and stop making trouble
                just then the light
changed   turning from red to green   we crossed
                the men clubbed us
threw their tears at us   they took out our wallets
                took everything we had
and left it on the sidewalk   with our streaming eyes   with the rain

From White to Black Campus

Omar Tyree

BACK IN THE SPRING OF 1989, WHILE ATTENDING THE University of Pittsburgh, some fellow African-American students and I were feeling generally alienated from campus life.

"Yo man, I wonder what brothers at Howard would be doing on a night like this," my friend said. A year later I found myself on the campus of Howard University in "Chocolate City," Washington, D.C.

Black universities have always offered some of the most beneficial assets for the education of African Americans, advantages which predominantly white universities lack. Professors, classmates, and a surrounding environment which reflects the identity of Black students are excellent helps socially and academically. And a prestigious Black college gave me the extra boost that I needed to finish my education.

In my first semester at Pittsburgh in the fall of 1987, I earned a 3.58 G.P.A. and joined the Phi Eta Sigma Honor Society. Pitt had television coverage in NCAA Division I football and basketball, and I was a member of Pitt's Big East track team. My college career was in order and the future looked very positive. But as the months moved on into the second semester, weird things started to happen.

I began to evaluate my purpose in life as a Black man. When my Jewish roommate used to ask me, "Why are Black people so violent?", at first I couldn't come up with a response. It was not until the completion of a cultural anthropology course in the spring of 1988 that I was able to respond.

The course in cultural anthropology detailed the devastation that western society has caused not only Black people, but also all people of color across the globe. Asia, Latin America, Australia, and Africa have all been carved up, raped, and controlled by western culture. The western world has not only practiced genocide on people of color, but also on helpless animals while destroying the natural environment. My eyes were opened that semester, but unfortunately my studies were affected. I just couldn't seem to concentrate on my work while walking around swallowing animosity toward white people.

My grades started to fall as I felt more alienated in the classroom. I became a "Black radical" and the entire world became polarized. Every part of life became either Black or white. Now I had a response to my roommate's interesting question.

"Black people are only a product of their environment, because white people are the real violent ones," I said near the end of that semester. "What about when six million Jews were killed in Germany? It wasn't Black people who did it." Quickly he got the message, but still he had a response. "Yeah, but Jews are not running around killing each other."

I was startled, with no response again, and this time I was criticizing Blacks all summer long for everything we seemed to fail in. Jews and Asians control our communities economically, a feat which African Americans fail to do. Are they better keepers of money than we are, or is it because they're more respected and can get more financial support from the government? I continued to ponder this question. We seemed to be failures, and I was mad and ashamed.

In the fall of 1988, I took an African-American literature course and I wrote a ten-page report on Malcolm X after reading his autobiography. The book made me realize the importance of a Black revolution. Black people should produce goods and services and begin to control their environment. Most importantly, African-Americans should have confidence in themselves. And if they have confidence in themselves, they should have no problem with attending predominantly Black universities.

I decided to leave Pitt after the spring of 1989. Nevertheless, money was a problem at Howard. In the fall of 1989, there were only loans to receive and the rest of the tuition had to be paid by my mom and earnings from an after-school job.

Most of the African-American students at Pitt, including me, were scholars from the inner city, and we were heavily recruited to raise Pitt's "minority" enrollment. "It's a white world and we have to learn to deal with white people," we would say. Pitt gave us lots of financial aid and college scholarship grants, and besides we didn't want to go to "dumb" Black schools anyway. But what we didn't realize is that we were accepting oppression by degrading the integrity of African-American people and Black universities.

I had to work for both school years at Howard and had a G.P.A. which rose each semester from a 2.6 to a 3.7. My average is now 3.25. And at Howard, I realized that it takes hard work to build confidence with skills to compete and to develop an educated "Black machine." A "Black machine" is one who is never tired of producing ideas to increase the awareness and the number of opportunities for African-American people. I feel that African-American college students should graduate with a plan to help our people. With one more semester and thirteen credits to go, Howard has created a "Black machine" in me.

Many African Americans graduate from large white universities, but a higher percentage graduate from Black colleges. It's you against the world in a large classroom at Pitt, and despite the importance of a college's reputation, the real purpose for being in college is to further one's education.

I remember a few experiences with white students at Pitt which were not at all tasteful, like the time a group of four white males secretly changed a correct answer I had supplied on a chemistry lab experiment. Or the time my friend Calvin and I were given invitations to a white fraternity party only to be stopped at the door and informed that there was no more room. The only two African-American members had given us the invitations, but maybe Calvin and I were "too Black." It looked like the party had plenty of room to us. Then again, maybe the white fraternity had decided that two African-Americans were enough already.

One Black friend who grew up in the suburbs with white students, and was an honor student himself, told me that his white study partners had done him an injustice as well.

"I was supposed to do this project with these white guys for class," he said, "and they changed the meeting and met without me, claiming that they couldn't get in contact with me. I couldn't believe that because they had obviously gotten in contact with each other, and we all have classes together." These are only small tastes of the negative events which troubled me at Pitt. It was time to leave.

A positive surrounding brings strength to the African-American student inside and outside of the classroom. Black professors can speak of their successes and hardships. Networks to African-American businesses and organizations are available. Students learn to believe that they can succeed. Furthermore, Black colleges continue to produce most of the nation's African-American teachers.

Because I will graduate from Howard, my awareness of African-American excellence and unity is enhanced. Not to say that the University of Pittsburgh is a bad school, but at Howard I have learned to love my people and to understand them. It takes hard work to build a "Black machine," and most white universities don't have what it takes. My mission is now to do all I can to increase the power of African-American people through education and the benefits which can be gained from it. I will graduate as a print journalist who plans to become a novelist, an entrepreneur, and a teacher, all in the cause of uplifting African-American people. Thank God for Black universities.

Eastley Echoes

Dayle B. De Lancey

For my mother, F. Elaine De Lancey, who puts me on the right road and outfits me for the journey, and for Miriam "Duchess" Harris, who tells the story wherever she goes, and who, through that testimony, made me remember stories of my own.

SEVERAL YEARS AGO, WHEN I WAS STILL SUBMERGED in Eastley life, Robert Ballard and various colleagues at the Woods Hole Oceanographic Institute discovered the *Titanic* lying lonely and forlorn on the ocean floor. The search had consisted mainly of meticulous sonar sweeps, a process through which signals were cast down from the research ship on the ocean's surface into the dark depths below, where they hit designated sections of the ocean floor and sent sonar readings bouncing back up to the mother ship. For months, all the sonar sweeps had done was give the Woods Hole scientists a detailed map of the ocean floor in one of the deepest parts of the Atlantic—a research boon in itself. But one day, they had thrown a clear, silhouette-like reading of the *Titanic* up to the monitors on Ballard's bridge.

The creatures who inhabit that dark world several miles beneath the surface of the sea had long since devoured any human remains, so Ballard and company found no trace of bodies. What they did find—in abundance—were the opulent relics of the *Titanic's* maiden voyage, preserved by temperature, darkness, and depth. Ballard had been in a quandary about what to do with the *Titanic* throughout the long months that he had spent searching for it. The French scientists who had donated men, technology, and time wanted to sack the ship and place its relics in a museum. The Texas oilmen who had financed part of the research wanted to find a way to raise the vessel so that all of its remains, including the ship's own rusted and worm-eaten carcass, could be auctioned. But Ballard mourned the *Titanic's* "two-thousand lost souls" and ordered the ship and its secrets preserved as a memorial to them. To gain support for his position, he photographed everything—from the gaping thirty-foot hole where a smokestack used to be to the china cup that rested unbroken on the sand of the ocean floor several hundred feet from the ship—and released the pictures to the world. People were moved.

I was one of those people. In fact, I was obsessed with the *Titanic* disaster during my last three years of secondary school. My mother tells me that this was part of a pattern of identification with violent suffering, especially violent suffering involving children, that she first noticed when, as a ten-year-old, I trembled and wept for the murdered children of Atlanta with an anguish that she was almost willing to swear was some type of psychic connection. When, five years later, the second MOVE house was torched and its adolescent inhabitants found charred in its ashes, my own flesh burned; I read over and over again the newspaper profiles of MOVE that had appeared in the days before the firestorm, studying the children's faces, learning their names. And when, as a seventeen-year-old helping my mother prepare a history unit for one of her classes, I at last learned the details of the story of the Chicago boy whose name I had heretofore heard only in passing, I felt Emmett Till's blood call out to me from the grave, and saw his smile flash and his amber eyes glow in months of vivid dreams.

When I saw the photos of the *Titanic's* remnants in *Time* magazine, I was especially struck by one of the head of a doll. According to *Time*, scores of children, most of them the offspring of second- and third-class passengers, perished when the *Titanic* sank. The doll's head, which was made of the delicate porcelain common to the period, was remarkably intact, with traces of red still visible on its cupid's bow lips, a few strands of blond hair still attached—by miracle or accident—to its pale pate, and its lashed blue eyes crusted open and staring into the darkness. From the very first time that I saw it, and I saw it many times in Eastley's "Library Two," I was inexplicably drawn to the *National Geographic* articles on Ballard's expedition. "Like a damned morbid moth to a flame!" my mother said angrily, when I smuggled the magazine home one night. The doll head was highly evocative. When I looked into her eyes, I saw the ship's stewards, whom Captain Smith had instructed to prevent the third-class passengers from entering the area of the ship where the lifeboats were kept (the *Titanic*, I had been surprised to discover, was transporting large numbers of poor European families to new homes in the United States). The stewards stood with their arms linked together before the desperately surging crowds of immigrant women and children, their blue-uniformed bodies a living and impenetrable wall that I could almost feel pressing against my own.

The longer I attended The Eastley School for Girls, a small private school in a wealthy suburban town twenty miles from the city in which my mother and I lived, the more I found myself making a concerted effort not to feel sorry for white people, or to identity with their tragedies. Nevertheless, the doll's head touched me.

Sometimes, lying in bed in the morning before I rose to make my way to Eastley, or resting in bed at night to renew myself after a full day there, I thought of that doll, of that ship, and of that water, dark and blue. Mommy and I had to get up so early to get me ready for school that when we left our apartment to head for the train station, the sun was only beginning to shake off the cover of night. It was the time of morning when looking up at the sky is like looking toward the ocean's surface from a vantage point deep in the water, halfway between the bottom and the top: it was just that shade of blackish-blue. Because Eastley required that each girl be involved in some sort of extracurricular activity, and I then went to my mother's office after taking the train back into the city every afternoon (so that we could eat dinner at the Faculty Club of the university where she taught), the sun was always either down, starting down, or nearly down by the time my mother and I arrived home. Thus, the end of my schoolday was also the blue of the deep sea. For five years, I awoke to cobalt and arrived home to cobalt; so was Eastley colored in my mind.

Much later, during my second semester of college, I was surprised when I began to cough little rivulets of rage. I couldn't figure out from what depths they had been pumped. It was then that I realized that, for five years, I had done nothing but go to school early and come home late, for day upon day, in a cycle so complete that I scarcely thought about its mechanics or remembered how it had begun. I knew, of course, how it would end—"COLLEGE" flashed forth like a beacon at the edge of the blue expanse—but I was so engrossed that I never thought to measure the distance to that point. Every day, though, I added a new, treasured hope to a chest nestled in the warm, dry bottom of the lighthouse from whence the beacon shone: I would do well in college, very well, so well that never again would anyone be able to question my right to the education I was getting, or attribute both my successes and my presence in their midst to my blackness alone; there would be boys in college, lots of them, lots of good ones, and maybe some or one of them would like me, or think that I was pretty, or become a friend; and I would have real friends in college, good friends, best friends, who would never drag a swift and sneaky glance over the top of my paper to see whether my grade was higher than theirs and get angry if it was, or hold my arm aloft next to theirs when they got back from spending Christmas vacation in Bermuda so that they could show everyone how deep a tan they'd gotten.

These hopes were not only all I ever managed of question and critique; they were also, quite simply, all I ever managed of deep consideration where Eastley was concerned. If I opted to analyze the particulars of my situation, I would perish; if I took a moment to think about the means by which I accomplished my feat, I would lose the power to achieve it. It was safer—and, of course, necessary—to study German, or Ancient and Medieval History, or Biology, or English Literature, or Sculpture, or Drama, or Latin, than it was turn my attention to the setting in which I learned these subjects. To contemplate would be to lose the ability to breathe water, and such was a loss I could ill afford. And so I rose and fell each day, putting off reflection for a date in the indeterminate future, storing reactions in some unseen place, always rising and falling, rising and falling, in the steadily wakening or weakening light.

White Friends

Jennifer L. Vest

After awhile
You don't want to explain anymore
You stop telling
Stop being patient
Close your eyes, hold your heart
And run like hell.

They call you narrow then
They want to know why you
No longer want to teach
Them to love you,
No longer want to hold
Their one hand
As they punch you
With the other
No longer want to wipe
The spit from your face
Turn the cheek
Be invincible
Be like granite
And smile
In the stinging
Onslaught
Which they call
Their innocent ignorance.

Untitled

Touré

"SHUT UP, TOURÉ!" MY CLASSMATE ROARED AN-
grily, his dark-skinned, middle linebacker frame and red, frat sweatshirt
looming violatingly in front of me and above me and around me. "You
ain't *Black*!"

I was shocked. My jaw dropped; the room fell silent.
In a heartbeat, cultural-nationalism had gone from an abstract concept
to a lyncher's noose and it was me being hung. If any of the twelve students standing around me screamed, I didn't hear it. It was Saturday
night. Time to go home and prepare for Sunday and the homework due
on Monday. The end of the weekend. But for me it was the Saturday
night of my college years. The bill for my two-year-old crimes against
the Black community was past due and my classmates had come to my
face to demand payment.

The lynch mob's footsteps had been audible behind
me for years. Because the only thing most Black people control is how
much we believe the illusion of our empowerment, we will reach out to
control anything. We abuse loved ones into submission, join gangs to
kill over turf we will never own, burn down our neighborhoods and call
it an insurrection. And in the subworld of collegiate cult-natism the
lynchers come quick, ready to slip the noose of cultural intimidation
over any neck that'll fit.

My freshman year at Emory University was spent
avoiding most of my Black classmates and their organizations. More
than a decade in a New England prep school and the conflicting lessons
of first-generation middle-class parents made identification complex for
me. Especially confusing were the lessons of Dad, who, thanks to hard
work and affirmative action, lived a bold class ascension that took him

from the streets of Harlem to the head of his own, now fifteen-year-old, accounting firm. It left him a firm believer in cultural submersion. "They *expect* you to be loud and unruly!" he would warn of my prep school teachers and classmates as he combed my little afro and zipped and buttoned me up for first grade. The answer he would order triumphant and dead serious: "*Trick 'em!*"

Dad and Mom drove me to college and left me sitting on the curb in front of the dorm with my stuff on my left and the rest of the world on my right. More used to being the only Black than one of many, I chose what I knew, opting for the supposed glamour of being the only Black. The glamour, I constantly lied to myself, was without tarnish. I did not wince at the irony of wanting to be in a white world yet being unwilling to be as invisible as they hoped. I wasn't bothered by constantly explaining myself, my race. I didn't mind dating thin-lipped blondes and brunettes with no resemblance to my beautiful brown-skinned Mother. I didn't know that while I understood racism so well in the institutional, the macro, I aided it in the personal, the micro. I lied so well.

While all this went on, the lynchers, baby cult-nats all, many still firmly entrenched in their parents' economic diapers, to clean up messes, were deciding they weren't Black but African-American. Or not Afro-American but Black. Or was it not American at all, but just African? I can't recall which it was, but neither can they. All they knew was that I, the sell-out, oreo, wanna-be, house nigger, incognegro would never play their cult-nat games.

I went home for the summer with a lot to think about. Talked to Mom and Dad, traveled to London and read. And then suddenly there was something in Public Enemy's *Fear of a Black Planet* I hadn't heard in previous listenings. Something that spoke directly to me. You're not being honest with yourself, it said. Look and listen deeper, it advised. Run and buy *The Autobiography of Malcolm X* and read, it demanded. I did.

If to be surprisable and impressionable is to be young, then I discovered how young I was that summer poring through *Malcolm X*. And the I who began the book at summer's open was not the same at either's close.

That fall I returned to school determined to stop paying lip service and to join my classmates where they lived, played, organized. But some weren't having it. To them, the community was a rigid religion I had sinned against. To them, I had not taken the sacrament of weekday protests and weekend parties; I had not worshipped at the altar of the Black woman; and, worst of all, I had joined another church when I joined a white fraternity. These were serious sins from which there was no salvation. But what all these newly-minted cult-nats missed with their heads buried deep inside Fanon, Nkrumah, and Karenga is that Blackness is neither a religion nor a choice. It is a race, culture, and nation we are born into and spend every waking moment constructing. We share a history but react individually: there have been as many Black selves as Black people, all valid, all Black.

I made Black choices, though unfortunate ones. When I began accepting my community—myself—and stopped lying to myself, I made another very Black choice. And when my classmates converged on me like warring crusaders with their crude, blunt, *You ain't Black!* they failed to see that I was only a boy at war with no one but myself. That war may have been as messy and conspicuous as the L.A. riots, but the only person I hurt or betrayed was myself.

Half Gold, Half Black: Thai Journals, 1979–80

Faith Adiele

When I was sixteen I spent a year in a small town in northern Thailand. The region is known as the Golden Triangle because of the heavy drug traffic in the area where Thailand, Burma, and Laos meet. In 1979 Thailand was not yet a popular travel spot, so the only other Westerner in town was a Peace Corps volunteer—a white man in his thirties. The first several months I lived with a Thai family on a rice mill forty-five miles out of town and commuted each day to school; later I moved into town. The school had girls in grades eight through twelve and a limited number of boys in the eleventh and twelfth grades. Except for the English teachers at school, very few people in the town spoke English. None had never seen a black person before.

TUESDAY, AUGUST 28, 1979. THE RICE MILL. MY host brother Loe delivered me to Mr. Pongchit's office. When I move into town in September, they will be my new host family. He had arranged to drive me to the immigration office to get my visa extended, and we took a beautiful route up to the border. On the way back to Chiangrai we followed a long muddy road into the hills, passing through small villages. We came to a temple built into the side of the mountain and near it a cave. The mountain rose straight up, covered with lush greenery. Monks were bathing in a stream that came rushing out from the cave. High in the trees monkeys chattered and leapt about. Large butterflies fluttered over the clear water and kept bumping into us. The air was quite cool.

Mr. Pongchit and I were very spontaneous, talking about a place and then going to visit it. We went to a village of Chinese refugees who live exactly as they did years ago in old China. The village was dry and the houses were geometric structures of adobe-like material—quite unlike Thai wooden houses. We stopped and had a Coke of course and talked to some people. A girl was there, very friendly, and we smiled a lot at each other. As she gave me the Coke she said "Thank you" in English.

We asked what the villagers were waiting for. *For Taiwan to win back the mainland. It will happen*, they assured us. *This is only temporary*. Has been temporary for thirty years now! In the meantime they cannot even go down the mountain to the movies without permission from the local officials.

Mr. Pongchit now suggested something I had only dreamed of: going into the mountains to visit the hill tribe villages! The view was superb as we drove high into the tangled green mountain on the muddy red road. We found a small dry village nestled on a rise in the ground. Scrawny, dirty children ran out to meet us. They had ugly wizened faces, the washed out faces of sixty-year old men. Light eyes, fine dusty skin, blond hair that fell in random, sickly strands.

We walked into the village and stopped at a small open-air school made of bamboo, with wooden stumps for chairs and small hanging chalk boards. A picture of the Thai king torn from some magazine hung on the wall. The teacher was a young Thai woman, the only twentieth-century thing in the village. Her hair was neatly held with barrettes and she wore a pale blue checkered blouse and a silver watch. On her lips were the remains of half-chewed pink lipstick. She explained that the government paid for the school, and that there were usually more kids but they were all sick. She did not seem particularly pleased to see modern city-dwellers. She answered our questions but stared straight ahead, past us, into something.

"How can you live here, in all *this* . . . ?" Mr. Pongchit asked. She said she would live anywhere for God, do anything. He turned to me with a shrug that held disdain. What can one say to that? She shifted a little as we left. We walked on, leaving her standing there, all fixed up for herself, staring ahead. Contemplating perhaps her heavenly reward.

We came to a low platform with a thatched roof in the center of the village. The village men reclined sluggishly, consuming opium, the children clustered around them. The women were off somewhere working. Everywhere were little black hairy pigs and large white butterflies. The men were too sleepy and stoned to notice us. The children followed us, asking for cigarettes or just for something to do. Mr. Pongchit turned to the boy who looked the oldest and who had been the most persistent and handed him a cigarette. "This one has been asking for a long time," he said. We smiled and walked on.

We looked around the low, gray, dry village and then went down the road to the car, which was surrounded by children. Someone began to play a drum with a single, monotonous note that fit perfectly with the slow heat of the day. "Better than the cannibals of New Guinea," Mr. Pongchit muttered, as we stumbled down the dusty road towards the car encircled with little old faces. Butterflies flapped by and the drum beat on. "Are you afraid?" he asked me as we approached the car and the faces turned and the sun was high and the drum throbbed again and again and I put my hand on the door handle. Are you afraid? Are you afraid?

We drove along the road and saw a sign pointing to Chiangsan, the Golden Triangle viewpoint, and took the turn. Nothing can stop us now! We came to a perfect stone ruin that didn't look Thai, perhaps Laotian or Burmese. It was a huge *stupa*, each level smaller than the one before, ending with a cone on top. The gray stone was surrounded by jungle. A Thai guide was showing a white tourist around, and they both nodded to me. At Chiangsan we actually found a sign that said *Golden Triangle* and followed to the left! We sat on the bank of the river with Laos directly across and Burma to the left.

I was overwhelmed, looking at the green mountains with mist curling down from them. "At the top is a temple," Mr. Pongchit said. A temple hidden in all that thick white mist, at the top of a dark mountain near red poppy fields in the Golden Triangle. Suddenly the impact of all northern Thailand hit me and I felt like crying. The thick creeping mist, the relentless sunlight, the drums, the fading dusty people, silver opium pipes, teeth black with *betel* nut, mountain streams, monks' saffron robes, hidden temples, chattering monkeys, bold butterflies, the red earth, children with glazed eyes, soldiers with machine guns at checkpoints, the mountains, the warm rain, villages hidden in jungle, the tall blond European backpackers hunched in the smoky interior of Fascination Coffeeshop. All this beauty and all this decadence. I think I must be here forever. I find it hard to believe I wasted sixteen years not being here. All my dreams and poems are here.

Wednesday, August 29. Went to the village doctor for my mosquito bites. Nothing works—not extra-strength repellent from the U.S., not Chinese coils, not local Thai remedies. I now have one hundred fifty bites on each leg and cannot sleep at night because my legs feel as if they're on fire. The doctor was a nice man who spoke excellent English. We talked for half an hour about Thailand's social problems while his wife, the nurse, flirted madly with my host brother. They invited us to dinner, and as we got up to leave I finally remembered why I came. I displayed my swollen, purple legs. "Oh, mosquito bites," the doctor said airily. "Buy some repellent!"

Sunday, September 2. The maid's daughter woke me up and brought me tea. I wrote letters home while she slept on my bed. After I got dressed, my host sister Gluay and I picked fruit from the garden. We hung around the rice mill, charging around after each other with a huge bunch of bananas and leaping over giant mounds of rice chaff. My host brother Loe got perturbed because the workers kept stopping to watch us and weren't getting any work done. He called me to his side and took me on a tour of the mill.

"Let this be your day to earn your keep," he said, handing me one of the long wooden hoes the workers use to spread and turn the rice on cement drying slabs. I stared at him, hoping he was joking. Mountains of rice stretched around us on cement slabs as large as football fields. "C'mon, I'll help you," he said, walking out onto the cement. We bent over and began to push our hoes through the rice. The mill workers gave a great shout and ran to watch us. They stood in clusters on the sidelines, their mouths open and looks of delight on their faces. Gluay held her stomach and screamed with laughter. We finally reached the end of the row. Already my face was covered in sweat from the midday sun and my arms ached. The rice was thick and not nearly as easy to smooth as it looked. I couldn't imagine laying and turning the entire field—hundreds of rows. "Isn't this fun?" Loe asked, and I had to laugh.

We started the next row, looking up to grin at our appreciative audience. One of the workers had run to get my host mother and father from the mill office. They ran out with the camera, eager and shouting encouragement. The mother couldn't stop laughing. "Oh, Faith," she would gasp out before giggles overtook her. After twenty minutes Loe took pity on me and we stopped. Two workers sprang forward to grab our hoes and immediately began plowing through the rows at three times our speed. The other workers applauded and nodded to me.

Next we went to where workers were loading unhulled rice from a truck into a storage barn. Barefoot, with scarves tied over their faces, they hoisted yard-high baskets filled with rice onto their shoulders and ran up a narrow plank from the truck bed into the barn. As we approached they stopped their work and stared at us, taking the opportunity to wipe their faces. Loe and I together managed to lift a basket after pouring out two-thirds of the rice and the workers chuckled. Inside the barn I understood the scarves. There was no oxygen; dust from the rice clogged the air. It was dark and still and a single ray of sun came in through the open door. I began to choke and had to run outside. I felt sure that ten hours a day of this must shorten the workers' life spans.

"Look how they have to fill each basket and carry it inside," Loe said. "It takes them all day, ten hours, to unload two trucks. If this were your mill, what would you do to improve it?"

I was glad to be asked. "I'm *sure* there's some machine—I don't know which—that could load it more efficiently!" I said, eager to be helpful.

"Hmph," he said. "A machine. That's an American answer. Always a machine." He sounded disappointed.

I stared at him, embarrassed to have come off like a spoiled American. *I'm not really*, I wanted to tell him. *I'm nothing like the Americans you read about or see in movies. I'm black. I was raised by a single mother and ate government beans and cheese until I wanted to throw up. I can only afford to be here because of this scholarship.* I was also disappointed that, with all the great cross-cultural understanding I thought I had, my thinking was so limited. Of course, Thailand had plenty of people, people who needed to work. Of what use was a fancy machine in the tropics? How had I not seen that? This was the real issue. Western "development" is not necessarily the answer in a country like Thailand.

Thursday, September 6. Didn't go to school. A religious holiday. The servants put flowers, fruit, and small pink and white cakes on the small wooden altars all around the house. I walked out into the living room to find mats spread out on the floor with a feast laid down! Ten bowls of rice, an *entire* boar's head, incense, tea, wine, a gigantic basket of tropical fruits, dishes and dishes of curries, noodles, and soups, those little cakes. Oh boy, I thought, a party! I sat down and waited for the guests to arrive. After twenty minutes I was surprised to see the servants come in and start removing the food. "Who will eat?" I asked in Thai.

"*Phii*" was the answer. They pronounced the word, which means older sibling, with strange emphasis, drawing out the vowel.

I was bewildered. My host brother Loe was in Chiangrai, a good hour away. "But *Phi* Loe is in Chiangrai," I said.

"Not *phi*," they replied, shaking their heads. "*Phii.*"

"But which one?" I asked, impatient. "*Phi* Loe and all his brothers are out of town. What *phi* is coming for the feast?"

"No, no," they laughed. "Not *phi*! *Phii.*"

Why did they keep emphasizing the word? I frowned. At my confusion they turned to each other and conferred. One of the young women tried again. Picking up a small cake she began to talk about how *phii* was already finished with it. She then took a bite of the cake and handed one to me.

I shook my head. "I'll wait till *Phi* Loe gets back."

Shaking their heads, they gathered the first load together and went downstairs. I went outside to wait on the steps. I counted the shoes neatly lined up on each step to see if anyone in the household had returned. The servants came back with one of the drivers. He too tried to explain the mystery and then began to eat a delicacy, gesturing that I should do the same. Obviously they were not afraid that someone in the family was going to come home and find them eating the feast. Every time I looked at them they would shrug and offer weakly, "*phii*?"

I tried saying the word the way they said it, pulling my mouth wide at the sides and letting the vowel rise up through my throat. All of a sudden I remembered the lesson on tones in my Thai workbook. Like Chinese, Thai has five tones: regular, high, low, falling, and rising. The book had said that the same word, said with a different tone, had a completely different meaning. As an example, it said that a *phii* in one tone meant sibling, while *phii in another tone meant ghost!*

Though I knew about tones, I had forgotten this particular example because I didn't have much use for the vocabulary word *ghost*! What the servants had been doing was just a larger version of the food put out at the altar each morning and taken away each night. An offering to ancestral spirits. I had to laugh at the picture of me sitting on the front steps waiting for the honored ghosts to arrive!

"Oh!" I shouted, grabbing up a pink cake and devouring it whole. "I understand! *Phii!*" The servants gave a great shout and began to laugh.

Saturday, September 15. The town. Had to go to school today. Woke up and found I didn't have any regulation socks. After breakfast my new host sister took me downtown to buy some. I got to school early and walked by the ping-pong table, and my ping-pong coach shouted my name. He then performed various balancing tricks with a bottle, delighted to have captured me so as to have captured a larger audience, intent on both me and the bottle.

Now that I'm living in town, there's no getting away from the crowds after school. I was mobbed walking through town. Ran into friends all the way to my new home.

I changed out of my uniform and waited for a friend to pick me up to go to the basketball game, but no show. My host sister and I went. My friend showed up a bit later, looking fiery with her odd mannish hair swept back and her thick feverish eyebrows. The sun was bright and hot. The three of us walked behind the stands to buy sodas and I finally saw why this is the Golden Triangle and why the village doctor had said that drug addiction was so widespread.

The air was thick and heavy from all the stoned, dull-eyed men. Here the excitement of the game couldn't be seen or heard. A low soundless whisper started up and I could fell every eye on me. The air was dark and quiet and electric. Men standing in shadows, half gold, half black. I recognized the very stoned friend of a worker at school. Here he looked sickly, staring at me as we passed. A girl was lying on a bench thrashing and howling. Cries of absolute terror or despair or pain coming from deep in her throat. Six girls carried her away, still struggling. The silent spectators drifted away without a word.

The Golden Triangle is behind the stands at a high-school basketball game. I found it in the green thickness of the mountains, saw it again in a dusty hill tribe village, glimpsed it once through the doorway of a coffee shop. It is in the air. Northern Thais say they can't breathe the polluted air of Bangkok. But they can breathe this drugged air. Back home, black folks must breathe both.

Tuesday, September 18. I miss the rice mill and everyone there. Life was freer there and I felt safe. But I am Thai now. So much has happened. I wouldn't even know how to tell them. My whole life has changed many times over in a few days. I have noticed that growing is just a nicer word for loss. That is all.

Accent

Damon Roberts

REMEMBERING JUNIOR HIGH SCHOOL WAS IMPOSSIBLE without thinking about the problems I had with my accent.

On the plane coming back to America, I was sitting next to a woman, as I always seem to do, and as we approached the land of the stars and stripes I could feel my accent becoming more American once again. I remember Patrick Forde, the Guyanese boxer who was beaten both by Eusebio Pedroza and Salvador Sanchez in his bids for the world lightweight crown, coming up to the front of the plane to talk to this brown-skinned, full-lipped, bourgeois-looking woman sitting next to me. Patrick and I were friends through my father, and we exchanged seats so that she could get to know the young lady. But even more clearly, I remember, in talking to her, having what felt like a physical sensation come over the middle part of my tongue and I was no longer able to control my accent. By the time the plane landed, I was as American as when I left to go home.

America was my environment now, and I was not foolish enough to think that in hanging around Americans I wouldn't sound more and more like them. Yet every time a Guyanese said to me that I sounded American, my first response was to suppress the desire to punch them in the mouth before a deep feeling of shame and betrayal would envelop me—as if I was not making my country proud the way my father had encouraged me to do. Accent was very much tied up with identify for me, and for those first two years in America had been a constant source of frustration.

Kami, my younger brother by two and a half years, adapted quickly and easily and had become quite a social butterfly. For goodness sakes, I was supposed to be teaching my baby brother the ways of this world, not vice-versa. I had tried to take him under my wing in Guyana, to introduce him to my friends, to tell him about girls so that he could sound like he actually knew something with his little friends. Here I had no wings with which to shade him, no cultural adaptation to perform my role as big brother. And I envied him, secretly. He would pore over the sports statistics, from baseball to hockey, even as I distanced myself from them, on the grounds that they were American sports.

He could afford to start over, because he had nothing, I reasoned. I had a reputation back home, and I wasn't willing to trade that in for any kind of new life. I knew why I was here, and that was for my education. *I can't take time off from that to try to get Americanized.* Yet still, at least for the sake of image, I had to be in style, with my Lee jeans of various colors. This was the kind of freedom for which I had yearned—freedom from the khaki pants and the white shirt with the Queen's College coat of arms and the Nobbs House colors. Out of the $27 a week I made from my job as a *New York Daily news* paperboy, $15 was spent on buying a pair of Lee Jeans per week. The sad thing was that the next year, in the ninth grade, for fear of being ridiculed with "Shout! Shout! Lees are played out," I couldn't bring myself to wear those same "high fashion" jeans. I was an unwilling slave to New York's 1985 teen fashions. Yet regardless of whether I was in or out of fashion, I felt out of place, like my spirit and theirs were different.

Neither could I protect my sister. I had been taught not to fight, especially with girls. No gentleman would ever do that. Grave hypocrisy when I consider my mother crouched in our kitchen corner with my father over her, hitting her. She had tried to stop him from leaving the house by attacking him with a knife and he had responded violently. We watched, my siblings and I, and I wished that I was big enough or forceful enough or courageous enough to pick up the stool that I was sitting on to break it on his back. I was scared, or perhaps too well-trained in a philosophy that was being broken right in front of my eyes. Do as they say and not as they do. But what was he supposed to do, and what was I supposed to do?

In a nearby elementary schoolyard, Miari came frantically looking for me, interrupting me from a handball game. Two girls and about three or four hoodlum-looking boys came hurriedly behind her. "Damon, Damon!" This was urgent. She proceeded to tell me that she had come from one of the girl's houses, and that the girls had set her up and tried to hold her down so that the boys could touch her and take off her clothes but that she started kicking them and ran away. She wanted me to do something about it, to slap one of the girls or something. The girl threatened me—"If you even think about slapping me, amma bring ma big brother to whup yo' ass." Why she was getting frantic, I couldn't quite figure. It wouldn't have crossed my mind to hit a young lady. Even in Guyana when I was younger, at some children's party, a girl got angry at me, took off her shoe, and started walloping my head with blows. I used my hands as a protective cover and accepted my punishment gracefully. She was a girl. I was a favorite target for the blows of teachers in Guyana because I was mischievous and I could take a good slap—perfect scapegoat to keep the other children in line. Mrs. Jagan, in standard four, seemed to get especial pleasure out of publicly berating me and humiliating me in that way. But it didn't cross my mind to retaliate, certainly not with a woman.

People gathered around expecting some kind of tirade in the schoolyard that day, but nothing was forthcoming. My father, fortunately, was in the country at the time and I told my sister that she would have to talk to him, that he and the girl's father would sort it out. He was who I had run to when the older boys in the army compound had gathered together and stripped me of my pants, making me run home with only a t-shirt, my hands covering my genitals. After I put on some clothes, I asked my younger brother whether he would have helped me. "Why? So dey could pan's me too?" My father gathered the boys involved together in our living room for a chat. And, simple as that, the problem was solved. They never even brought it up again.

As I returned to the schoolyard from walking my sister home to my father, I approached Nicole, a big girl who was somewhat of a friend, and asked her what I should do. She looked at me forebodingly, full of disdain, shook her head and walked away. I ran after her and tugged on her hand to slow her down. "Get the fuck off me."

"What did I do?" I asked innocently, not understanding her anger.

"Did you see your sister coming to you crying. . . . Sheeet, you 'pose to fuck them up! Man, for your sister, you 'pose to throw rocks, stab and shoot people. Wha' kinda fuckin' man is you anyway?" Her fiery rhetoric took me aback. She could definitely take care of the problem. "Please take care of the girl for me, and you beat her up if she bothers my sister. I'll take care of the guys."

Nicole, before agreeing to take care of my sister, broke down to me a principle of American manhood, something which actually helped me to understand the backlash against Dukakis when he gave his 1988 response to what he would want done to hypothetical rapists of his wife. She explained to me that you never let anybody take advantage of the women in your life, your mother, your sister, your girl. Fight to the death if you have to, but never let anyone walk all over your sister. That was a different philosophy. Even without religion, I had grown up believing in turning the other cheek. Here, it was you and your family against the world, and I started to understand why those first two girls had reacted the way they did with me. And even though I shuddered with horror at a black audience's loud cheers when Ice Cube's character avenged the death of his brother in Boyz 'n the Hood, by then I understood. Nice guys finish last here in this dog-eat-dog world. This was no place for a gentleman.

All this served to intensify the already stark differences I sensed between myself and the people around me. It was symbolic of the alienation I felt, the outcast status I clung to, because I preferred to be an outcast than to betray my father's command—make your country and your father proud. I could never understand these Americans—why even try.

The transition was traumatic. Even LeRon and Marlon, friends as they were, would stand around and laugh at my accent. Damon, Damon. Say this. Say that. And stupidly enough, I complied. "Damon, Damon, Say three." "Tree," I said, not pronouncing the "h." And they would laugh. Then they would gather a few more people together and ask me to say it again. "Tree." As they all laughed I would join in with an insecure snicker, not quite sure at first of whether they were laughing with me or at me. When, soon enough, I figured out the problem, I would try to overcompensate. "Say it again." "Thhhhree," I said, almost biting my tongue in the effort. And, of course, they would laugh even harder.

Once a girl, perhaps the ugliest girl in 226, approached me and said that she liked me, that she wanted me to be her man. I looked at her in disbelief, this ugly, overweight, indiscreet girl loudly asking me in the hallway to be her boyfriend, when we had never even met.

"Tuh te' yuh de trut', ah doan really wan' a relationship right now."

"You wanna what?"

"Lewwe jus' be frien's."

"Wha'?" and turning to a girl behind her, "Yo, come tell me what dis nigguh is sayin.'"

"Whatchoo said?"

"All ah trying to explain to she is dat I in whan' no gyurlfren' now, dat I awright jus' how I stay."

"What?"

"Ah say I awright jus' so, dat how I in whan' no gyurlfren.'"

"What?"

And, as usual, people were gathering around, watching me like I was some kind of clown. And there I was, trying to repeat what I wanted to say in different ways so that I could be understood, failing at the same time to see that they were asking me over and over again, not only so that they could understand, but so that they could laugh at my expense. Finally, somebody in the crowd got tired of the game and ended it with an insult: "Monkey, go back on your banana boat." It pained me inwardly first of all because it hurt, but also because I thought I was better than these black rabblerouser American kids and yet they were laughing at me. Did they know who I was? Did they know who my father was? And then I caught myself . . . they don't give a damn about my father, and furthermore they don't give a damn about me. All my supposed knowledge was of no consequence to these people—they have got to find somebody to put down to feel better about themselves. And I started to get a sense of what Jewel Denny had felt in Guyana.

Jewel was a brown-skinned American-born girl of Guyanese parentage who had come into school with us in Georgetown. We were merciless with out imitations, in front of her face, behind her back, anytime, anyplace. We stuck out our lips and overdramatized the whole American style. We imitated her bow-legged walk, sticking our little chests out to mimic her developed breasts. And we laughed at Mrs. Blake, the Jamaican schoolteacher at Queen's College. I thought that Jamaican accents were horrible, as did all my friends, and ironically enough, people in New York were mistaking me for a Jamaican when I opened my mouth. Forgive them, Lord, they know not what they say.

The Guyanese in New York, I came to believe, was a persecuted individual. I thought of how inhumane the whole ordeal had been, and that I would never do something like that again if I was ever in the position. By the middle of the spring semester, when my Guyanese accent had lost its sharp edge and I wasn't being made fun of as much anymore, another West Indian came into the class. Though I was sorely tempted to make fun of him along with the rest of the crowd, I restrained myself and made friends with him, remembering how I had felt.

So when I returned to Georgetown, bearing in my body the marks of humiliation for my alien status, the ultimate insult was to be laughed at by my own Guyanese friends. I remember a friend accusing me in a derogatory way, "You t'ink you'se a Yankee boy now, nuh!" My acquired partial American accent was ridiculed in much the same way that my Guyanese accent had been laughed at in New York.

Every Guyanese had a "friend" who wanted so much to be American that even when he was refused entry at the airport, he still returned with a thick American accent. Needless to say the "friend" was despised. I had always laughed. Now I felt uncomfortable, even empathetic for the "friend," not because I wanted to be particularly American, but because I recognized the involuntary nature of my own speech adaptation.

Language meant identity for me, and therefore to be told I had an American accent meant that I carried with me the marks of evil that singled Americans out in the third world. The accusatory nature of my father's attitude toward "those blasted Americans," as if they alone were responsible for all the evil in the world, put me in the position of defending and explaining America, whereas in America itself I was strongly antiexploitation, anticapitalist, and gung-ho about the rights of the downtrodden. Nobody had to tell me to support Mondale over Reagan in 1984 when I had just come to America—it was automatic. In Guyana in 1986, I felt afraid that I was beginning to sound like the very conservatives I disdained.

Field Trip

Kevin Young

Not enough
was the lunch I brought
but I didn't trade, stuck
to my small fare. While

others passed peanut
butter & pickles, I ate
my soggy sandwiches,
the one with mustard

first. No dessert.
The field held on
to its secrets, the words
we kids got sent here to find,

names of trees & birds, Latin,
scientific. We gathered
samples, stirred under rocks
to study the world pale & blind

as the black albino
able to enter Cotillion, to pass
the brown paper bag
test at the door but still get

talked about. To this day
my father won't wear
baggy pants or carry his
lunch in bags—both remind

too much of teenage
times, of days Negroes
had to lug lunch to town,
chicken grease or hocks

seeping the paper, making
the bag a newborn's caul,
the veil that lets you see
ahead. After all, who knew

when you'd end up downtown,
walking past miles of WHITES
ONLY signs or the thin disguise
of Gentlemen's Clubs. No one

had to wink or hint what
Members Only meant. Just head
out, hungry, past the boulevard
towards the dock or boardwalk

or fields that chain
& label nothing except
food. Alone, devour cracklin
& drumstick till no meat

or marrow is left, just
bones & grease
& fossil enough to feed
a father's fire.

Part 5

You Ask Me
What Hip Hop Is

Art and Aesthetics

Billie's Blue

Yao Bhoke Ahoto

for the love of my heart
strings plucked
till my fingers blistered up
inside wounds worked
way a chain gang man's chains
grind
on his mind

welded voice
quilt of me/mine/mystery
patched pains and psalms

sages soaked my heart
in the deep blue of Harlem
water

i must drink
coolness, swishing
songs behind the swallow

        what have i done

                i feel a million songs

                    prick my tongue

You Ask Me What Hip Hop Is

Godffrey Williams

CREAMY NITES. A HOUSE IS REQUIRED, DEEP & AN-
cient, filled with vapors (Egyptian Musk above O.E., above sweat,
above years & years of BLACK LOVE incense poured slowly into ceil-
ings) rising from the center of black shadows wrestling with light emanating from a dense, smoke-filled bedroom of laughing, leaning bodies.
Walls shrouded in dark, invisible, stirring people: sisters pout, breathe
visibly, sweat beading on their silky necks below golden earrings. Eyes
glow. Against them, strangers, boyz, angry sentinels of muscles poured
against bones sleeping beneath gentle buttondowns, shifting silently,
searching desperately beneath their indifference, the unspoken code.
Bodies envelop as fixtures. Wall of flux sustains the center, from which
the bass line reels like Sab's spinning plastic. Subtext—bass throbbing
percussion above the muted guitar & growing ripple of synthetic cymbals. First layer of deep pulsing cannons settled, shoulders sink: fading
into the gunmetal blackness. Connected to invisible cords, we are flesh
marionettes, whose muscles explode in metered bursts. Soon, the violent eulogy, or nu style, or street psalm manifests. Soon, bass line drifts
beneath lyrics as stars disintegrating from blue skies into darkness suspended below the wrinkled, leafless veins of trees outside Rombay's on
any Friday night.

The backdrop incomplete. A sharper call is needed
& atop this, voice to articulate. Upon the bass, against the pretense,
finer sounds implode. In seconds rearrangement, & sent forward, the
slow culmination of intent. Air has thickened, punctuated with curling,
electric tones: punching forward like the LED display on the Sab's table:
red, green, gold. The instrumental struggles eagerly. A door swings

open, sampling the bitter language outside beneath the rising ash foam of KOOL cigarettes, of Newports.

Regular heads: Rog struts inside & Dial & E., covered in pillowy coats tossed on the sofa aside the nervous whispering statues. Their faces neutral: sharp beige noses, eyes piercing. Heads, dispersing as atoms through the crowd, they flow unconsciously. Bodies soon removed from the wall, coming into union in twos, in threes, deposited easily in the center. Instrumental. Something faint. Something unexpected: burning staccato cadence of a cello. Something Jazz. Something your Pops listened to. Something Ron Carter.

Layers. Cadences of bent seventies Pop Funk, of Parliament backbeats, of Pop 40 backdrops, removed, enmeshed together in a plastic alloy above the streaming arms & bobbing heads. Check the re-vision. Jazz cats. Dizzy. Miles. Something Rick James. Be-bop mix against faint Blues frag. Our invisible revolution. History fluxes, pulsing in fragments, in samples. X. X. Malcolm head. Check the paradox. We are the avant-garde. We are the remix, spewing a violent montage, constructed in the subtunnels, below the city, below walking monkey suits, below hot dog vendors, below the sweet exchange of money, below three-piece suckers rising gently in elevators from the street to their cubicles. Tell me.

Of Black on Black, of Crack, of Gangbanging, of Midnite beat downs hate/love/history, of Slavery burned into winding plastic, tell me. A nu upheaval is upon us, violent as our jumping bodies. Hearts quicken to a nu economy of rhythm erupting from the speakers. tell me. Two bones in my pocket & mind asleep: I'm nice, buzzing, but tell me. Az's dead, so tell me. Tell me, old man in a sound fragment. E-LECTRICITY: Malcolm lives. The foundation set. Voices forming—melting of near-gospel chants into the flow. Tell me, Umar Bin Hassan: *I love Niggers / I love Niggers / I love Niggers / Because Niggers are me / And I should only love that which is me / I love to see Niggers go through changes / Love to see Niggers act / Love to see Niggers make them plays / And shoot the shit / But there is one thing about Niggers I do not love / Niggers are scared of the revolution.*

Shifts in samples, the house beat, traces of broken meaning. Voice: hard & self-contained erupts, beating against the ceiling. Neutral & masculine, burns with bass line, exploding in low techno-drums (cello drives, vanishing.) Words, at once obscure, stream together above the bass: meaning. A voice deeply conscious of the gospel melt, of the drumming, of those in the center, of those affixed to the walls as wax statues, wearing deep grins, of quiet promises, & later the grinding union of hips: rub-a-dub.

Tribal litanies bullet from the speaker, heads respond as lips mouth lyrics with the familiarity of repeating your last name. The circle complete: meaning bent behind the rhymes, metallic pounding, & the angry scratching (the protrusion of fingers upon a turntable, pistons driving plastic in a sharp zig-zag.) In the kitchen, voices are mellow; drinks are sipped, intentions hidden behind a 64, a Mad Dog, St. Ides, behind a Blackberry Cisco. "Five Thousand," lips open softly. Eyes are neutral to the outflow of bodies into the street, who will soon crowd into cars, will soon fall into the comfort of pillows.

The Battle

King (J. Phillip Pringle IV)

IT WAS FRIDAY NIGHT UPTOWN IN BOOGIEDOWN, AND the moon found Geronimo in front of his speakers, caught up in a storm of sound. The music poured into the bedroom of his small Bronx apartment in waves. They bounced and reverberated off the walls, until he could feel the air around him shake, and his mind drifted into a meditative state, and he was deep asleep, but still awake. He sat motionless except for the nodding of his head, which could not be helped, as he strained his brain trying to describe in words the sounds that he felt.

The low moan of the bass line seduced his mind. He imagined a woman drawing him into the core of the storm. The deep, mean, full tone, embodied in the rugged features of her voluptuous form. The woman had a child who was hyper and wild. He rushed from the speaker, bringing with him the rhythm, causing Geronimo's head to nod as each blow hit him. A piano flowed over the violence of the drumbeat. Its sublime designs carried his mind to the heat of a scorching hot flame that was the guitar line.

"Yo! I heard that nigga said that money's shit was dead and stinking." Voices from the street below flowed through Geronimo's window and interrupted his deep thinking. He jumped to his feet and ran to the window. He looked down into the street, expecting beef; wondering what brotha was going to release, and who would be at the receiving end, catching grief. But all he could see were two brothas yelling at each other in amplified conversation.

"Damn!" He slammed his window. "Niggas is always hanging out talking about nothin'." He recued the record on the turntable, hoping he would again be able to dive deep into the music.

"RING!" He was startled by the obnoxious sound, and he leaped to his feet, looking around for the phone, before it rang again.

"Yo!" He barked into the phone.

"Geronimo!?"

"That's me. Who dis?" he replied, unable to recognize the voice on the other end.

"Yo, it's me, G!" said the voice, also annoyed at going unrecognized, and raising its tone.

"Oh, shit! What's up Chief!?" exclaimed Geronimo, as he realized it was the voice of his D.J. Shank, who got his name because he could always find the deepest cut on a record.

"Yo!" Shank yelled into the phone.

"What happened Bro?"

"You remember Preacher Man, from Rock Steady park?"

"Yeah. What about him?"

"Money got a record deal G."

"You bullshittin' me!" said Geronimo. "How did that shit happen? That peasant . . ."

"Buss it," said Shank, cutting him off. "Money's a puppet though. Youknowhati'msayin'? He don't write his own lyrics, and he don't even have a D.J., to spin records when he's playin'. In fact, they didn't even pay him. They just leased him a jeep to ride around in."

"He went for that shit?!"

"That's what I said. They're just pimpin' him bro."

"Well come on. I already knew money was a little trick. That's all you called to tell me?" Asked Geronimo.

"No."

"Well, what is it?"

"Money wants to battle you G!"

"BATTLE!!" Geronimo felt a head rush at the mere mention of the word.

"Yeah G," said Shank. "He wants to battle you, at the jam at Riverside Park, downtown. He said your rhymes were whack, and that he was going to take your crown."

"What is he doin', smokin crills?" asked a disgusted Geronimo. "What is money thinking?"

"I don't know. But whatever it is, money said your shit was dead and stinking!"

Geronimo's eyes opened wide as he realized that the gossip he had overheard from the two brothas in the street below was about him and how he allegedly couldn't flow.

"We got to go show and prove G!"

"True indeed," Geronimo agreed. "Yo! Do you have 'Give Me Your Love' over there."

"Yeah. I got that record. Why, you found a break?"

"Yeah," said Geronimo. "Where the guitar starts, and all the way up to where they break it down with the horns. All it needs is a phat drum beat. Bring it with you to the park."

"We in there," said Shank, and hung up the phone.

Geronimo stood quietly in the dark, remembering his first encounter with Preacher Man at a jam at 98th and Amsterdam; Rock Steady park. The jam had blasted into the early morning hours of the night. But when Shank took his turn on the one and twos, he unleashed a sonic beast, made of break beats and turntable feats, and Geronimo knew from the loud roar of the crowd that the party would go on till the break of dawn.

He stepped to the mike and started to recite. He prowled back and forth in front of the crowd, like a lion on display in a cage, and collected the panties that girls threw on stage. But this duo had come to rock Manhattan from Boogiedown, and the natives could not let this invasion of their borough go down without a battle. That's when Preacher Man stepped on stage and challenged Geronimo. Each one took their turn on the mike, and at the end, after all the lyrics had been dropped, it was Preacher Man who had been burned; by the laid-back voice and the smooth criminal style of the Boogiedown kid with the gold-toothed smile.

Preacher left the park, and Geronimo and Shank stayed and moved the crowd; until the sun started to rise, removing night's dark shroud, bringing light to the city streets. Now Preacher Man was signed to some white record label. He didn't even write his own rhymes or use turntables. He was a puppet, and someone had pumped him up to feel that since he had a record deal he could go to any jam, and his rhymes would appeal. The fool!

"So I'm dead stinking?" he said to himself in a voice filled with anger and disbelief. Then he laughed at his unnecessary anger, and went to the bathroom, to get ready to go downtown.

He jumped into the shower, lathered up, and ran shampoo through his short afro. Then he jumped out and put lotion on his dark skin, so he would not look pale on stage at the show. He grabbed his toothpaste and toothbrush and brushed his gold teeth. Then he took his Johnson's baby powder, and poured some down his briefs. He opened his closet and pulled out his freshest Adidas suit. Then he carefully oiled and cleaned his nine millimeter, in case he'd have to shoot. He placed his toolie in his pants, in the small of his back, and picked up his newest Adidas kicks from off his shoe rack. He went to his bureau and put on his thick gold ropes. Then he grabbed his leather Kangol Lido and his brown suede coat. He stepped in front of the mirror, to make sure that the gear assembled on his gaunt frame looked dope. Last he grabbed some cash, as he left his apartment to go wrap the mike cord around Preacher Man's throat.

Geronimo stepped into the street and started walking towards the D train. As he walked down the Grand Concourse, he began forging an arsenal of rhymes in his brain; wondering which one would be the mental slug he would put in his verbal gun and fire at his opponent once the battle had begun. He walked oblivious to the constant hum of the traffic speeding down the Concourse, except for the occasional blaring of a horn and screech of tires, which would quickly lift his head.

Small crews of Brothas and Sistas, Blacks and Bordiquas, would cross his path; hanging out, and enjoying the clear Friday night. As Geronimo crossed Kingsbridge Ave., a jeep passed, and the whole block got hyped. The people danced to the Hip Hop that blasted from its speakers. The music pounded so loudly that it could be heard long after the jeep had driven out of sight.

As he walked past Poe Park a shout blasted out of the dark. "Hey yo!" He turned, and recognized his boy Nana, who sat on one of the benches. Nana's cloudy eyes were fixed on the Concourse and the traffic speeding by. His mind was locked in a slow motion state by a dust-induced high. Nana was a Puerto Rican who spent his days smoking leak, and from his bench in Poe Park, peddling bags of marijuana to potheads, who wanted to get sparked.

"What's up bro?" greeted Nana, his speech slurred and slow.

"You are," Geronimo replied. "You diesel kid?"

"You know it," said Nana flashing a prideful smile. "Where you goin'?"

"Downtown."

"That's right, you going to throw down. Money was around here the other day."

"What did he say?" asked Geronimo. He could feel himself becoming angry as he waited for the quote.

Nana coughed, clearing his dry throat.

"There was a bunch of us here in the park, and money pulls up right there, in a jeep with a bunch of his boys," Nana said as he pointed toward the curb. "But money rolls up on us like we gonna get served. KnowhatI'msayin'? Like he's about to do a driveby."

"Yeah," Geronimo replied, already sorry he asked a question of this dusted mind, which existed in a world devoid of time.

"Anyway," Nana continued, "you know I'm the man. You know that, right?"

"Yeah," said Geronimo, his patience waning.

"I got up and walked over to money, and asked him what's all this, and that if he was looking for beef he was gonna get dissed. Anyway he got scared. I could see it in his eyes. He starts thinkin', maybe he made a mistake putting on his little show. So money tells me he's looking for you, and to tell you that he wants to battle."

"He say anything else?" Geronimo asked.

"Oh yeah," Nana laughed, roaring, so that everyone in the park turned and looked at him. "He said your rhymes was dead and stinkin'."

"Yeah!" Geronimo snapped. "I'm about to show and prove right now."

"I don't know," said Nana, flashing a demonic smile.

"Money's got a record deal, maybe he's got some styles."

"Shut up Bro," snapped Geronimo, trying to end the conversation at its present point. "Yo. You got skahms."

Nana pulled two bags out of his pocket and held them in his palm.

"Is that shit booms?" Geronimo asked, looking at the two bags.

"This shit is Indica. So you tell me." Nana said. The money and narcotics exchanged hands, Geronimo gave Nana pound, and turned to step to the jam. As he walked, a sinister thought entered his head.

He turned and said, "Yo buss it. Watch yourself bro, cause you know that it's an election year, and I hear that 5-o is on the rampage."

Nana said nothing, as he stared with unblinking eyes which betrayed a paranoid rage. Geronimo turned and walked away, happy that he had ruined Nana's high, as the dusted Puerto Rican sat waiting anxiously for 5-o to drive by.

Geronimo quickly walked to Fordham Road, and descended the stairs into the D train station. He stopped at the turnstile and cautiously looked around before he jumped over it.

"Hey!" yelled the token clerk, from behind the thick bulletproof glass of his booth. "Pay your fare!" Geronimo casually raised his middle finger in the air and ran down another flight of stairs to the platform.

A homeless man walked up and down the platform shaking a cup filled with change, asking for a handout from the people who stood waiting for the train. Most of them looked away from him, trying to maintain the peace of their own individual private worlds. Their consciousness shut out this man, who carried the reality of life in the city like a heavy load upon his hunched back. Geronimo walked to the end of the platform and began breaking up the hemp in his hand. His head shot up as he heard the approaching change cup of the homeless man.

"Spare any change?" the man asked as he slowly passed. Geronimo dug into his pocket and pulled out a dollar.

"Here chief," he said, placing it in the cup. Then he directed his attention back to breaking the buds of Indica up. The buds were green and moist, and he smiled in anticipation of the high. He pulled out his blunt, split it, dumped the tobacco, and breathed heavily on the leaf, so it would not get dry. He poured in the medicine, rolled and sealed the blunt, then discreetly bent over while he lit it, using his body to conceal it.

He lifted the blunt to his mouth and inhaled deeply, pulling the sweet smelling smoke into his lungs. Its heat burned his chest and throat, and like a black dragon he coughed up the smoke. He wiped tears from his red eyes and took another drag. He exhaled, and began to feel the restraints of time slowly fading.

The train rushed into the station, and as it clacked by he inspected each car, making sure that 5-o was not along for the ride. He stepped onto the last car of the train and took his seat. He lifted his blunt and took another drag. He exhaled slowly, coughing a little, and sat back. He closed his eyes, letting his stoned mind become lost in the rhythm of the train as it rushed down the track. He fit words together into coherent lines, then dissected and inspected them, making sure they rhymed; creating the composition that would be his ammunition, while the train rolled along, keeping time.

As the train pulled away from the 179th Street platform Geronimo left his seat and walked to the door. He was eager to perform and hear the crowd's roar. He could feel himself shaking with nervous excitement as the train neared his destination, the 145th Street station. He lifted his blunt and took another drag. Then he reached behind him and adjusted his gun, which had been knocked out of place by the hard plastic seat during the ride. The train reached the station and Geronimo stepped outside of the car and on to the platform.

"Hey!" A loud shout startled him, and as he turned around his eyes fell on a transit cop. He dropped the smoking blunt to the ground.

"You been smoking on my train guy?" the police officer asked in a condescending tone, as if he were speaking to a child.

"You saw me with the blunt. What you think I was doin? . . ."

"Hey, hey, hey," the officer shouted nervously. "You watch your fucking mouth guy." Geronimo looked down at the cop's gun. Suddenly all he could feel was the cold steel of his own gat, hidden in the small of his back. If the cop searched him, and found it, he would spend the night in the holding cell for sure. He had no choice but to run.

"Get your hands in the air guy. We're goin' to the precinct." The cop reached for Geronimo's arm. Geronimo leapt back, and then with all his strength attacked; planting his shoulder in the cop's stomach, and knocking him to the ground. Then Geronimo leaped down onto the track and ran across to the platform on the other side of the station.

The officer regained his footing and pulled his gun. He hesitated as he aimed across the track. He could not get a clear shot as Geronimo weaved in and out of the crowd of people waiting for the uptown train. He bounded up a flight of stairs that led into the street. He could feel his chest about to burst from the pounding of his heart as he stepped into the night air of 145th Street. The police officer's pursuing footsteps echoed through the stairwell. Geronimo dashed across the street, dodging the oncoming cars. As the nervous transit officer reached the street, he again drew his weapon, but couldn't find his suspect. Like a chameleon, Geronimo had blended into the Harlem backdrop of black skin. He jumped on to the back bumper of a departing bus, hanging on to the black visor which covered the back window. The bus pulled out into the street, weaving itself into the river of traffic. Geronimo smiled as he looked behind him, at the police officer who stood in the street unable to find him.

Muffled sounds drifted into the Harlem sky and became the clear intricate rhythms of record breaks and drum beats, as the bus drove by Riverside Park. Geronimo leapt off the back of the bus and entered the park. He listened to the drums, which seemed to talk. They told him the direction in which he should walk, until he found himself looking upon a dense ocean of bodies in motion.

The powerful sounds erupting from the speakers were like the invisible forces of the moon, which cause the tides to rise. Its power pulled and pushed the souls of the Blacks and Puerto Ricans, and moved them from side to side. The D.J. stood on a stage controlling the loud sounds, and the crowd. Their pleasure was in his hands, which viciously attacked the records on the two turntables. B-boys in hoodies bounced up and down, hawking the girls, as they moved their bodies seductively to the beat.

As Geronimo pushed through the crowd, looking for Shank, he began to feel the heat of someone's stare. As he looked around his eyes met those of two hardrocks, who sat on top of one of the speakers. They were hunched over, like two predators analyzing their victim, and Geronimo recognized the message in their eyes. He reached behind him, feeling the steel in the small of his back, while he looked at the two hunters, countering their visual attack. They turned away, acknowledging Geronimo's own silent message that he was strapped. As he continued the search for his D.J., he began to wonder if the predators were two stickup kids who had their eyes on his gold chains, or if they were a part of Preacher Man's gang.

The deep ocean of dancing bodies surrounded him on all sides. He could feel the sweaty heat of backs and the sharp thrust of elbows in his sides, as the people danced unaware of anything except their musical high. The D.J. began fading in the deep bass line of Eric B and Rakim's musical massacre. Suddenly Geronimo found himself at ground zero of an explosion of human energy. The crowd's roar of approval blasted into the air. He felt a head rush of excitement as he looked at the mike stand that sat on the stage. He was eager to take it in his hands and control the power which moved around him.

He continued to push forward and stepped into a ring of people, who formed the arena for a battle between two breakdancers. Geronimo watched as the two Puerto Rican combatants walked around the circle, stalking each other to the rhythm of the music. One of them turned his Yankees cap to the side and sent his body flying through the air, trying to kick his opponent. The dancer being attacked did a flip back, and his adversary dropped to the floor and went into his routine. From his audience he drew a scream as he supported the whole of his body on one arm. His elbow was tucked into his stomach, and his forearm formed a perpendicular line from his body to the floor. He took his hand from under his body and with his other hand caught himself before he hit the ground. His body weaved and spun around in imitation of the sound.

Geronimo looked across the circle and recognized Shank, who stood cheering the dancer on. He walked around the circle and stepped beside him.

"What's up money?" said Geronimo, as the two gave each other pound.

"What's up bro?" said Shank, his eyes still fixed on the events in the circle. "Oh shit!" he exclaimed suddenly, as the other dancer who had been waiting on the side leapt into the circle, kicking his opponent and sending him tumbling into the audience's feet. Then he stepped around in a top rock pattern, catching the beat before he went down, and began spinning on his head. "Oh shit!" Shank exclaimed again. "Wait until I get on the stage. These niggas won't know what to do with themselves."

Geronimo was glad to see that Shank was as eager as he to take the stage.

"You brought the records?" Geronimo asked, looking at the backpack which Shank wore.

"I wouldn't be here if I hadn't," Shank replied.

"You seen Preacher Man yet?" Geronimo asked.

"Yeah."

"Where?"

"Over there," replied Shank, looking up from the battle for the first time. He pointed across the crowd to a fence.

Geronimo looked up, and saw his adversary. Their eyes locked in an intense stare, and the tension of their silent competition charged the air. He recognized the two hardrocks from the speakers. They stood next to Preacher Man, one on either side, like two bodyguards ready to protect their boss if anything was tried.

Geronimo could feel anger beginning to ignite inside him, as he realized that his suspicions had been true. The two hardrocks who had hawked him from the top of the speakers were a part of Preacher Man's crew.

"So let's go set this off," Shank said, his voice quivering with anxiety. The duo began pushing through the crowd, making their cautious approach. Geronimo stepped to Preacher Man with clenched fists. He was ready to inflict pain, and make this fake M.C., who had disrespected his name, feel the flame which flowed through his veins.

"You been looking for me," he said between clenched teeth. The stocky young man who stood against the fence pushed his thin dreadlocks out of his eyes.

"Yeah I been looking for you."

"So I'm right here bro," Geronimo barked, driven to the point of trembling fury by Preacher Man and his nonchalant remarks. "State your business Nigga." The two hardrocks stepped to either side of Geronimo, reacting to his angry shout. He quickly reached behind his back, wrapping his finger around the trigger of his gun. The tension in the air was thick, and hearts beat rapidly on both sides, in anticipation of beef.

"So this is how you want to settle this bro?" Geronimo asked, motioning to the two hardrocks, who stood ready to attack. "What's up? You afraid to take the stage?"

"What?!" Preacher Man snapped. "Your shit is dead and stinkin' YouknowhatI'msayin'? I gots mad styles G. That's why my shit is on wax," Preacher Man bragged of his record deal. Geronimo slowly took his hand off of his steel. He dug into his pocket, and pulled out four $100 bills.

"I got $400 here says your rhymes got no frills. So put your money down, and we'll see who's got skills. YouknowwhatI'msayin'? Or is that record contract of yours not payin'?" Suddenly it was Preacher Man's face that showed irritation at the suggestion that he had received no compensation for his rhymes, but instead had been given a jeep that he could ride around in for a short time. Preacher Man matched Geronimo's $400, and raised him $200, bringing the bounty up to a yard. They entrusted the money to the stage manager of the jam, who gave his word that he would place it in the winner's hands. The music stopped and the crowed faced the stage, becoming the jury to the trial, which began as Preacher Man took the stand.

As he walked to the mike Preacher Man handed a tape to the sound man.

"SeewhatI'msayin'," said Shank with a disgusted scowl. "This peasant don't even use turntables when he's playin'." The music blasted forth, molesting the crowd. It was a montonous and preposterous blend of noises created from sample machines in some Manhattan studio. The Preacher Man grabbed the mike and started to yell into it, but his voice was barely audible over the bass and treble.

"You see this shit?" said Shank. "This nigga didn't even check his levels." Preacher Man looked out at a sea of blank expressions and a few people at the foot of the stage who jumped around in mockery of the rapper. As he finished his harsh vocal display he threw up his hands in self-applause. Shank and Geronimo wasted no time in taking the stage, as the crowd expressed in boos and jeers its rage.

Shank approached the two turntables and the sound man and began making his demands.

"Yo. Turn up the levels," he commanded, as he inspected the mixing board, which controlled the volume of the speakers.

"There's enough power now," the sound man protested. "Anymore and the system might blow."

"I don't give a damn! Turn the shit up, so we can get on with the show."

"Can't do it." The sound man answered Shank curtly, expecting him to leave it at that. Shank grabbed the small man and slammed him against the back of the D.J. booth.

"Turn the levels up, or I'm going to give you proof that I'm not playin'." He lifted his fist in the air "SeewhatI'msayin?" He loosened his grasp, and the small man resentfully turned up the levels on the mixer, trying to avoid Shank's wrath. Shank reached into his backpack and pulled out a small drum machine, which he hooked up to the system. He touched the key for the bass drum and listened as the speakers erupted, sending a loud explosion of bass through the park. The chatter of voices began to rise from the crowd.

Shank took out the two identical records that his M.C. had requested and placed one on each turntable. With his hands, he began sliding each record back and forth under the turntables' needles. He listened, making sure that the system could take the weight of the heavy sound he was about to create.

"Check the mike," he yelled to his partner, who stood on stage rolling and lighting his second blunt.

"Oh shit," said a voice from the crowd.

"That's right," said Geronimo. "I'm about to get nice, so I can get nice." He took a deep drag of the blunt as he stepped to the mike. "A one two, a one two. Turn the mike up," he said, exhaling the smoke from his lungs. He tried it again. "My mike sound nice, check one. My mike sound nice, check two." He listened as his voice boomed through the speakers and travelled through the air. His ears amplified and crystallized every sound. He walked to the edge of the stage and knelt down before the crowd, while Shank continued to scratch behind him.

"Buss it," he addressed the crowd. "I was chillin' at my house mindin' mine, when boy calls me, and tells me that this peasant," he pointed at Preacher Man, "has been talking shit." He took another drag of his blunt. "You people know what he's been sayin', right?" The crowd roared. "What did he say?"

"He said that your rhymes were dead and stinking!" Geronimo laughed, flashing his gold fronts.

"Alright. Buss it. The D.J.'s about to make y'all move. And me? I'm going to show and prove, and when we're done this crumb will be rethinkin', whose rhymes are dead and stinkin'."

Shank began cutting the record, unleashing a barrage of cuts and scratches. He improvised and flowed to a rhythm which existed only in his mind, testing the crowd to see if they could catch that same rhythm.

"Yeah," Geronimo said, nodding his head to his partner's abstract drum line. "Can y'all hear that shit? Can you feel that? See my D.J.'s doing y'all a favor by giving you just a little taste of this flavor. You gots to get your mind ready to be rocked steady. 'Cause I guarantee that on the mutha-fuckin' sound there is no equal. And if y'all can't handle this, then you better leave now, cause the rest is scandalous."

On that cue, Shank touched a button on the drum machine. An explosion of bass, snares, and cymbals turned the world inside out. The outside world ceased to exist, and the only reality was that of the music's effect on the mind.

Shank let go of the first record, and a guitar, piano, and the low moan of the bassline flowed over the drum line of Shank's design. As the break on the first record began to near its end, he began cutting and scratching, keeping in time with the drum line, and getting blend in the same break, from the second turntable. He would go from one to two, and back from two to one, blending each identical thirty-second break into the other; creating a song that could last as long as he thought this musical world should live on. Geronimo stood on stage ready to give words to Shank's display of raw feeling.

> Yo buss it. You wanna know the meaning of dope?
> I'll tell ya.
> It's a rhythm and a rhyme combined,
> that won't fail ya.

As Geronimo started to flow, his words wound up and down and around the tempo.

> I'm your pusher man nigga, yeah you know me.
> I'm the one you run to when you need a hit,
> So I dig into my pocket and I pull out your fix.
> But this dope is legit.
> I don't fuck with no junk.
> I peddle tapes of bass, cut with lyrics of funk.
> You rush home,
> And break it down, section for section,
> And tap your vein,
> And take your injection.

Lyrics flow through your bloodstream,
and hit your brain.
And when I enter your mind,
I'll soothe your pain.
Now you're ready to comprehend,
The lesson I'm going to send,
To your body and mind,
Through this musical blend.
You lose control of your thoughts,
And you know that you're caught,
Up in the one-two one-two of the music time.
This rush will take you to your depths,
And there you'll find,
The bassline,
Before you like a woman,
moving so sexy and mean,
You lose control and wanna scream.
So you make your approach,
But you can't handle her scandal.
You want to taste her lips.
Throw your hands on her hips,
And feel the power of the bass at your fingertips.
You can feel the low tone vibrating your dome.
And when she whispers in your ear,
You hear her low moan.
She'll press her breast on your chest,
Feel her soul pounding?
And when she whispers I got you,
You know that it's true.
She's seduced your ear,
And she's all you want to hear.
But she steps away,
And makes room for the next dimension,
A new invention,
In this composition,
That the D.J. fades in,
With a sniper's precision.
The drums start to speak,
In metaphysical speech.

And when they bring the beat,
Your knees get weak.
You're in the ring,
When the drummer starts to swing.
Hits you with a wicked combination,
And you feel the sting.
Like a raging storm that can't be contained.
This is controlled abandon.
You won't be left standing.
You're down for the count,
Face down on the canvas.
The piano comes in with sublime designs.
Takes you out of the ring,
and puts wings on your mind.
You think you can fly.
You wanna touch the sky,
And reach this guitar line,
That burns as hot as the sun.
But you can't reach that high,
Cause you ain't the one.
Now your rush is over.
It's finished, you're done.
You fall back to New York.
You can't even talk.
Already plottin' and schemin' for another fix,
Of a heroin rush found in a musical mix.
You're hooked and addicted,
And I've exposed ya.
Ya lost your composure,
And I'm gonna hold ya.
Fiendin' and droolin' for my musical diction.
You shouldn't have fucked around,
Cause I'm an addiction.

Geronimo threw his hand in the air as he looked out over the hyper crowd. He was like the graffiti image of a king, standing before his subjects, who shouted and screamed his name in applause.

"That's right. Y'all been rocked, and Shank and Geronimo are the cause." Geronimo turned to Preacher Man, who hung his head in defeat. "You can come with your white industries, your sample machines and fancy Manhattan studios, but you can't fool the people. Cause they know that I'm real Hip Hop, and I can't be beat. Cause I'm a product of the jungle called the Boogie Down Bronx, and those New York streets."

This Poem

Ta-Nehisi Coates

As testimony to just how ignorant they really are
here he comes talking that shit . . .

"Really digged your thoughts,"
AND
"the vibe was like flowing,"
AND
"man those images"
But then came the clincher . . .

"And by the way can I buy that poem?"
Seems he's always confusing my values with his
Taking jigsaw portrayals of sinister demons
and pasting them over majestic portraits of righteous Afrikans
   cause we're all
the same, right?
so can I buy this poem?

Maybe do it up in a pink prom dress,
erase the drab colors of oppression.
steal the clouds from the storm reality brews
and replace it with sunny days that never existed on this side
(that is the darkside)
Black warriors slain in battles of racial integrity
scream deadly warnings from these verses
but let's silence the grave tones,
gag the middle passage voices
that bleed harmoniously from the sea,

and slice the tongue that dare say freedom or death
Can I buy this poem?

buy this poem like buying niggers at the dock,
buy this poem like buying Black womanhood for 2 minute arousals,
like niggers buying wine on Friday night (just to feel alright),
like devils buying tickets out of hell,
like you buying warplanes,
like you buying battleships,
like you buying guns and bombs and bombs and guns,
like you buying death a full course dinner of fricasséed niggers
Can you buy this poem?

like buying handkerchief heads to do your bidding
like buying our heroes a 6 foot buffet
of grass, flowers, and permanent silence
like buying your death certificate back from the grim reaper
who wears a Red, Black, and Green robe
Buy this poem like buying
the sun,
the stars,
the moon,
the night,
the day,
the way niggers talk when you tell them
you just bought their latest song.
their latest painting,
their latest poem . . .
Can you buy this poem?

Maybe a billion for every ancestor honored,
a sweet mill for every baby lobotomized,
and a cool G for every nigger who's died a foolish death

Can I buy this poem?

Rape it of all its pain,
and send it walking in a new shade of red, white,
but no Black folks' blues,

It's got a nice original concept
but if we can do some fixing

Perhaps a few moral operations
and maybe just maybe
it'll pass for a white boy's hippie ballad
written somewhere
in the vicinity
of Harlem . . .

Hazy Shade of Revolutionary

Adisa Sebaku Banjoko

All change is not growth; all movement is not forward.
—Ellen Glasgow

"1, 2, 3, I'ma G—as in guerilla, see I'ma killa." Da' Lenchmob in their new cut on the *Menace II Society* soundtrack. It really made me laugh when I heard it. 'Cause when I first asked one of my homeboys if he had peeped their first single, he said, "Oh yeah, you mean them Muslim gangstas right?" "I guess I neva thought about it that way," I told him. "Well, that's what they are man," he shot back. And with that, we just rolled down Van Ness Ave bumpin' some Jamalski.

But it wasn't until I heard "Guerillas Ain't Gangstas" that it really made me think about it. So I played "You and Your Heroes" and got amped checkin' them just destroy the myths about those European society labeled "greats," from U.S. presidents, to music, to boxing. Feelin' it deep when one of them yells, "I'll snap your redass neck you mutha$%&*@!# perpetratin' biiiatch!!!" "Hell yeah, buck 'em down y'all!" I say to myself as I nod my head to the kick drum.

But then I'm checkin' out tracks like "Buck tha' Devil" and I'm like, "O.k. lemme get this straight, in one line brothas givin' Salaams (peace) to one another, but, in the next I'm hearin' them refer to themselves as niggas." Now being a former Orthodox Muslim and a frequent reader of the *Final Call*, I was caught in the paradox. Because from all of my accounts of revolutionary thought, speech, and action, the words "nigga" and "African" have never been synonymous. Especially from a brotha who claims that he's tryin' to civilize the 85'ers (the ignorant). And although malt liquor and marijuana are *known* destroying agents used in African communities coast to coast, you hear references to blunts and barley laced throughout the album. Granted the fact that I was pleased to hear no degradation of African sisters, I was still disappointed in the overall slew of contradictions.

I remember how angry I was after finding out that Ice Cube had done ads for St. Ides. Then I read an interview where he was sayin' how St. Ides donated $100,000 to the African community in AmeriKKKa. He asked the question to the effect (I'm paraphrasing), "Where is the Black community gonna get $100,000 from?" I dug his point of view for a minute, and then I contemplated it and said, "Lemme see, split $100,000 dollars between Los Angeles, Detroit, San Francisco, Seattle, Oakland, Washington, D.C., Miami, Houston, and New York. Assuming that there are at least three or four organizations that are in need, that comes out to about squat." "Man," I said to myself, "that $100,000 ain't shit compared to what St. Ides makes in a day, and it doesn't pay for the years of permanent psychological and physical damage done to African families across the country."

That triflin' hundred g's ain't doin' *Nothin'* for the sister who's got an icepack on her eye because her boyfriend socked her while intoxicated on the stuff Cube said would make his jimmy thicker. Or for the young African boy whose father would rather get his "buzz on" than teach his child how this spiritual, social, and economic system is built to destroy him.

The main difference I see in listening to Da' Lenchmob, as opposed to say Easy E, is that instead of pointin' the A.K. 47s at me (like Easy would) these brothas are pointing them at white folks. Which really does not bother me, but, what I'm sayin' is that there is still a lot of work to be done in terms of revolutionary thought, speech, and action before I would ride with these brothas into battle with the "devils." First of all, I'm not a believer in the "devil" philosophy, because I know of Europeans like C. F. Volney, John Brown, and, more recently, Michael Bradley, who have done and written positive things in regard to the African. But I won't try and deny that in the overall scale of history the Europeans' deeds of evil by *far* outweigh the good. "Hittin' devils with a bat" has its benefits at certain times and places, but if you're drunk and blunted how do I know that you won't bust me up in the midst of your intoxicated rage? 'Cause I've seen alcohol put the best of friends at each other's throats.

So then I begin to contemplate the violence factor. I think about all of the times my parents opened my bedroom door only to be greeted by Bushwick Bill yellin', "I walk around with a smirk / fuck school, fuck curfew, fuck homework!" In shock at the dinner table they say, "How can you listen to that raunchy music all day?! It's *filthy*!" And I'm like, "Wait a minute, first of all, both of y'all have and continue to use language like this regularly. Second, are these the same parents that watched Richard Pryor and Red Foxx videos, and who spun Millie Jackson albums till the wax was ragged? Y'all ain't heard nothin' new." They sit there silent for a moment and bark, "I don't have to justify why I don't like that music being played in *my house*." I tell them, "I'm not asking you to justify *anything*, but, please, don't you people of the older generation look at the Hip Hop nation with a holier than thou attitude. If you use foul language don't think your children won't." "Well, I still don't like it," they say.

Up and down the streets of the Bay Area, long rusty buckets creep along tha' Ave. With their hats pulled down to the bridge of their noses, smokin' a thick blunt, these brothers bump the likes of Too Short, E 40, 51/50, Totally Insane, R.B.L., Mac Mall, and Dre Dog. "Yeah man, this some *real* shit I'm playin' right here, you know? Dats why I like these niggaz man."

The sad thing about these many reflections of reality is that there is such an influx of violent Hip Hoppers that what used to be a smooth reality check has become a contest to see who can talk the craziest. Now it's about how many niggas they can blast, bitches they can fuck, and who has got the longest firearms checklist. Everybody is a blunted, 40ed, black boot stompin' beanie wearin', hooded, Glock down, not givin' a FUCK ass NIGGA. Many have become caricatures of the true gangstas that roam the streets. And most can't tell the difference between "street knowledge" and gangsta ignorance.

Street knowledge comes in the form of tracks like Ice Cube's "The Product," which explains from day one the odds against an African male in AmeriKKKa before he exits his mother's womb. Or songs like "The Streets of New York" by Kool G. Rap and D.J. Polo that take you through a no frills tour of the underground. And even recent cuts like Spice 1's "Trigga Gots No Heart" spell out the mentality of many young African men in sets coast to coast. But many of today's rappers come with this: "I'm *so hard* that if you stepped to me I'd. . . ." Fill in the blanks with your favorite gangsta fairytale. Most of these brothas have never even held a Glock in their hands, let alone "peel a propa cap."

A sadder thing is that now a lot of sistas are tryin' to imitate us men. Callin' themselves bitches, claimin' Glock status, and beatin' down hoes at the drop of a hat. You ever give time to think about the fact that we Africans in AmeriKKKa are the only group in the history of the world, as I have observed, that makes music about killin' each other, debasing our women and our men? You ever think about how deep that really is? We seem to be in the final stages of a self-destruct mode that has existed in the ghettos for generations. But I'll tell ya I never thought I'd see the day when the mother of humanity would be singin' songs about destroyin' the father of mankind. Whatever happened to African women singin' songs like "Strange Fruit"? Or African men singin' songs about what "Black Is"? What's Black now? Jackin' for loot on the Ave? 40-oz.'s? Wearin' beanies when it's 96 degrees in the shade? What kind of ancestors will *we* be to look at 2,000 years from now? What kind of musical legacy will *we* leave for our children to follow? "Bitches Ain't Shit"? "You've Been Played"? I think that it's dangerous that a group like Da' Lenchmob can be seen in the eyes of most as revolutionary.

The original draft of this work was published in July of '93. Since then J-Dee (the lead rapper of Da' Lenchmob) was booked on murder charges; 2pac as I write is waiting to go to trial on some drama with two undercover cops in Georgia and a charge of forced sodomy in New York. Snoop Dogg is waiting to go to court on a murder charge and so is Public Enemy's Flavor Flav, who is allegedly addicted to crack cocaine as well. Sometimes brothas and sistas see me walkin' up Telegraph Ave in Berkeley and ask me, "Bishop man, why do you think they do this kinda stuff? Why are so many African men goin' to jail over stupid things and killin' one another? It seems as if the Black man is losing his mind" and I try to give them an explanation as best I can. But then I read a book by Frantz Fanon, who summed it up by writing that in looking at the African male in AmeriKKKa's actions you must understand that "his customs and the sources on which they were based were wiped out because they were in conflict with a civilization that he did not know that imposed itself on him." What you are witnessing is a psychological and physically violent reaction to that trauma. No more, no less. And it's sad.

At the same time I would like to say that Da' Lenchmob is not the only group guilty of balancing on the progressive/regressive Hip Hop wire. Brand Nubian, Grand Puba, and a host of others have projected similar contradictory lyrical imagery in their music. Sister Souijah, KRS ONE, and The Coup have been the only groups in *my* opinion that have attained and maintained positions of revolutionary thought, speech, and action. Jamalski has positive vibes to share as well. Hip Hop, when really observed by those who seek its pure essence, will be seen as nothing but the Blues of inner city youth; whose parents couldn't afford piano lessons, saxophones, or flutes. All doubters listen to Schoolly D's "Another Sign" or even Ireland's group Sacry'eire, with their phenomenal track "Lost For Words." Masta Ace's "Slaughtahouse" is an excellent album to get to gain an aspect of the complete essence that is Hip Hop.

Some of my friends told me that I shouldn't have this essay published, fearing that I might get rushed at a Hip Hop gig or something. But I told them, just like I'm telling all of the groups involved, that what I am striving for is bigger than Da' Lenchmob, it's bigger than Brand Nubian, St. Ides, or anybody or anything mentioned. What I am fighting for is the global freedom of almost one billion Africans suffering from oppression here and abroad. These people mentioned above seem to be heading in the same direction I am, but there can be no half-steppin'. Being a revolutionary is kind of like being pregnant; either you are, or you aren't. Many have a hard time dealing with the true *personal* sacrifices one has to make when they involve themselves in the struggle. But it's all for one and one for all, right? If that is the case, then let no egos be bruised and remember that no one is beyond questioning—*ever*. Not Cube, not Farrakhan, moms or pops, Dr. John Henrik Clarke, not me, not anybody. Like KRS ONE said, "Remember that the truth can always be questioned, yeah, that's how I'm livin'." You see, if a man is speaking truth, he will not mind being questioned because he will have the facts to back it up. Then the truth can be seen by all. On the blood of our ancestors I have sworn to speak and act on the principles of Maat, which are the oldest known principles of positive living in the world. If the brothers listed above are aware of these principles and operate on the constant stride to uplift themselves and their people, all that has been written should not be a problem. In ending this "sermon" I leave you with the words of Spock, the rational Vulcan, "I object to intellect without discipline; I object to power without constructive purpose." Learn how to live long and prosper, African man and woman. HOTEP!!!

This essay is dedicated to the memory of John G. Jackson, who passed away on October 13, 1993. He was a master scholar of African civilization. His works such as "Christianity BEFORE Christ" and "Man, God and Civilization" had a profound impact on my life. His death was a great loss to those who knew of him, and perhaps it's an even greater loss to those who never did. Luckily, his works live on, and with them his legacy of the search for truth. I'm sure the ancestors greeted you with open arms. You did not work in vain, brother, believe me.

Pimp 4 Life

Lichelli Lazar-Lea

A WEEK OR SO AGO, I WAS INVITED TO AN INDUSTRY record release party at Prince's new club, Grandslam, in Los Angeles. The festivities were in honor of two Oakland rap artists, and as a resident of the "Town," and a hip hop fan, I was happy to attend. However, once I was in the club I witnessed events I found so intense that it became more of a case study for me than a party.

Inside the club, as inhibitions dropped with the aid of the free-flowing cocktails and L.A. "chronic,"* I witnessed how most of the brothers turned into snarling beasts, pulling and grabbing at me as I walked across the club. At first I stopped and explained to them that being pulled by my hair went out with cavemen, and that it was a poor way of getting anyone's telephone number. For the most part their approaches changed just long enough to ask me where I was from due to my accent. I explained that I was born in Trinidad but raised in England. They nodded their heads, then put their hands back on my "ass" and asked for my number again. Needless to say, I tired of dead-end explanations to brothers who had no intention of respecting me, and so I stopped explaining myself and was called a "bitch" for not giving up my seven digits.

I am a little ashamed to admit that during the three years that I have been living in the (not so) United States of America, I have become desensitized. When I first arrived in this country, I would have been so offended at being called a "bitch" that I would have been made sick to my stomach. The pain was particularly potent, as in England I grew up for the most part in the white community where white

---

* Chronic: *L.A. street slang for marijuana.*

men did not respect me. Now, in the U.S., I was surrounded by brothers who were equally disrespectful. Yet, after three years of hearing the word "bitch" used as frequently as the word "the," the word tends to roll off my back, as I know that I am not one. As rapper Ice Cube put it, "a bitch is a bitch," and if you are not one he is not talking about you.

However, at this point in the party, my shallow rationalizations were rising to my throat. I was not a "bitch," but I was being called one by men who did not even know me. I was not even dressed in a way to suggest I was interested in being sexually harassed, although as I scanned the room, I saw that the majority of the women were. I decided to head for the restroom to see how the other sisters were dealing with the situation. In the restroom I softened my choppy British accent so as to blend in with the other women present, a technique I learned early on during my stay in the U.S. so as to avoid isolation. I also wanted to make sure their prejudices against foreigners were not held against me.

The sisters talked freely. They were warm and extremely open. A beautiful woman with a dark complexion walked into the restroom, fitted in a transparent black lace bodysuit, with a g-string and four-inch heels. As she put on her shocking red lipstick, she complained about all the brothers touching her. I wondered what she expected as she was all but naked, but she went on to explain herself. "They can play with my shit all day, just let me see some rent up in here, O.K." There was a chorus of approval. I looked around at the other women, all beautiful and all but naked, with butts hanging out here, and breasts hanging out there. Another sister told me she had seen Doctor Dre, an L.A. rapper, in the club. "I'm gonna get me some of that," she proclaimed, and offered to show me where he was. I later saw her having an intimate conversation with an Oakland rapper. As I studied the women I realized what they all had in common: they had all made careers out of being disrespected; careers out of using their bodies to get money out of men.

Later on, I danced with a brother I will call "A," whom I had met on several informal occasions and was attracted to. Exhausted and dripping with sweat, we retired to the lounge area with drinks to talk. Things were going well until I had to go to the restroom. When I came back another woman was sitting next to him. I thought nothing of it, as I have a number of male friends, and I thought this could be the case here. As I sat down, he turned to me smiling. "I know what you're thinking," he said. Interested, as I was not thinking anything, I said, "Really?" He went on, "You're thinking: 'I'm finer than that broad.'" What! Shocked, I looked up and evaluated the situation. His homeboys started surrounding him, looking me up and down and nodding their heads. I looked at the girl as she sat flirting with him shamelessly. She had a light complexion, with long curly hair. I looked at myself, light complexioned, with the same kind of hair. I cringed, realizing that I was his type. I then looked around the room. All the rappers had several women hovering around them, showing off their goods like they were produce in a market, melons to squeeze and test for ripeness. Aware that "A" expected me to compete with these women for him, I felt sick to my stomach, a feeling I had not felt for some time. "A" had not heard a thing I had said to him during our prior meetings. He had not heard that I was a writer, determined to make my own way in screenwriting and journalism. Nor had he heard that I practiced photography, or that I worked as a visual arts director for a foundation. He had not even heard that I was a film student, or that I worked as a production assistant on music videos and independent films in preparation for my own feature film. I might as well have been saying, "Blah, blah, blah, blah!" for all he heard. He had not deduced from all of this that I was an independent woman who expected to be treated with respect.

I had a flashback to the day in England when it had finally 'clicked': at fifteen years of age, I realized that my white boyfriend had been using me to justify his being in the hip hop scene. Now a black man was using me, and it hurt more, much more. Completely surrounded, I saw how brothers looked at me, like a "ho." When "A" broke out into a free-style rap about being a "pimp" and a "player," I watched as the girl, declared by "A" as my competition, sat smiling vacantly, in total denial about the sexism she and I were a part of. All the girls were masters of the same technique: of removing their souls from their bodies while they were being degraded. They saw their beauty as a gift enabling them to be around famous men whose wealth they (the girls) could easily tap into.

At that moment, like in many others in my life, I cursed my looks, tired of being propositioned by men as a f**k before I could be judged as a human being. Damaging both for a woman's psyche and career goals, I thought back to the three types of men I have come across in the entertainment industry. Type number one makes sexual advances, but if the woman is not interested in him, he refuses to deal with her on any level, business or otherwise. Type number two thinks the woman is playing hard to get when she turns him down, and he continues to sexually harass her on every subsequent meeting. Type number three, the rarest of the three types in my experience, is content to maintain a business relationship with the woman, even if she is not interested in a sexual relationship with him. Yet it is important to note that all three types make sexual advances first, if they find you the slightest bit attractive.

As I cut out and left "A" to his fantasy, a few brothers made passes at me. Even though I wanted to cuss them out with all the obscenities I had ever learned in my twenty-one years, I knew better. Most of the brothers in the party would not have thought twice about slapping a "bitch." So I moved on, wishing with all my heart that I had "crew" with me: brothers that I knew "had my back," and were sympathetic to my plight. As I walked to the door I received a sympathetic look from a brother I shall call "B," who sat back against the wall. He represented one of the more conscious brothers in the party, aware of the ill treatment being inflicted upon his sisters, but doing nothing about it. "B" was a coward, unwilling to risk being made unpopular or alienated by his homeboys for disagreeing with them on any level. So he sat back and smiled, did not directly participate, but did nothing to stop it.

When I saw "A" later on, I was sitting, resigned, talking to my homegirl. He passed me walking up the stairs and summoned me to follow him and his boys, rather like one would call a dog, or more to the point, a "bitch." I assumed he thought that I would be honored to hang on his arm while he talked business, after all I had won over the other girl. But I declined and kept my "ass" right where it was. It is hard for me to pinpoint how I felt at that moment, but I do not think it too far off to say that if a freak earthquake had caused a ten ton boulder to fall on him, crushing his groin, I might have smiled.

In my experience, and in a condensed form, this is what the urban black hip hop "community" has become, much to the distress of the founders of the music. Men who aspire to be "pimps," have as many women as they can, and clock as many "g's" (thousands of dollars) as they are able. Women who call themselves "bitches" and don't mind being used as long as they get what they can out of the guy, which on the low end is a night with a famous rapper, or on the high end is being the number one wife in the harem enjoying his money.

As I drove back to Oakland I wondered which came first. Did men first start disrespecting women, forcing them to be materialistic because, let's face it, they are not getting love or commitment from these brothers? Or did these men start treating sisters badly because the sisters first made too many demands? Despite a more egalitarian relationship between male and female enslaved Africans during slavery, I came to the conclusion that this behavior might have more to do with the black man's need to have power over someone or something in a white patriarchal society where he has been made to feel inferior.

Black men and women blame each other, however, instead of seeing how the situation has been produced by this social system. One brother told me he had been in love but he had been dumped, and so he vowed never to love again. "It didn't amount to shit. I ain't gonna go through that pain again, for what?" Now he says he goes out with all kinds of women, "black, white, yellow, pink with purple spots," it does not matter to him as long as he can use them for something— food, money, and/or sex. As he told me this, I wondered what he had been like prior to the love relationship, and what had caused the sister to leave him, as I doubt that one woman could turn a good brother into a dog, on her own.

Many of my girlfriends who used to be in monogamous relationships now see many guys at a time. When asked why, they usually reply with one of two responses. Some say that it is 1994 and that they are equal to guys so they can do what they do. However their need to be equal to men has drawn upon the most negative and yet glorified male pastime of sexual conquest and domination. Others are simply hurt from being dogged by the men they "love" and suffer from intensely low self-esteem. Doing to other men what has been done to them makes the women feel powerful and thus momentarily eases the pain. However, liaisons such as these can open a Pandora's box full of negative repercussions such as unwanted pregnancies, venereal diseases, depression, and sometimes suicide. It is 1994, granted, but as women we must realize that even if we choose to have casual relationships with men, sexism dictates that we are not going to have the dubious honor of being seen as "pimps," but as "hos" by men and women alike.

Inner city blacks are afflicted with what El Malik El Shabazz (Malcolm X) called "a paralysis of analysis," as they are unable to see how their behavior has been created by the power elite. As slaves we were commodities essential to the white economy. Today we are still commodities as entertainers and athletes, making money for the few. I firmly believe that the United States creates borders for all its people. These borders are race-, class-, or sex-related, and the largely white middle class is allowed a passport by the white male elite with which it can travel with relative ease. If, on the other hand, you are born in the ghetto, and in this case are probably black, you are not given a passport, as the power elite wants you to stay right where you are, killing your brothers and sisters, or yourself. Only if you have something the power elite wants or can make money out of, will they give you a passport to the American dream of fame and riches. These passports are definitely not given to everyone, as the economic system does not allow for everyone to be rich. Even those that are selected for the passports are kept sexed- and drugged-out, so that they will not organize to challenge how they are being used, or how the system is destroying their community.

A great many of the rappers I have described do see the power relationship. However, as they are being used in a way that they find gratifying—"they are getting paid"—these rappers do not care. More than that, as the type of rap that degrades women makes more and more money, its economic success validates the ignorance in the songs. As these young black men see it, they took one of only three options open to them growing up on the streets, entertainment, the other two being sports and selling drugs. Anything has to be better than selling drugs, right?

There is a price to pay for going from poverty to extreme wealth. When enslaved Africans, negatively affected by the legacy of racism and capitalism in the United States, try to play the game the way the hegemonic society lays it out, they are destined to lose every time, unless they begin to understand the rules. History and the current headlines bear me out when I say that the money made by these young rappers does nothing to improve them as individuals; nor does it lead to the transformation of the system. All it does is make it easier for them to destroy themselves, as now that they are rich they believe they can do anything they wish.

As a woman I firmly believe it is upon us to take the steps to make changes. Never before in history has the dominant group changed, unless pressure has been put upon it to do so. In the U.S., the dominant group consists of wealthy black males. We black women must stop underestimating ourselves, for we have the power to stop men from disrespecting us—each and every one of us. Look carefully at the men

I have described. Watch how, when these young black men make money, they buy the best car on the market, dress as sharply as they can, and buy the biggest house or apartment they can afford. Why? To attract women! Men do not do all this simply to impress their home-boys. So, if this is true, what would happen if we said, "*no*"? If we refused to appear half naked in videos, stopped tolerating verbal and physical abuse, and generally said "no" to being disrespected in any way, shape, or form? What if we applied a condition, that the situation has to improve, otherwise these men would not be permitted to touch us! One would be stupid to think that ingrained sexist attitudes would disappear overnight, but brothers would definitely stop and think about their actions.

We as women must stop abdicating our power and use it. We must also stop competing against each other over men who do not care about us, and we must ask ourselves individually, why do I want this bastard? Do I have low self-esteem? *Yes*, and when we discover this, there is no excuse for us to sit back and say, "Oh, well," because now is the time to get on with our lives. When we are whole, then and only then will we find a brother with whom to form a meaningful relationship. We must also stop continually undervaluing ourselves, believing that we do not deserve more than we have received from our men. I believe we are actually complimenting our men by expecting more from them than they are giving. We are treating brothers like boys if we allow them to disrespect us, and they are definitely not boys, even though this racist society teaches them they are. They are men, strong men who have survived a kind of hell here in the United States through which we have been by their side, for better and for worse.

However, now it is time for my generation of black men to grow up, so that we can work together on creating a strong black community for our children to grow in. Black men must realize that all the qualities they look for in their homeboys can also be found in a relationship with the right woman. In us they can find trust, companionship, support, strength, love, and much, much more.

Part 6

Coming into Myself

Establishing Black Identity

Untitled

Jennifer L. Vest

Tossing between
Yesterday and today
The bed sheets are short
My feet cold
And the sunlight is
Piercing/is cruel
Is taking away the peace
That never came
With night time.

Day is nagging me
Is pretty
Is sharp
Is scary white
Is luring me
Out of myself
My warm bed
My uneasy acceptance
My unbalanced life
As if
I should get up
Today and live
Really live
And the hope and promise
Of today this day
Is irresistible
Is mine

A B C

Faith Adiele

I WAS EIGHT YEARS OLD BEFORE I REALIZED MUSIC EX-
isted. It was the summer of 1971, and I was staying with my grandparents on our farm in eastern Washington state. My mother was away at
summer school in Seattle where she wrote to us regularly from a rented
room. A few weeks into the summer she sent a package.

I had been playing outside in the yard when
Grandma went to get the mail from the big mailbox across the road. The
red flag was down, indicating that the mailman had come and gone, zig-
zagging his way across country roads from right-hand boxes to left-hand
boxes like drunken farm boys on a Saturday night. On the times I was
allowed to cross the road to get the mail with Grandma, I surveyed the
distance in both directions, noting with satisfaction that our mailbox
was the largest one for as far as I could see. When the county rezoned
all the rural routes and we were upgraded from Route 1 to Route 2,
Grandpa took the opportunity to buy a new mailbox. I sat on a stool in
his workshop while he painted the huge box a light, pearly silver and
handlettered our new address on the side: *Hansson, Route 2, Box 2704*.

That particular day Grandma came running down
the gravel driveway, a thin cardboard package in her hand, calling that
my mother had sent me a present. I jumped up and tore open the box.
Inside was a letter and a record album by a group called the Jackson
Five. My mother's letter explained that she had come across it while
searching a used bookstore for textbooks.

I stared at the album cover. Except for my old Dis-
ney storybook records, I had never had a record of my own before. To
be honest, I had never particularly wanted one. I was surrounded by
music—from Grandpa's country western radio out in the workshed, to

the music my grandparents played on Saturday nights before going squaredancing; from the musical comedies my mother sang along to when she cleaned house, to the stacks of classical albums she put on the stereo each night to help her sleep—but paid it little attention. At that moment, however, studying the record sleeve in my hands, its psychedelic red and yellow splotches fairly quivering with big-city excitement, I realized that I had been missing something. My mother's letter claimed that all the young black kids in Seattle were listening to the Jackson Five.

Mine had been a childhood spent waiting for information and clues in the mail. Periodically my father, an African who lived in Africa, sent letters about our family. My only other link to black life was through my mother's subscriptions to *Ebony*, *Essence*, and *Jet*. Each month these magazines arrived, a bit worn and battered, from New York City, a place that seemed as mythic and faraway as Africa. And now there was this, a letter from my white mother informing me that the Jackson Five were sweeping the nation without me. *All the young black kids in Seattle are listening to them.*

Heart pounding, I carefully slipped the white inner sleeve out of the cardboard cover and opened it. A heavy record—broken into three neat pieces—slid into my hands.

The next few weeks dragged. My mother had promised to send another record once she had some extra money, but I was inconsolable. I read the liner notes over and over, learning that this was the group's third album and that the Jackson Five were wildly successful. Using Super Glue, I tried to resurrect the record. The break lines were so clean and the circle of plastic fit together so perfectly that I wouldn't believe it could not be saved. I played the album—with its three ridges of hardened glue—anyway, spending hours hunched over my grandparents' large stereo console, trying to decipher the pained gurgles of sound trickling from the speakers, trying to imagine what the real Jackson Five sounded like. What the rest of the black world was hearing.

Finally another package arrived. Grandma and I hugged each other with relief: the record inside was unharmed. I ran to put it on the stereo. "*Stop!*" a voice on the album commanded and I froze, aghast. A loud, terrible noise flooded out of the speakers and filled the room: the sound of boys yelling and screaming and howling in the street. "Hey!" they shouted. "Oh! Oh!" Occasionally the crash of cymbals could be heard over the terrible racket. This wasn't music! I looked to Grandma for guidance, but she appeared equally horrified. I thought I had chosen the wrong speed and adjusted it to 45 rpm. The screaming sped up; I switched to 78, it slowed down.

"Whatever was your mother thinking?" my grandmother muttered, going back into the kitchen. I remained in the living room, staring at the record as it spun on the turntable. I sat down on the floor directly in front of the built-in cloth speakers and listened hard. The noise was fast, disturbing, and confusing. I studied the album cover carefully. Five young black boys, dressed in wide pants with bright striped and flowered shirts like the ones in *Ebony* magazine, climbed out of giant letters on a bright blue cover. The pastel letters spelled *ABC*; it was their first major album. Maybe it was good that the other record had been broken in the mail, I thought. I liked the symmetry of having my first album be their first.

When the record finished, I restarted it, and suddenly all the screaming, all the terrible noises were gone. "*Stop!*" young Michael sang this time. "The love you save may be your own." I jumped up from the floor and stared at the turntable. Somehow, without having done anything, there was now music where before there had been only noise. The album looked exactly the same. I checked the controls; the settings were the same. I settled gingerly on the floor, afraid to break the spell.

The music was like nothing I had ever heard. There were high and low voices harmonizing against a rhythmic, infectious beat. Some of the lyrical melodies were peppy, others were more soothing. The voices bubbled up happy and excited like a party was going on inside the stereo. "Let me show you what it's all about," they beckoned. I realized that they were not yelling in chaos or anger; they were singing, chanting. "2-4-6-8. Who do you appreciate? *Hey!*" The shouts punctuated their emotions.

The exhilarating sounds spoke to me like my family's music had never done. The words were simple, the emotions honest; when the drum beat I could feel it throbbing against my neck. "Hey girl," Michael's clear voice called to me. "I'm-ma gonna teach you all about melody. Sit yourself down and take a seat. All you gotta do is repeat after me." I felt as if I were learning a new way of communicating. "A-B-C—it's easy as 1-2-3, as simply as do-re-mi. Baby you and me."

My grandmother popped her head back into the room, surprised to hear me replaying "that noise." She stared at me with curiosity. I stared back, equally confused. Didn't she notice how sound had transformed? How noise had become music? What I had learned to hear? "*Listen*," I urged her. "Can't you hear the change?" She couldn't. To her the Jackson Five remained noise.

Excited as I was, I could sense something was wrong. What, I didn't know. I didn't know that I had started to speak a new language, with new sounds, that this music promised an entire world somewhere else, a black world. I couldn't know that the problem, this first difference between us, was not a generation gap but a culture gap. That I was a black child in a white family, soon to be a black woman in a white world. And that, no matter how much I loved my grandmother, we would never again listen together and hear the same thing.

Coming into Myself

Riché Richardson

I AM SO THANKFUL FOR ALL OF MY MOTHERS, EMPOW-
ered and sustained by God, who have blazed the trails and made my
journey into black womanhood a matter of accepting a powerful legacy
and undertaking a meaningful struggle. In spite of the crosses that so
many of my maternal ancestors have carried, they have bequeathed to
me the knowledge that I, too, can strive to carve a space, however small
or limited, for love and wholeness in a society that has historically aimed
to erase, displace, or misrepresent Africa's daughters. Each day, as I
learn more about what it means to be a black woman, I think about who
I was when college began, and who I am becoming now. In my mind
and heart, Spelman College will always be a metaphor for the bonds of
sisterhood that can stitch black women together and inspire us to love
and know ourselves completely. It was there that I gained a conception
of self-actualized womanhood. As a young scholar, I feel privileged to
know myself in terms of race *and* gender. However, it took me a long
time, in the spirit of the philosopher David Hume, to learn that there
is a necessary connection between the two. Coming into myself has
largely meant realizing that a healthy black woman cannot divide herself
down the middle in terms of race and gender. On her quest to better her
black family locally and humankind globally, the black woman must
necessarily bring herself together.

Initially in college, I prioritized my racial identity.
In the traditional sense, I was an ardent black nationalist. Therefore, as
a black woman, I was somewhat of a masochist. I primarily associated
black social ascendancy with the reclaiming of black manhood; dreamed
of meeting my Malcolm X-like man for all seasons and having sons in
his spitting image; conceded that there is primarily an urgent need for

black male schools; and, blind to the realities of violence faced by my sisters, I lamented the black man as an "endangered species" and the primary target of racism and violence in society.

Today, I do not negate the struggles of my brothers. However, I do insist that weighing oppression is unhealthy, and that the narrow vision of what constitutes real pain and struggle among blacks has turned deaf ears on the cries of my sisters. No healthy, progressive people can have a one-sided agenda, and seeing the tears of my sisters, I refuse to endorse incomplete objectives. And even if black women initiated the mud-slinging, sexually politicized battle to claim the status of primary black victim, they could easily identify with the Vanity 6 concept of female tribulation: that for a female, 3 [the given load of pain as a human being] x 2 [the added load as a woman] = 6. I still long to meet that special black man if he exists. But now I know the dangers of buying into notions of Western romantic love, and my quest to become a woman for all seasons is my priority. Also, I am now quite aware of the typical status of women in most so-called progressive nationalist organizations.

Fortunately, I never slipped far away from myself as a woman. I did not internalize essentialist notions of female inferiority, for in school through the years I excelled as a young scholar and as a leader. No one could have told *me* that boys were better or smarter. I knew that was a lie. I didn't accept the biblical explanations/rationalizations for woman's role as helpmeet when some college associates resorted to scriptural ammunition during the "woman's place" debates, either. Just as I knew that black people were not made to be enslaved, I knew that I as a female was not made by a God worth serving to be anybody's satellite. My high school religion classes taught me to see womanhood as an abstract entity on the road to becoming fully human and whole. Therefore, from ninth grade on, I knew that as a female it was my calling to strive for a higher ground. But back then, I never would have thought that coming into myself would be this complex or beautiful.

It was during my sophomore year of college that my evolution into self-actualized womanhood gained momentum. That year, the writer Shahrazad Ali was criticized in numerous scholarly circles for most of the ideas in her controversial book, *The Blackman's Guide to Understanding the Blackwoman*. The debates about Ali's book were heated. Some brothers wholeheartedly agreed with Ali's position, even down to the notion that an "out-of-line" black woman deserves a sound slap across the mouth. Their compliance was frightening and hurtful. I began to see that a black man's desire for power, privilege, and progress in society could also make him want to assert authority over my sisters and me. To be called a queen Eldridge Cleaver-style and silenced in the name of love did not sound reassuring at all. It was then that I began to develop a healthier definition of what it means to love and support black people as a black woman. I also began to realize that a people in love with its daughters would not put them on sacrificial altars as martyrs for the race. A man completely in love with a woman would not seek to silence her either.

My journey into womanhood became more grounded as my scholarly investigation of gender expanded. Role models in the Spelman community such as Dr. Johnnetta B. Cole, our Sister President, and others sent me further into myself. It was from the visiting scholar Paula Giddings that I learned of the "Hottentot Venus" and of intracontinental African female enslavement. I had believed all daughters of Africa were accorded respect before the arrival of European enslavers, and that our African past was more ideal. When Women's Studies became my second minor at Spelman, two beautiful mentors, Dr. Gloria Wade-Gayles and Dr. Beverly Guy-Sheftall, supported me in my new discipline.

The theoretical perspectives that I gained really pushed me home. For instance, as a result of Dr. Wade-Gayles's class on images of women in the media, I began to hold black men more accountable for their media depictions of black women. She opened my eyes and ears and gave me the skills to deconstruct the world around me. The reactions that I got when I first shared the knowledge with male associates convinced me that some men, even when aware of how patriarchy poisons humankind, adamantly refuse to renounce male privilege. I was pushed into the ranks of black women activists who know that some black men, who have been willing to engage in political action to eradicate racist hegemony, simultaneously disavow the plight of the black woman. They downright refuse to see how race, gender, and other variables of oppression coalesce, and they willfully abet the commodification of misogyny. And I will not play the martyr and pardon them because they know not what they do. Many do, but they just don't care. And on top of it, they still demand black women's allegiance to eradicate the black man's burden.

And when some of those guys finally conceded that there *is* a problem, they did not problematize the prostituting of black women in the media by black men; instead, they fetishized women who dress provocatively and dance to the music as the ones to blame. Those women who internalize oppression must certainly be held accountable, but so often I have told my brothers that every way of seeing is a way of not seeing. I want them to summon the wholeness to realize that how a woman carries herself or behaves is irrelevant to the centered man. No centered man bases his personhood on the level of respect that a woman accords herself. In spite of her self-destructive actions, he loves himself enough to do the right thing. He loves himself enough to respect her still. He loves himself enough to hate misogyny.

Sometimes, I was even criticized for taking the music and the world around me too seriously. Many times, I have wondered why some black men expect black women to accept degrading songs (like "Pop that Coochie," "Baby Got Back," "Rumpshaker," "Shake What Yo Momma Gave Ya," and "Dazzey Duks") that objectify black women. I think of the progressive negation of black women in terms of sexuality. Today, some black men have assumed the role of the Europeans who paraded Sara Bartman around as the "Hottentot Venus" to display the prominence of her buttocks. Upon remembering the museum where Bartman's sexual organs were made a spectacle posthumously, I take the analogy further and wonder if those men preserve the walking (un)dead black women in their videos for the media tourist's gaze. And some of my brothers (*and sisters!*) think that the songs are actually elevating and celebrating us. How could a rational mind construe "bop that thang, freak" as an affirmation? I'll assume that black men and women would not dream of embracing racist songs, but, still, some of them have no problem with dancing to "bitch" and "ho." Because I have finally brought myself together as a human being, I will not apologize for insisting on being accorded respect as a human being. And the struggle is more meaningful now that I have broken the chains of psychological masochism that narrowed my vision when I was lost.

Spelman taught me to value my mothers and sisters even more completely. The community that exists among black women is so beautiful to me. Sisterhood is alive in my heart today. Moreover, I love my maternal role models who have supported the struggle. They have also supported me as their girl child on my journey into self-discovery and womanhood. As Destiny's child, I feel empowered enough to face the long struggle ahead.

Living Out Loud

John Frazier

*I am an invisible man. No, I am not a spook like those
who haunted Edgar Allan Poe; nor am I one of your
Hollywood-movie ectoplasms. I am a man of substance, of
flesh and bone, fiber and liquids—and I might even be said
to possess a mind. I am invisible, understand, simply
because people refuse to see me. . . . When they approach
me they see only my surroundings, themselves, or figments
of their imagination—indeed, everything and anything
except me. . . . So why do I write, torturing myself to put
it down? Because in spite of myself I've learned some things.*
—Ralph Ellison, *Invisible Man*

For some time now, I've postponed completing, or rather beginning,
this endeavor. I've attempted writing a piece about the ramifications of
being black and gay on several occasions but ceased after only managing
to write a few lines each time. Perhaps this process has been so difficult
because, in undertaking it, I must realize that neither the ideal I have
constructed nor the reality I am living can ever entirely free me from
the masks I've spent so long laboring to mold. Like Ellison, though, I
am compelled to write because in spite of my experiences, or more accurately because of them, I have also learned some things.

      I have adopted a new Bible of sorts since coming out.
Essex Hemphill's *Brother to Brother* was my first exposure to the lives of
black gay men, not just the lives of the effeminate queens or the hyper-
sexed mandingos which are all too often spectacles in white media, but
black gay men—men like me. I read the entire anthology in one night,
searching for the images which had been denied me for so long—search-

ing for my reflections which had been silenced the first time I heard my father say "faggot," and silenced the first time I was called "nigger."

Like Essex Hemphill, I, too, have spent a substantial amount of my life constructing and affecting masks in the gay community, in my own ethnic community, and even in my own home. But, perhaps, unlike Hemphill the greater portion of my adulthood has been consumed with attempting to deconstruct them but not knowing entirely how to remove these masks so thick and seemingly impermeable they have rendered me a different person. Indeed, my invisibility has been in part my own undertaking—or has it? Did I have a choice? Do any of us really have the choices and freedom we boast of? Who can claim total volition and free will when submerged in a world of prejudice and homophobia? For me, coming out to my ethnic community, as well as confronting racism in a predominately white-influenced gay community, have been matters of reclaiming my life from those who would deem it invalid.

I will never forget the moment I told my mother. She simply said she had suspected—that there had been clues over the years. I wanted to talk to her. I've wanted to talk for the past twenty years, but once again silence took its place in my world. My heart screamed and yelled and cried and cursed and shouted, but my lips remained pursed as I fulfilled my duty and remained the silent, voiceless brother, lover, friend, and son I had become. I remember my first lover almost as vividly. I remember our first kiss and the way his body seemed to overwhelm my own. And I remember feeling very alone and scared when he left me to be by myself again. He had promised to call the next day, but a week passed before I heard from him again—a week full of anguish, pain, and tears. Maybe he felt pity for what he thought must be a lonely boy crying at home. Maybe from his own home he could hear my tears crashing to the floor. At any rate, he called and I listened as my life slowly spiraled. That I should seek love, no not really—maybe confirmation, in the arms of a white man much older than myself seemed so tragic. My second lover, a true brother, was not true at all to himself or to me. He resented his own sex and his own inescapable blackness so how could he not resent me? And I don't think he ever loved me, and I know I never loved him. I loved what I thought he could do for me—what I thought I couldn't do for myself. I thought that only these men could save me, but I feared that there was nothing left to save. The masks I built should have cracked in the presence of a lover and fallen at my black feet. But I only needed to hear one insincere or mis-placed "I love you" to make them thicker and even more impermeable.

White hands embracing black hips. White lips part-ing black lips. Black arms wrapped around black legs caressing black backs melting into blackness. Black hands always wiping black tears alone. Always black hands wiping black tears on black cheeks in the blackness alone. My black hands won't ever stop smoothing black tears on my black face in the darkness. Always black. Always alone.

When will this agony end? Why must I still affect these old, heavy masks which have shaped my face in the way only a lifetime of sorrow and pain could? Sometimes I look at my eyes, my old brown eyes, and I cry because I know it is not over. I am tired, but a road still lies before me.

It has been a tough battle with a mother who is ashamed of her son because he's a faggot. It has been a long struggle with both a gay and an ethnic community who now more than ever need me but neglect to confront this reality. More importantly, there has been an internal battle fought on uneven terms. There has been a battle that, up until now, I thought I had lost—believing that I deserved the embar-rassment of my family, the scorn of my ethnic community, and the re-jection of my gay community.

Somehow, amidst all this confusion I have managed to deceive myself that I have reconciled my sexuality in terms of my religion and my ethnicity. Somehow, amidst all of it I have been duped into fighting battles which are not mine, defending agendas which ad-dress either my ethnicity or my sexuality exclusively. At times, I have had to choose my identifying marker, black or gay, sacrificing one for the other. Indeed, it has been an unfortunate situation of always at-tempting to identify where my loyalties should lie.

And I hope that I haven't discovered too late that they should lie with me first.

As I turned the page of a local gay newspaper, my hands fumbled across the obituary section, one which I had grown ac-customed to dismissing because of fear—not really fear of AIDS or car accidents or tragic deaths, but fear of death itself. After all, they are all the same, because each in its own way brings forth death, whether un-anticipated or too early or too late. Anyway, I immediately recognized the face of a local black gay poet, essayist—man. For, indeed, it is a feat simply to survive as a black man or a gay man today, much less a black gay man. But here before me was a glimpse, ever so brief, of a black gay life lived and lost. I thought of the times I had met this man and how a light seemed to issue forth from his eyes, eyes which were to say to me then, "Praise God, for I have made it this far" and eyes which say to me now, "Work swiftly, my brother."

I was deeply moved by what seemed like such an important life. Despite my adoration, no, because of it, the sight of his eyes and the peace of his face and the accomplishments in print frightened me. I was afraid that one day my own life would be taken or given away—maybe abruptly or maybe agonizingly slowly hour by hour. I wondered, "Will my house be in order? Will I be able to honestly look at myself?"

What do I see when I look in the mirror? Honestly, I think when one examines oneself in a mirror one not only sees the body self but also one's state of mind, one's point in life—one's masks. For indeed, my face changes little from day to day. Hair comes and goes, is cut and grown. Color comes with the summer sun and fades with the inevitable encroaching winter. But my spirit! If this is the answer, then it is why I can look at my face now and see a beauty I have never before seen. I can see a shimmer of light which must have been dulled many years ago like a camp fire smothered with dirt. But I can also see the invisible lines which will never entirely be smoothed out. I can see masks full of hate and pity, hope and joy, sadness and pain.

Sometimes my own image scares me now for the same reason his picture did and still does. They are testimonies to the masks we affect, endure, and hopefully one day relieve ourselves of as black gay men.

We do accept our responsibility in this scheme. I accept my responsibility. Indeed, every lie I tell contributes to my invisibility, but the lies have been essential to my survival. Now I must, for my own sake and the sake of my brothers, at least try to reconcile these issues and risk a life without the deception. We are strong. I am strong. I am a strong black gay man. Despite our strength, this dream, however, will not be easily transformed into reality. If in the interim I cry, and I will, it is because I know that each morning I must begin to dress myself, not only with clothes but also with masks I have spent much too long constructing and in turn demolishing. I pray I won't have to die to escape them.

How It Was for Me

Sarah Van't Hul

Nineteen seventy-two, the year abortion became legal, was the year of my birth. It was also the year that the Black Social Workers Association decided that white people should not be allowed to adopt black children. They said that it is more damaging for black children to be adopted by white parents than to be placed in foster care, because the adopted children would be stripped of their identity and culture. As a result of the BSWA's position, many black children have been left with no family and very likely a poor sense of identity.

When I was two months old I was adopted by a white family and brought from Toledo, Ohio, to Ann Arbor, Michigan, right around the time that the BSWA made its recommendation. There were few other black or biracial kids in the white middle-class community in which I was raised. Unsurprisingly, my first reaction toward white people was positive. I loved my parents, my sister, and my brothers. The friends I had were white, and if I didn't like somebody, I never associated my dislike of them with their appearance.

I distinctly remember when the difference in my appearance became an issue for me. On my first day of kindergarten all the other girls except me had on dresses and had long straight hair. I had on jeans and had a very short Afro. It was instant alienation and embarrassment. The girls didn't want to play with me; they told me I had fat lips and a big nose, and that my skin looked like "pooh." The only friend I had at first was a boy who was black like me, and he was just as shy as I was. We played with each other during recess because nobody else would play with us.

My first lasting friendship was with a girl named Laurie. I think part of what attracted us to one another was simply that we were the same color, and she had been adopted by a white family also. We were both different, and if one of us was teased by anyone for our color, we no longer had to bear it alone; they would have to deal with both of us.

It was in these early years that I heard one of my mother's friends say, "Oh, what a beautiful girl!" If she had only known know much I cringed when she said that! I though she was crazy, or just trying to be polite. Someone black can't be pretty, I thought; she should *know* that.

It wasn't long before I did have a lot of girlfriends, maybe just because I was friendly. But racism became a definite reality for me in the later years of grade school. I had a group of very close girlfriends and always seemed to get along with boys very well. Boys liked to play with me, because I was good at sports and didn't act "girl-ish." Wearing dresses was never my thing, and I was never afraid to fight. But when my girlfriends were beginning to date and have boys who had crushes on them, I found myself left out. The few boys that had the courage to date me soon let me know they didn't want to "go out with me," because I was black.

It took me a long time to feel comfortable about dating any boys, and I became the "feminist" amongst my friends. Girls began to see me as a source of strength, for I appeared confident and self-sufficient. What my friends never understood was that my so-called feminist strength was much less a choice on my part than a method of coping with prejudice.

Family outings, too, were often much more pain for me than pleasure. What I believed was my quirky family drawing so much attention in restaurants, I later realized was really subtle racism. Going out to dinner and on vacations was much like pulling teeth for me. In diners on the road (my father's favorite eating establishments) and in restaurants outside of Ann Arbor, I had to deal with seemingly endless silence, when my family of four white people and two black kids (one of my brothers is also black) entered a restaurant. Everything seemed to stop, except the music. The stares and the screaming silence filled me with shame and left a permanent scar.

When I was twelve years old, I lived in Switzerland for a year with my family. My self-consciousness hit its peak. Everybody stared at me. At least in Ann Arbor there were havens where I did not feel alienated. In Europe, it seemed like I was the only black person on the whole continent. I could not blend in. The school kids petted my skin and hair, as though I were an exotic creature. It was one of the most frightening experiences I have ever had.

The prejudice from white people was subtle, however, compared to the overt hostility that came from other blacks. My first exposure to groups of black people was in junior high, and, to my surprise, they completely rejected me. I quickly found that if the black kids have a problem with you, they will get in your face and tell you exactly what's wrong. They immediately let me know that my problem was that I thought I was white. Before I even opened my mouth, the black kids told me who I was: a "white wannabe." (This was kind of ironic, because *they* had bone-straight hair, and I had a natural.) I talked funny, I dressed funny, I thought I was better than anyone else, and why didn't I straighten that nappy do? Black girls frequently wanted to fight me for simply being me. They wanted me to be ashamed for being different and to hold my head down instead of up. My retaliation was verbal. I would try to show them that they were acting much worse than I was and it was stupid for them to want to fight me when I had done nothing to them.

L'Tonya was a big black girl who tormented me throughout junior high and until the eleventh grade in high school. Every time I walked down the hall, she loudly made fun of me—about everything, from my hair and clothes to the way I stood. Because I would never respond, teasing became unsatisfactory for her. One time when she and five of her friends caught me and one of my friends in the gym, she threw a basketball at my head, and then a chair. She called me all kinds of names and more than anything wanted to fight me. I told her I wouldn't fight her, and I didn't understand why she hated me so much. I don't remember everything I said, but I remember I left her speechless for the first time. She continued to harass me, but I began to recognize my strengths and her weaknesses, and I began not to cringe or care as much.

In the eleventh grade, I had to take the California Achievement Test; I was put in a room with the other black kids. I wasn't on my own turf, and I was awaiting the teasing and snickering. Instead, one black boy had the courage to approach and talk to me in front of the rest of the kids. L'Tonya was in the room, and she didn't look too happy, but after the boy walked away, she came up to me and, to my amazement, apologized for all the times she had made fun of me.

I felt triumphant: for once I was appreciated just for being me. But I didn't say, "That's o.k."; I didn't say anything at all. For three years she had made me feel completely disowned and ugly, when I had given her nothing but respect. Now she wanted my respect, and I didn't have any for her.

Through all of this, I learned not to take my true friends for granted, for I knew they had to like me for me, and they often had to deal with name-calling from others just because they were friends with me.

Before I could even put into words what I felt, I knew I was different from other people who looked like me, and I struggled a lot with how to bridge the gap between me and them. I wondered what I had missed out on and what made me so different. I learned to accept the only position available to me when around other blacks—the observer. In that position I gained another kind of insight into black culture, one that has helped me become more understanding as to why I posed a threat to them and they to me.

It was the hostility of black kids that first made me conscious that being black means a lot more than having darker skin; it carries a whole history and anger. I resented those kids for punishing me for being black and confident, but I was also attracted to them for having more knowledge about black culture than I did.

In recent years, I have become very curious and interested in black awareness and identity. I have mainly taken the responsibility of educating myself both through reading and listening to others speaking about black issues.

Black history, past and present (in particular, the history of black women), has been one of my primary interests ever since I have been out of high school. I am starting to learn many of the answers to the "whys" I had growing up. It has been both a relief and empowering to learn about black culture. It is the whole other half of history I was never taught in school.

The racist attitude of whites was more inconspicuous than the overt anger from blacks, but they both were equally powerful and disturbing. Yet, since the rejection from blacks was obvious, I initially attached my immediate feeling of oppression to other blacks. As time has gone on, I have become more understanding (though not accepting) of the black kids' resentment and more aware and less tolerant of prejudice from whites.

Dancing saved my sanity. It has been my coping device. Often when I felt there was no one I could talk to or who would completely understand, dancing was the closest I could get to peace. I didn't start taking classes on a regular basis until late high school, but I would always dance in one of the free rooms of my house. My mother tells me that I started doing this as young as two years old.

As an aspiring dancer, I was not exposed to the latest moves in the black community, and although I would take classes in modern and ballet technique to strengthen myself, I never found a form of dance that I felt was completely my style. Instead I made up my own style and created movements that felt right for my body.

Now as a dance major at the University of Michigan, I don't just dance for pleasure, but with purpose. I find that through my choreography, I can finally speak and be heard. I have connected with black and white people (both in the audience and fellow dancers) at a level I could never reach verbally. Through my dance I found mutual respect.

One of the most significant questions I am frequently asked when people see me dance is where did I learn those moves, and if I could teach them. I tell them that I made them up. Although their interest is flattering, I have begun to realize that the real question they want to know the answer to, once again, is how to classify me. I believe I have started to define my own class, in dance and in the rest of my life, which grows out of both black culture and white culture.

Although I sometimes wish that I had been raised in a black community, I am still very grateful for having been raised as I was. Having a family at all, and especially one that loves and supports me, is far more important to me than being raised in a specific community.

I experienced some of the best and worst of both cultures, which has given me a wealth of insight that I only recently have begun to appreciate and hope that I can pass on to others. When I was growing up, I often felt like I had no place. Now I have come to realize that by not having a comfortable place, I had to create my own, which at times seems to serve as a bridge. In this world, full of so much hate, I believe we need all the bridges we can get.

Becoming the Third Wave

Rebecca Walker

I AM NOT ONE OF THE PEOPLE WHO SAT TRANSFIXED before the television, watching the Senate hearings. I had classes to go to, papers to write, and, frankly, the whole thing was too painful. A black man grilled by a panel of white men about his sexual deviance. A black woman claiming harassment and being discredited by other women. . . . I could not bring myself to watch that sensationalized assault of the human spirit.

To me, the hearings were not about determining whether or not Clarence Thomas did in fact harass Anita Hill. They were about checking and redefining the extent of women's credibility and power.

Can a woman's experience undermine a man's career? Can a woman's voice, a woman's sense of self-worth and injustice, challenge a structure predicated upon the subjugation of our gender? Anita Hill's testimony threatened to do that and more. If Thomas had not been confirmed, every man in the United States would be at risk. For how many senators never told a sexist joke? How many men have not used their protected male privilege to thwart in some way the influence or ideas of a woman colleague, friend, or relative?

For those whose sense of power is so obviously connected to the health and vigor of the penis, it would have been a metaphoric castration. Of course this is too great a threat.

While some may laud the whole spectacle for the consciousness it raised around sexual harassment, its very real outcome is more informative. He was promoted. She was repudiated. Men were assured of the inviolability of their penis/power. Women were admonished to keep their experiences to themselves.

The blacklash against U.S. women is real. As the misconception of equality between the sexes becomes more ubiquitous, so does the attempt to restrict the boundaries of women's personal and political power. Thomas's confirmation, the ultimate rally of support for the male paradigm of harassment, sends a clear message to women: "Shut up! Even if you speak, we will not listen."

I will not be silenced.

I acknowledge the fact that we live under siege. I intend to fight back. I have uncovered and unleashed more repressed anger than I thought possible. For the umpteenth time in my twenty-two years, I have been radicalized, politicized, shaken awake. I have come to voice again, and this time my voice is not conciliatory.

The night after Thomas's confirmation I ask the man I am intimate with what he thinks of the whole mess. His concern is primarily with Thomas's propensity to demolish civil rights and opportunities for people of color. I launch into a tirade. "When will progressive black men prioritize my rights and well-being? When will they stop talking so damn much about 'the race' as if it revolved exclusively around them?" He tells me I wear my emotions on my sleeve. I scream, "I need to know, are you with me or are you going to help them try to destroy me?"

A week later I am on a train to New York. A beautiful mother and daughter, both wearing green outfits, sit across the aisle from me. The little girl has tightly plaited braids. Her brown skin is glowing and smooth, her eyes bright as she chatters happily while looking out the window. Two men get on the train and sit directly behind me, shaking my seat as they thud into place. I bury myself in *The Sound and the Fury*. Loudly they begin to talk about women. "Man, I fucked that bitch all night and then I never called her again." "Man, there's lots of girlies over there, you know that ho, live over there by Tyrone? Well, I snatched that shit up."

The mother moves closer to her now quiet daughter. Looking at her small back I can see that she is listening to the men. I am thinking of how I can transform the situation, of all the people in the car whose silence makes us complicit.

Another large man gets on the train. After exchanging loud greetings with the two men, he sits next to me. He tells them he is going to Philadelphia to visit his wife and child. I am suckered into thinking that he is different. Then, "Man, there's a tone of females in

Philly, just waitin' for you to give 'em some." I turn my head and allow the fire in my eyes to burn into him. He takes up two seats and has hands with huge swollen knuckles. I imagine the gold rings on his fingers slamming into my face. He senses something, "What's your name, sweetheart?" The other men lean forward over the seat.

A torrent explodes: "I ain't your sweetheart, I ain't your bitch, I ain't your baby. How dare you have the nerve to sit up here and talk about women that way, and then try to speak to me." The woman/mother chimes in to the beat with claps of sisterhood. The men are momentarily stunned. Then the comeback: "Aw, bitch, don't play that woman shit over here 'cause that's bullshit." He slaps the back of one hand against the palm of the other. I refuse to back down. Words fly.

My instinct kicks in, telling me to get out. "Since I see you all are not going to move, I will." I move to the first car. I am so angry that thoughts of murder, of physical retaliation, of separatism, engulf me. I am almost out of body, just shy of being pure force. I am sick of the way women are negated, violated, devalued, ignored. I am livid, unrelenting in my anger at those who invade my space, who wish to take away my rights, who refuse to hear my voice. As the days pass, I push myself to figure out what it means to be a part of the Third Wave of feminism. I begin to realize that I owe it to myself, to my little sister on the train, to all of the daughters yet to be born, to push beyond my rage and articulate an agenda. After battling with ideas of separatism and militancy, I connect with my own feelings of powerlessness. I realize that I must undergo a transformation if I am truly committed to women's empowerment. My involvement must reach beyond my own voice in discussion, beyond voting, beyond reading feminist theory. My anger and awareness must translate into tangible action.

I am ready to decide, as my mother decided before me, to devote much of my energy to the history, health, and healing of women. Each of my choices will have to hold to my feminist standard of justice.

To be a feminist is to integrate an ideology of equality and female empowerment into the very fiber of my life. It is to search for personal clarity in the midst of systemic destruction, to join in sisterhood with women when often we are divided, to understand power structures with the intention of challenging them.

While this may sound simple, it is exactly the kind of stand that many of my peers are unwilling to take. So I write this as a plea to all women, especially the women of my generation: Let Thomas's confirmation serve to remind you, as it did me, that the fight is far from over. Let this dismissal of a woman's experience move you to anger. Turn that outrage into political power. Do not vote for them unless they work for us. Do not have sex with them, do not break bread with them, do not nurture them if they don't prioritize our freedom to control our bodies and our lives.

I am not a postfeminism femisist. I am the Third Wave.

Part 7

MOVE

Revolution and Solution

Youth

Jennifer L. Vest

Autumn is intoxicating
When you're young
Everything dying
And you so alive
With the end of each summer
There is another
Is it any wonder then
That we start revolutions?
That death has no meaning for us?
That our dreams seem so real?

For All the "Think-They-Conscious" Writers Who Applauded Wilson Goode at a Conference Celebrating Black Writing

Jennifer E. Smith

is this aaanotha MOVE poem?
anotha poem to be read at readings/
publication parties to be marketed
to brothers/sisters who think
cultural aesthetic the correct/only
response to white oppression?

is this aaanotha MOVE poem
for anotha book of poetry/essays/
documentaries to be sold for profit?

yes, there is money to be made off
the torching of them dreadhead
back-to-nature niggers over
there on Osage Avenue
by bourgeois negroes pim
ping the continent pim
ping the cause

ask any bookseller
ask any philly tourguide

or is this a poem to cause you to squirm
in yo seat/strip you naked/shame you/
skin you to the bone/gut your spirit/
make you slam yo soul up against the wall
ask yourself where the hell you were
on May 13, 1985, when 14 black

men women children were eaten by flame
in a house C-4 bombed by the state police?

or is this a poem written to say
'oh isn't it a shame'
aaanotha poem demanding
    no retribution
    no justice for
Birdie & Ramona Africa?

no, this ain't just aaanotha MOVE poem
to be politely digested with reception/
handshakes/autographs to follow

this poem is free is a free MOVE poem
whether you ask for it or not

2,190 Days in the Life of a B-Boy:
A Freestyle Chronicle of a Culture

Jelani Cobb, Jr.

The following is a quasi-autobiographical polemical soundbite history of collegiate politics and Black pop culture.

Nineteen eighty-seven. Seven years of Reagan's cowboy capitalism, that vulgar mix of laissez faire and super-Darwinism, had turned America into one surreal, all-encompassing white sheet. That summer Ron's "I ran the contras" scandal dominated tele-culture and marked my eighteenth year spent in that sprawling Hades on the Hudson known as New York. In spite of its rep as a teeming pool of eclectic liberalism, that city practices its own curious brand of racial politics, and 96th Street is the unspoken barrier between cosmopolitan New York, gemstone of Western civ. and capitalist gluttony, and Uptown, a never-never land of primordial ghetto-dwellers. Refracted through the media prism, the Black community became a hazy caricature of itself, colored by decay and decadence. The ghetto has no zip codes—at least not in the existential sense (picture Bed-Stuy 90210). It is a seamless, borderless grey area ruled by a fierce pan-urban code of survival of the quickest. At least it is in the minds of the uninitiated. I came of age as a soul survivor against a background of Reaganesque vulgarity and trickle-down con games.

And for those die-hard ghettocentrists, the powers-that-be initiated a freestyle exercise in urban demonology, complete with rogue welfare queens plundering the economy and roaming packs of wilding youth playing Attila to white America's Rome. The exorcism took the form of beat-downs administered by overzealous five-O and reduced "entitlements"; meanwhile gruesome spectres wandered the streets in crack-crave dementia and AIDS jacked life from the unsus-pecting. . . . The eighties, it's been said, were an ugly decade to be young, Black, and unarmed. And between the guerrilla journalism that hyperbolized the Black community—to the glee of Anglo voyeurs in the burbs—and demagogue politicians, a grim new menace arose. Sud-denly Euro-New Yorkers had license to kill, and the exorcism took a grotesque new turn as Bernard Goetz proved it was o.k. to blast Black boys who act up on the subway. And now new jack lynching was in vogue, as demonstrated by the good citizens of Howard Beach and Ben-sonhurst in the late eighties.

Hip Hop also came of age amidst the me-centric ap-athy and societal wreckage of the eighties, its funk-inflected, soul-drenched poetics providing the soundtrack for the urban apocalypse. But in 1987 Hip Hop was still wallowing in its own narcissism, domi-nated by a cult of hyperbolic self-exaltation. By the late eighties, partly due to Reagan's polarizing politics, Black America had become a more insular community, which happens whenever the political pendulum swings to the conservative side. But this time the neocons had run a mad powermove that had white kids bumrushing anything with melanin on campuses across the country.

My response was to choose a hysterically Black col-lege. In 1987 I migrated to Washington, D.C., and Howard Univer-sity—the "capstone of Negro education" as race-conscious strivers dubbed it years ago. I flowed onto campus with a mini-crew of similarly displaced b-boys, Brooklynites, and boulevardians and immediately de-nounced Howard as a sea of neo-negroes and buppies-in-training. How-ard became the site for the strictly hardcore urban *Zeitgeist* that was im-posed on what we saw as a cultural wasteland. The consequence of this was a legion of funk-fakin' ghetto poseurs livin' just enough to front like they was from the city. Now everybody wanna be a ghetto bastard. Style politics dictated our agendas, and we were on some old school un-derground type flava. Every party, same shit. Check my man Rudy from the Boogie Down—flattop sculpted to perfection, executing a flaw-less floor glide while Super Lover Cee's "James Brown" booms in the background. Peep that kid Crazy Mike aka Absolute Zero from Flat-bush: the wild-haired, wild-eyed master of ghetto eurythmics. Known as Absolute Zero 'cause he's blunted/fortied himself to the point where his thought processes are nothing more than a series of commercials flashing past at light-speed on the screen of his mind. An illicit haze, whose source is a Cypress Hillian blunt-a-thon in the corner, envelops the spot, contributing to a communal high. Damn. Back in the days.

But implicit in all our urbanisms was the need to pull elements from a world we knew in order to color our new environment. Calling college "a different world" was an understatement. Try parallel universe. The H.U. world was defined by the hi-yella tradition and deviation from the accepted standards of bourgieness was a social offense. Sorry, though. As my man Lou put it, "You can take the kid out of the projects. . . ."

But beneath the posturing of H.U.'s Afrostocracy was a community of young minds engaged in a type of ideological trial by fire with the fates of African-Americans hanging in the balance. The political scene ran the spectrum of rebels without a pause to rebels without a clue and everything in between. Competing for ideological supremacy was a sea of ultralib/cultural nationalist/neocon/born again/ radical muslim/vegetarians—each with its respective panacea for the damnation of the Black. It seemed to me that while the conservative set was mouthing meaningless platitudes about self-help and bizarre remixes of Booker T-ism, the more liberal squad was content with mindlessly championing the Democratic Party's *messiah du jour* and its crew of high-profile, low-influence "leadership." By far the most colorful set was a fringe which, absent any actual ideology, could come up with more conspiracy theories than Jimmy Hoffa at an Oliver Stone film festival. ("Contrary to what they tell you, my brother, the Council on Foreign Relations, along with the Masons and the A-Team, killed J.F.K.") While this made for interesting screenplays, it created a smokescreen in which the real conspiracies were colored in with much fiction and fantasy.

Two Years Later: 1989 was the year of living vicariously, plundering the cultural archives for images of Black Power whose relevance had been rediscovered. Hip Hop's iconography sampled the Blackspeak and posture of a bygone era. Note the ascendancy of funk-orishas X-Clan, hyperblack urban oracles with a dress code that spanned 4,000 years of Black aesthetics as proof.

That year Va. beach proved what we had always known—that Black America was a police state, only now we dropped terms like fascism and neocolonialism to categorize it. It was Black steel in the hour of chaos. Our politics were shaped by the post-Public Enemy wave of nationalism; our actions informed by contemporary Hip

Hop rage prophets and retro-sixties icons. Malcolm X, resurrected and sampled, reminded us we were "Too Black, Too Strong," and KRS-One elevated street corner pedagogy to a hardcore national cult phenomenon. That same year saw Lee Atwater get played by an insurgent H.U. student body determined that he would not sit on the board of trustees. Afrocentrism quickly became the dominant "ism" of the era. At its best, it was an attempt to redefine ourselves as subjects rather than objects of history; at its worst it was an eclectic blend of fact, fiction, and pop metaphysics. The movement converted legions of committed b-boys (myself included) into beaded braided urban apostles, and dangling around the necks of us newlydreads were elaborate glyphs where gold medallions once reigned supreme.

With few exceptions, Farrakhan's melodic polemics were the binding thread between the "new" nationalism that had bumrushed both the campus and the boulevard, and the chaotic sixties, which had become a symbol unto itself. Not surprisingly, several friends joined the Nation. Also not surprisingly, my nationalist politics clashed with those of my parents' generation who were products of the civil rights movement. But to us, the politics of Jesse & Co. were out of touch, and integration was the bullshit philosophy that left us urbanites stranded while a select few got to sit next to dick and jane in suburbia. By now I was into Pan-Africanists like Fanon and Nkrumah; Harold Cruse and John Henrik Clarke were gospel. Reagan had passed into history, but his spirit lived on, embodied by his evil half-brother who cruised into the oval office in '89. Chuck D urged us to "Fight the Power" and Spike warned to "Do the Right Thing," but Bush dropped a race bomb named Willie Horton that scared his negrophobic electorate to the polls. Decoded, Bush's ad campaign used Horton to paint himself as the last hope of a republic besieged by welfare queens and ghetto-dwellers who relentlessly plundered the national reserves (sound familiar?).

Ironically, somewhere in this repressive haze, Black anger went crossover.

1991. I tripped off Malcolm becoming a pop phenomenon—"Buy Any Means Necessary." Remember when the artists used to give the most insightful critiques of society? In its endless machinations, late capitalist America managed to commodify Black discontent. Straight up: the revolution got televised (by MTV no less). X-wear became a depoliticized trend while a crew of sociopathic A&R execs decided that nihilism was the flavor of the month, so Hip Hop backslid into a wasteland of misogynistic gangsta bravado. Soul Poison. And those who weren't enticed by the lure of electronic drivebys by the faux hardcore opted to conjure up banal b-boy audioporn for voyeurism in stereo.

Amiri Baraka said the state of Black aesthetics/politics was locked in a "retrograde trend." Self-styled rage-prophet Chuck D put it even better two years earlier in his signature lyrical fury: "You singers are spineless." But wait, it gets better. Even the writers went out on some new and improved shit that year. In the introductory essay to *Breaking Ice*, Terry McMillan (New High Priestess of Black Pop Lit) talks of Black writing evolving to new forms, "the best of which are not didactic." And while she doesn't negate the works of preceding writers whose books are characterized as "Protest Literature," she asks, "How much sense would it make in the nineties if folks were still writing we hate whitey stories, . . . or why we should be proud of our heritage (we've known it for a long time now—our children know it too)." But while McMillan was giving Black protest lit. its eulogy she forgot to check out the status of the things we'd been protesting. Consider this. The opening chapter of *Native Son* was a vivid protest/exposé of housing conditions on Chicago's Southside during the 1930s. Last year, Cabrini Green dominated the news media for at least a month. Life in that sprawling eighty-four-building monument to urban imperialism is an extrapolation of the one-room rat trap that housed Bigger Thomas and his family. But no one writes/rights to affirm the humanity of the deferred dreamers of Cabrini Green.

But McMillan wasn't alone. Trey Ellis's definition of a "new Black aesthetic" dictates that "We are a new breed, free to write as we please, in part because of our predecessors, and because of the way life has changed." He also informs us that the new Black artists are no longer "shocked by racism like the writers of the Harlem Renaissance, nor are we preoccupied with it like the writers of the Black Arts Movement. For us, racism is a hard little-changing constant that neither shocks nor enrages." Dig that. The old struggle stuff is played; the new shit is talking about how hard it is to survive the trials of buppiedom. Ellis just gave the go-ahead for Black writers to abandon the issues of the masses and sink into the grey pin-striped ambiguity of whiter America. Unfortunately, as my man Ras Baraka put it once, "No matter how you decorate it, hell is still the thief of souls," and if racism no longer "shocks or enrages" we'll be a generation that coolly watches Rodney King catch a pay-per-view beatdown while we compose abstract bullshit poems about the beauty of a tree. In short, we'll praise the aesthetic merit of Nero's fiddle while L.A. is burning.

In the wake of postpolitical rap, and the reign of buppie literature, Desert Storm raged on the horizon, raining death on Bush's enemy of choice. Bill Clinton and Dan Quayle took turns dropping political pimp-slaps on rap artists, and most of my '87 crew has left college for the surreal world. Last year Los Angeles erupted into a furious freestyle of consumer anarchy.

In spite of L.A.'s baptism by fire, none have been able to address the systemic ills that caused it to explode. The restored icons of past radicalism are now mute and discarded ex-tokens (pop culture is now mining the less threatening seventies). I've spent most of this year in some sort of weird purgatory suspended between theory and practice. In retro, I wonder how much of political Hip Hop and the accompanying Black nationalism was legit and how much of it was commodity Blackness—the type that has KFC cashiers draped in Kente, Mickey D's hustling Black history, and Shaft hawking meal deals on late night Burger King commercials. Major labels have succeeded in spoonfeeding us our own self-contempt. Camouflaged by genius production and the infectious flow of Ice Cube, many of us are going back for seconds. The "nigga," for all his contemptuous glare and emotional exile, is a marketable commodity; his inhumanity can be packaged and sold, even emulated by negrophiles trying to break up the monotony of the burbs. But the move to come to terms with the "nigga" as a construction of warped white supremacist minds has evaporated from music specifically, and Afro/Urban culture in general. Having exhausted the trendiness of the sixties, Hip Hop's cutting edge may be defined by Digable Planets—a group of neo-beatniks. To complicate matters, too much of Afrocentric thought has been subverted into Blacker-than-Thou orthodoxy and chauvinist feel-goodism. The movement is in danger of replicating the ideological flaws (romanticism, etc.) that did in the cultural nationalist movement twenty years ago. The nineties have also witnessed a rebirth of the notorious weed culture. Check Cypress Hill: their sophomore release "Black Sunday" unleashed the pan-ghetto anthem "I Wanna Get High," which firmly ensconced these grand disciples of the cannabis atop Hip Hop's ever-evolving hierarchy. The burning issue (literally) of my generation has become ensuring the right to remain blunted senseless. Somehow it seems like the Black community has bigger battles to fight. If Jesse and his squad of Democratic Party backup dancers seemed out of touch in the late eighties, they're miles behind now. Having lost consecutive bids to become the nation's H.N.I.C., the good reverend has settled for a career as a human quote-a-tron. See Jesse run (from anyone the Dems deem as questionable). See Jesse flip from issue to issue like a mad cable junkie going thru channels. See *everyone* denounce Farrakhan.

And while Hip Hop provided a cultural soundtrack for the political resurgence of the late 1980s and early 1990s, a lot of the underlying ideas were embraced and romanticized, but not dissected and drawn to their logical extensions.

The post-college years haven't exactly been conducive to this task either. The realities of rent, car notes, and student loans don't lend themselves to the spare time for political theory that is so abundant in college, and I'm hoping Mr. Bill hasn't put us back to sleep. Oh yeah, and this year, seven years later, they just released "The Absolute Last Investigation Report of Ron's I ran the contras scam." Surprise! He knew everything!

As for me, I'm getting used to this role as boulevardian-turned-college-grad-still-looking-for-a-real-job-and-thinkin-about-gettin-a-Ph.D. But right now I'm deep into *Race Matters* and working on getting past the theory-practice blues.

The Darker the Berry

Tracy E. Hopkins

She should have been a boy, then color of skin wouldn't have mattered so much, for wasn't her mother always saying that a black boy could get along, but that a black girl would never know anything but sorrow and disappointment? But she wasn't a boy; she was a girl, and color did matter.

> —Wallace Thurman,
> "The Blacker the Berry"
> (1929)

It's summer 1991. I'm sitting in a quaint, semi-enclosed Cajun restaurant with my mother, on a typically muggy afternoon in New Orleans, trying to stay cool despite the fact that my tongue is on fire. On my fourth day in the "Big Easy," I made the mistake of ordering buffalo wings from a chef with an unnatural affection for Tabasco. So there I sit, chasing the hot wings with multiple glasses of water, not feeling particularly glamorous, when I feel eyes upon me. I glance over my mother's shoulder and there they are—a very seductive pair of dark brown eyes, attached to a fine specimen of a man.

"Nah, he couldn't be staring at me," I think to myself and abruptly look away, expecting to see a Halle Berry or Vanessa Williams look-a-like waltzing by. I mean, if I were a guy, the sweaty, chicken-eatin', hot sauce–fingered sight of me would not have prompted flirtation. But I'm not a guy, and I could feel the "Prince" eyes of the attractive stranger. This time, in that totally obvious way of hers, my mother turned to look.

"He is looking at you, Tray," she said in a giddy schoolgirl voice. Blushing, if that's possible for an African-American woman of my hue, I decided to see how far he was willing to take the seduction act. Coyly, I stood up to pay the check. The mystery man sat five feet from the cash register. I said "Hi" with a smile and a nod, paid the tab, and prepared to walk away, immediately feeling stupid for being so shy, but before I reached my seat, he motioned for me to come over.

"Hello," he said, then asked my name. I replied, then asked his.

"Cam Bermuda," he said.

"That's unusual. Is that your real name?"

"Yup, there's only one Cam Bermuda," he said in a Harry Connick, Jr., accent that drove me wild.

Hardly paying attention to the trivial "I don't know you but I'd like to" conversation, I found myself sizing him up from head to toe. Cam was about six feet, fair-skinned but tan (definitely mixed with something), had thick, black wavy hair, a muscular build, and well, I've already mentioned the eyes. The Cheshire grin on his face suggested that he too was concentrating on more than the convo.

"I'm sorry for being so forward. You must think I'm a gigolo or something, but when I saw you I just had to get your attention," he said, breaking my momentary lapse into fantasy.

Say what? Did I just fall through a black hole and land in the pages of a Harlequin romance novel? "Oh come on. I bet you sit here and flirt with women all day," I said, trying to get him to cut the act. "No, I don't. I mean, I was like—this girl is gorgeous. I just love dark women."

Now wait one minute. While I never heard from Cam again, outside of three, unexpected late-night phone calls three months after our chance meeting, and our New Orleans flirtation is still a most pleasurable memory, I didn't find that "I just love dark women" comment altogether flattering. Why is it that every time a "brother" gives a darker "sister" a compliment, it's as if they're insinuating that being dark and attractive is unique, or an exception to some standard of beauty?

Even in 1993, Black men and women alike have not been able to shake the color complex that has, as a result of the divisiveness of slavery, plagued our community for centuries. Attitudes of superiority and inferiority that developed when white slave masters allowed lighter-skinned slaves to do household chores, and consequently climb from the lower rung of society's ladder above their darker-skinned peers, who labored in the fields, still linger. Many Black men prefer "high yellow" or "redbone" Black women because their skin tone and features are closer to those of white women, whereas darker Black women—although many, like myself, do not have pronounced Negroid features—are considered "too Black."

Cam's intentional compliment opened up a Pandora's box of sorts, out of which one of the Black community's deepest and darkest secrets was unleashed. I can't count how many times a "brother" has qualified his attraction to me by saying something like, "You're pretty for a dark-skinned girl," or "Most of my friends only date light-skinned girls with long hair, but I find dark women so attractive."

Although Cam and others have good intentions, their comments imply that they feel the need to justify their attraction to me. And their confession that they tend to gravitate toward dark women is usually rooted more deeply rather than simply an issue of preference; it usually stems from an identity crisis or poor self-image on the man's part. I think that mixed or lighter "brothers" like Cam somehow feel more accepted and "Blacker" in my presence.

I had a boyfriend, whom I broke it off with mainly because of his rejection of Afrocentric values. Lawrence is extremely light and has green eyes. Early on in our relationship he'd boasted that "Some people can't tell whether I'm Black or white, so I leave it up to them to decide." Then he'd ask, "What do you think?" *Ohhh that pissed me off.* Lawrence claimed he was on this "color doesn't matter" trip, but once, while we were riding on a subway train in Washington, D.C., holding hands, he chuckled and said, "This is like the *Jungle Fever* ad." *What nerve.* So I barked back, "Which one of us is supposed to be a white woman?"

My shrink, whom I saw during my junior and senior years as a Howard University student, for counseling on how to be more assertive and how to break a cycle of detrimental relationships, even made comments like, "You don't have a problem getting men, but because you're dark, and so damn sexy, you will have a problem keeping them off of you." Thanks a lot, doc. I'm struggling to find a man who will take me seriously and make a commitment, and a professional tells me that my "sexual chocolate" might hinder that mission.

It seems that now that Black men can admit that darker "sisters" are attractive, they feel obligated to diminish that attraction to one of physical or sexual interest. The stereotype of the dark Black woman as the sexual superwoman once again harks back to slavery, when white slave masters raped Black slaves and justified their actions with the theory that Blacks were primal savages, who were sinful and carnal by nature.

Still suffering the backlash of that imagery, a close friend of mine, who is also dark, has concluded that "we" are good enough to screw but not acceptable enough to marry. However, for darker men, the opposite is true. The fact that Denzel Washington and Wesley Snipes, two of Hollywood's hottest commodities, star in the fantasies of Black and white women alike is a testimony to how desirable it is to be tall (or short in Snipes's case), dark, and handsome. For "sisters," dark men are synonymous with vitality, and white women find them attractive because of the "Mandingo" myth of sexual prowess.

When I was in elementary school, I was most conscious of my complexion. Children can be brutal, and I remember a female bully calling me names like "Blackie"; it was only after I continually ignored her that she stopped taunting me. And I thought I was over the paranoia. But just as was the case when I was eight, because others go out of their way to mention my complexion, the paranoia has crept back. Recently, I went to the beach with two of my cousins, who happen to be very light. It was close to 100 degrees outside, and they wanted to tan. Needless to say, I don't need one. I don't usually mind sitting out in the sun, but that day I was very self-conscious. Perhaps it's because I had mentioned my weekend plans to a co-worker, and he had jokingly warned me not to come back "too Black."

After forty minutes or so, without giving a detailed explanation, I expressed my discomfort with the whole beach scene, and with sunblock in one hand and a towel in the other, I made my exit for the shade. My cousins seemed concerned, and one tried to console me by saying that she understood my not wanting to sunbathe, but that her sister "liked to get Black." I cannot express how frustrated I was that the same contemptible pattern of thinking I scold others for exists within my own family. And the sad thing is that my cousin, like my co-worker, saw nothing wrong with her statement. Maybe I'm wrong, but I thought the term "Black" was representative of a race, and not a negative description of skin color.

Other insufferable comments that I've endured are: "God bless you for being so Black" (said by a drunkard on a bus no less); "As dark as you are, you must be from Africa" (said by a man darker than me); and "I don't know why I like your Black ass" (said by a man who is sweatin' me). I've almost become immune to the ignorance and insensitivity of such remarks, but the fact that my people say such things without thought bothers me. Although I know that lighter Black women put up with asinine comments too, they are certainly minuscule by comparison. I doubt if any man ever said to Vanessa or Halle, "I could really go for you if you were a little darker." Light skin is celebrated because of its approximation to whiteness.

Spike Lee, who in his film *School Daze* addressed the color complex that exists among African-Americans, was quoted as saying, "Whether Black men want to admit it or not, they feel light-skinned women are more attractive than dark-skinned women, and they'd rather see long hair than a short Afro, because that's closer to white women. That comes from being inundated with media from the time you're born that constantly fed you the white woman as the image of beauty."

Although I may sound it, I'm not ashamed or bitter. I realize that I am attractive, both internally and externally, and if the level of melanin in my skin brings me that much closer to my ancestry, I'm grateful. I just wish that we African-Americans could accept ourselves for who we are and where we came from, and not become so caught up in labeling and meeting a standard of beauty not set by us. In what other race can you find such a wide variety of hues? We are all beautiful. The lightest no more so than the darkest.

The Straight and Narrow

Tiya Miles and Keiko Morris

> *In America, African hair and skin became the badge of slavery, so that the adjectives "nappy" and "kinky"— instead of being purely descriptive . . . became synonymous with "bad hair." Straight and wavy hair—identified in America with privilege—became "good hair."*
> —A'Lelia Bundles,
> "Lost Women"

In "Lost Women: Madam C. J. Walker Cosmetics Tycoon," A'Lelia Bundles describes the early techniques black women used to straighten their hair. During the 1800s, African-American women pulled sections of their hair tightly across their scalps, twisted them, and tied them with string. This approach was so unhealthy that it caused hair loss.[1] In 1905, African-American cosmetics pioneer Madam C. J. Walker introduced a hair care system for black women which included cleaning instructions, a pomade that promised to grow hair, and the use of the "hot comb" as a hair-straightening method.[2] As historian Paula Giddings has documented, during the time that Walker's business flourished, black women were compelled to work at strenuous, low-paying jobs as domestics for survival. Although they earned as little as $8 to $20 a week, these women often spent large portions of their incomes on Madam Walker's hair care products.[3]

    African-American women were willing to risk baldness and to sacrifice needed funds to straighten their hair because African hair was undesirable. From the 1600s to the mid-1800s, being born a person of African descent in the United States customarily meant being a slave. After Emancipation, it often meant being poor, uneducated, degraded, and exploited. Blackness was an unquestionable handicap. So in order to function more easily and more powerfully in an American society controlled by whites, black people often had to be "less black." Some biracial and lighter-skinned African Americans had the dubious honor of being able to "pass" for white. As a result, they were more acceptable to white America and allowed greater, though still limited, access to educational and employment opportunities.[4] For darker-skinned blacks, however, being less black meant struggling to alter specific physical features that were devalued in America.

Many black women found that hair was the feature most easily altered, although such alterations could only approximate those traits prized by the dominant American culture. As African Americans maneuvered carefully in a society where nonwhiteness equaled disadvantage, some began to internalize the idea that whiteness was tantamount to superiority. Thus they prized near-whiteness among themselves. As part of the attempt to survive in an oppressive, racist society, black women tried to model themselves in the image of another race, thus devaluing themselves as people of African ancestry and heritage. In the essay "Not Color But Character," published in *The Voice of the Negro* in 1904, activist Nannie Helen Burroughs criticizes this trend: "What every woman who bleaches and straightens out needs, is not her appearance changed, but her mind. . . . If Negro women would use half the time they spend on trying to get white, to get better, the race would move forward apace."[5]

Today the "race" has moved forward, but Burroughs's hope that black women would stop "trying to get white" has not been realized.[6] In 1990, as in 1904, many black women, including the authors of this essay, have straightened their hair with a hot comb or chemical process. Many of the racial barriers and societal pressures that forced black people to adjust and conform historically remain. African Americans are still denied the respect and choices available to many European Americans. Systemic racial prejudice consistently exists within primary cultural and societal institutions which perpetuate the concept of African-American inferiority and limit African Americans' access to opportunities. In addition, blatant racist rhetoric and behavior seems to have come back in vogue, if indeed it ever really subsided.

For black women, the necessity of adapting to a climate of disdain is complicated by the narrow margin of movement afforded to us by both the dominant culture and male-biased black communities. In American society, success is defined by the limited and often exploitative variables of high income level and professional status. While some black men can move beyond their physical characteristics and become successful (if not accepted) by rising to the head of their professions, black women, like all American women, are consistently judged by our physical appearances. We are told to be beautiful within a narrow, Eurocentric definition of the term. We are then told to find a man, for American society is only willing to bestow limited legitimacy and power upon women who fashion themselves as objects of male desire. When we seek employment for fulfillment, accomplishment, and, more often, economic stability, we are not to let our commitment to the pursuit of beauty falter. Thus, hair straightening along with other "enhancements" of our faces and bodies seem to us to be necessary. Okazawa-Rey, Robinson, and Ward explain the impulse behind women's quest for beauty in "Black Women and the Politics of Skin Color and Hair":

> Feminist psychology of the last decades has helped us to understand why personal beauty is frequently considered the most important attribute a woman can possess. Personal beauty holds for women the same importance as do intelligence, political influence or physical strength for men. However, unlike the male attributes, which almost assure the holder real power in society, beauty does not buy women real power. A woman's attractiveness buys her only the ability to secure male companionship.[7]

In *The Beauty Myth*, Naomi Wolf describes the strength of this ideology of beauty and suggests that it maintains patriarchal society's control over women's lives. She writes:

> Recent research consistently shows that inside the majority of the West's controlled, attractive, successful working women, there is a secret "underlife" poisoning our freedom; infused with notions of beauty, it is a dark vein of self-hatred, physical obsessions, terror of aging, and dread of lost control. . . . "Beauty" is a currency system, like the gold standard. Like any economy, it is determined by

politics, and in the modern age in the West it is the last,
best belief system that keeps male dominance intact.[8]

If you doubt that the ideal of beauty and promise of
its rewards is reinforced and upheld in our society, recall the plot of the
recent blockbuster film *Pretty Woman*. The woman whom the title describes is a poor, beautiful (i.e., with long red hair, milk-white skin,
"delicate" features, and a thin but voluptuous body) prostitute who is
commissioned for a week by an affluent businessman. In the tradition
of Cinderella, the prostitute is transformed into a polished, sophisticated, soon-to-be wealthy wife. Her beauty has paid off for her in ways
that little girls are taught to dream of.

Although Wolf's book and the film *Pretty Woman* fo-
cus on white women's experiences, they demonstrate the psychological
expectations and compulsions concerning beauty that are doubly detrimental to black women. African-American girls are socialized to participate in the fantasy of Cinderellahood, but they are crushed by the
weight of this dream. For, unlike white girls, their chances of ever being
considered beautiful and reaping the approval and rewards society des-
ignates for girls are next to none. Okazawa-Rey, Robinson, and Ward
point to this intersection of racism and sexism in the following observation: "Hair-straightening and skin-lightening, despite the pain involved, achieve little degree of true success in approximating the white
ideal of beauty. Femininity is out of reach for the black female; and the
despised and debased darker sister is relegated to the status of ugly duck-
ling."[9] Black women's literature and spoken experience support this conclusion. Toni Morrison's first novel, *The Bluest Eye*, traces the path toward madness taken by a black girl who craves blue eyes like Shirley
Temple's, symbols of white women's beauty and privilege.[10] In bell
hooks's collection of essays *Black Looks* she describes the confusion and
pain of a preadolescent black girl:

> *Her skin is dark. Her hair is chemically straightened. Not
> only is she fundamentally convinced that straightened hair
> is more beautiful than curly, kinky, natural hair, she
> believes that lighter skin makes one more worthy, more
> valuable in the eyes of others. Despite her parents' effort
> to raise their children in an affirming black context, she
> has internalized white supremacist values and aesthetics, a*

way of looking and seeing the world that negates her value.[11]

As little girls we experienced the feelings which Morrison and hooks describe. We saw white women, not ourselves, in the images that America chose to project. We heard family members comment that so and so's baby had been born with good hair and they hoped it would stay that way. We became so used to these words and images that we failed to notice their impact on our perception of ourselves as we snuck yellow towels from the linen closet and bobby-pinned them to our heads. By the time we arrived at college, having endured years of hot combs and chemicals, we had learned too well to veil, and even despise, our hidden hair and selves. Once we voiced our feelings and found confirmation in the testimony and writings of other black women, we were able to see implicit meanings in our decision to straighten our hair. Our experiences echoed the words of Alice Walker—"oppressed hair puts a ceiling on the brain."[12] And we decided, together, to set our hair free.

We have argued here that actual as well as internalized racism and sexism influence black women's hair-straightening choices. In this analysis, we intend to assert that black women's hair has personally transformative power and political importance, not that it has fixed meaning. Like our skin, eyes, and bodies, black women's hair types refuse singular categorization. Similarly, the act of hair straightening cannot have only one impulse or only one effect. As M. Jean Harris uncovered in a study of fifty black women entitled "Identity and Aesthetics in African American Women's Hairstyles," many black women straighten their hair for reasons of convenience and personal style; others change their hair continually over a lifetime, alternating between natural and straightened modes.[13] In addition to this, some hairstyles that involve chemical straightening, such as fingerwaves, are culturally unique and reflect a black aesthetic. Given these facts, our choice may not be yours. But the suggestion of resistance that natural hair symbolizes in our lives and the culture at large is clear. Those who had hoped to confine and create us find themselves thwarted. It is no accident that with our braids and close-cropped hair, we sometimes pass people who whisper speculations about us: radical, militant, feminist. The tremor in these voices is undeniable.

Notes

1. A'Lelia Bundles, "Lost Women: Madam C. J. Walker Cosmetics Tycoon," *Ms.* (July 1983): 92.
2. Edward T. James, ed., *Notable American Women* (Cambridge, Mass.: Belknap Press, 1971), p. 533.
3. Paula Giddings, *When and Where I Enter* (New York: Bantam Books, 1985), pp. 48, 146.
4. Margo Okazawa-Rey, Tracy Robinson, and Janie Victoria Ward, "Black Women and the Politics of Skin Color and Hair," *Women's Studies Quarterly* (Spring/Summer 1986): 13–14.
5. Nannie H. Burroughs, "Not Color But Character," *Voice of the Negro* 1 (1904): 278.
6. Ibid.
7. Okazawa-Rey, Robinson, and Ward, "Black Women and the Politics of Skin Color and Hair," p. 14.
8. Naomi Wolf, *The Beauty Myth* (New York: Anchor Books Doubleday, 1991). pp. 10, 12.
9. Okazawa-Rey, Robinson, and Ward, "Black Women and the Politics of Skin Color and Hair," p. 14.
10. Toni Morrison, *The Bluest Eye* (New York: Washington Square Press, 1970).
11. bell hooks, *Black Looks* (U.K.: Turnaround, 1992), p. 3.
12. Alice Walker, *Living by the Word* (San Diego: Harcourt Brace Jovanovich, 1988), p. 69.
13. M. Jean Harris, "Identity and Aesthetics in African American Women's Hairstyles," conference paper, University of Pennsylvania, Philadelphia, October 1993.

Acknowledgments

Special thanks to *The Rag* feminist collective and journal which first gave us the space and inspiration to pursue these ideas, as well as to Eva Nelson, whose oft-spoken phrase assessing others' views of her—"radical, militant, feminist"—stuck with us.

Nia Song

Jennifer E. Smith

moon whispers dark clouds drone
sun bleeds rain
wind beats drum

hear again, stephen biko
hear again, stephen biko

nothing is/can be/will be
the same as yesterday

your words run dark veins
flow black rivers as
we ride waves of bloody canyons
we are one

hear again, stephen biko
hear stephen biko
stephen   biko
stephen
biko

On Generation X

Samuel Frederick Reynolds

In 1965, Ossie Davis eulogized Malcolm X as "our shining, Black prince . . . and our manhood, our Black manhood." But when I picked up the leather-bound black sneaker, outlined with red stripes and the bright green X on the sides, I wondered why our prince had fallen so low and whether we were wearing our manhood on the soles of our feet. However, to be honest, the "X" sensation was really nothing new to me. I knew that Spike Lee would soon grace us with *Malcolm X*, the movie; that we already had Malcolm X T-shirts, hats, jackets, schoolbags, watches, and potato chips; and that we were only missing Malcolm X action figures, a Malcolm X float during Macy's Thanksgiving parade—and sneakers. But when I saw the X on the sneakers, I wondered what other spots that X marked.

The X in Malcolm's name has been made to be a lot of powerful things to many people. Malcolm X's earthly exit acted as an inspiration for the creation of the Black Panther Party, one of the most noted Black radical groups of the twentieth century. Malcolm's *staged* photograph of himself looking out his window with a rifle in hand has been reproduced (with the added caption of "By Any Means Necessary") on almost enough posters and prints to take over that X on the wall of many homes that was once marked for the Jesus portrait; and with a fitting gesture of poetic irony it's usually placed right next to some print of Martin Luther King, Jr., probably headlined with something about America and a dream. According to Paula Giddings, author of *When and Where I Enter: The Impact of Black Women on Race and Sex in America*, and a host of other women "revolutionaries" from the sixties and early seventies, that X was room enough for many Black male "revolutionaries" to make Black nationalism synonymous with Black manhood and chauvinism. White radicals, usually socialists, have made use of that X by publishing most of the books we have on Malcolm to propagate their ideas that Malcolm was moving toward being a socialist and belongs to all comrades in the Revolution, not just the Black ones. And even still, those who know little about Malcolm X (White or Black) take the X to point toward a man who crossed out all hope of Blacks and Whites achieving cooperation and integration. They feel he steadfastly believed, to his death, that Whites were blue-eyed devils and that Blacks should be free "by any means necessary," including acts of violence (although Malcolm never led a revolt and was involved in far fewer violent situations than was M. L. King). And for that shopkeeper who was selling the "X" sneaker, the X equals its price.

However, Malcolm's X may indeed indict all of us and serve as a symbol of our times. In fact, this generation, my generation, has been marked "Generation X." On closer examination, however, the X encompasses more than just one generation: it could be said to mark an era. Many avant-garde academics, critics, and artists proclaim our era the postmodern era: the era that has exposed modernism—structuralism, marxism, nationalism, romanticism, and most other -isms (except postmodernism)—as fraudulent. The most critical scholars of our time have come to realize that the Western Enlightenment "project" and the triumph of rational thought toward progress was really nothing of the kind. It was at best a dreamy, romantic prelude to a horrible nightmare that would buttress the most virulent forms of oppression in this millennium: racist slavery, colonialism, industrial capitalism, fascism, Nazism, and the Reagan/Bush years. Postmodernism, essentially, is the Western moment of the "X": the moment of indecision ("What do we do now in a postindustrial/postcolonial world?") and the moment of dread ("At the point when we are most able to destroy ourselves and the planet, that is, to face global extinction, how do we find meaning and community now that God, Marx, and even Plato are dead?"). Postmodernism, especially in America, is faced with the horror, as Harold Cruse in *The Crisis of the Negro Intellectual* states, that "the 'crisis in black and white' is also a crisis in social theory wherein American capitalism, the racial exploiter, has, by its own inner dynamic, swept everything before it by its power of rapid development and ability to recover, adjust, and absorb and institutionalize *even anti-capitalistic features* [italics in original]."

At bottom, and thus at risk, our country has pushed its insistence on material gain and acquisition to such an end that all our best ideological opiates—religion, Marxism, and even liberalism—are almost so exhausted (perhaps from our overconsumption of the rhetoric of each ideology) that our urban areas have become bundles of raw drives and nerves. In fact, postmodernism, by its very intention to relentlessly usurp and upset all manner of "power games" and structures that secure privilege, is predicated on a sort of violence and has paved the way for a harder violence.

In fact, if postmodernism, this great X, crosses out the necessity to embrace previous "truths" such as Christianity, socialism, and even ideology itself, then it's not hard to understand why many urban Black youth, those who cherish the "X" most, would be so nihilistic—so blatantly without hope of adding meaning to their lives. In this "reign of quantity," as the mystic Rene Guenon calls it, why shouldn't a homeboy blow your head off to get your $75.00 sneakers? He's getting his like you're getting yours. In such a world marked by an X, we would, logically, have such young souls who are atheists before they know they are, as Richard Wright points out in *The Outsider*, and who succumb to satisfying their drives for reckless sex and violence because they have no reason not to. In such a world, many would, logically, choose to abandon pursuing tightly wrapped ideological opiates in relative safety to market real ones on street corners at herculean risk, because they know they still will be able to take home as much cash as any bourgeois Black nationalist or socialist academic; and, most horribly, because they realize that this congenital condition, Blackness, marks them for life and can only make them cross—and crossed out.

However, the postmodern age attached to our metaphor, the X, should not be viewed as the source of all our urban evils. In fact, the X paves the way for us to have a unique kind of experience that has not been afforded to previous generations: the chance to become what every fanatical Christian has dreamed of being in (but not part of)—the Last Generation. Since the X called postmodernism allows for no truths (including the tongue-in-cheek one I just gave), then there are no correct histories and there can be no more "one" ways—the very heart of the racialist ideas like Eurocentrism (the supposed consistency of the ideas that form Western history, from ancient Greece to the present) and Afrocentrism (its response). History is more like a CD player than a cassette player: it's all about random access and not going from side A to B. Our differences, our multiplicities—the hallmarks of postmodern thought—do not allow for making sweeping generalizations or homogenizing communities. So how can we still seriously talk about generations, especially a "Generation X"? And how can we seriously talk about a "lost generation," as Betty Shabazz called this "generation" in a recent *USA Today* article?

We are not lost. This X does not mark a loss, but the place where a great treasure waits to be excavated. However, there are some things to which we are lost. We are lost to shrill Afrocentrists whose insistence upon "correcting history" and reconstituting the Black community outweighs their ability to be sympathetic to and respectful of its internal differences and the needs, drives, and pains of each individual in it. We are lost to Marxists and other "rhetorutionaries" who abuse their powerful laser-like insights into the class dimension of American hegemony to cut around or dismiss the critical issues of race and racial formation in American politics. And we are lost to postmodernists who take multiculturalism and difference as an occasion to test the boundaries of their banal palates and to determine whether their intellectual stomachs can digest the vertiginous assortment of people who have been spewed out by too many monsters to name. They should learn to be strong enough to swallow their own pain and stop being afraid in the name of being sensitive, *à la* political correctness.

But besides these things, one grave matter must not be lost in our discussion about the X: Malcolm. Yes, we can celebrate our X and the implications of it; but we have again put another man on a cross to pay the penalty for our pain, and again, we, like Roman soldiers, sit at the foot of it casting lots and selling the man's garments to each other. Malcolm was no sellout, but we sure are. In our enthusiasm for his story, we have forgotten that, ultimately, Malcolm's story is his own. True, we often identify with him, but he had his own personal mission and had to find his own meaning—his own answer to his X. He did. He died El-Hajj Malik El-Shabazz. He was willing to take risks, suffer his own personal pain and anguish, and die while trying to live his own life. But the X granted to us by the shattering of rigid ideologies like racialism, Eurocentricity/Afrocentricity, Marxism, and the like, forces us to acknowledge that our communities are as diverse as each of our own personal psychological wounds and tragedies. Malcolm had his

X and each of us has our own, which probably has nothing to do with the man who died El-Hajj Malik El-Shabazz.

At this juncture (the X again) we should have enough courage and strength to bear our own pains and heal ourselves. We shouldn't have to sell out brothers and crucify them on crosses and then put on "his" sneakers at the foot of them. We should be able to bear our own crosses and be "hard" enough to give meaning to our own X's.

African-Based/African-Centered African Females and Males: Messengers and Manifestations of MA'AT

Cecil Gray

THE PURPOSE OF THIS ESSAY IS TO OFFER A PERSPECtive and model of African personhood that can equip and empower African females and males to navigate the life journey—to navigate the life journey *effectively* and with *integrity*—from birth through adulthood. The core intent of this essay is to posit one model—not the only model—of African personhood, which, if utilized, can serve to produce, protect, and propel healthy, contributing, authentic African adults. The primary goal of this essay is to inspire, encourage, and catalyze African females and males, so that we survive, thrive, and offer ourselves in profound service to the African community.

This essay is the work of an *Africalogist*[1] and a *NTRlogian* (NETERlogian).[2] That is, this essay ascends from an *African-based/African-centered*[3] perspective. Further, this essay is undergirded by spiritual-ethical—as differentiated from dogmatic-religious—insights derived from KMTic (KEMETic, ancient Egyptian) theology. Of course, integrity requires that presentday NTRlogians admit to being relatively influenced by contemporary theologies—and I admit to such influences. As a mature and maturing NTRlogian, however, I am not de-based, de-centered, co-opted, confused, or confounded by such influences; rather, I have achieved and am vigilant to maintain *harmosis*.[4]

This essay, therefore, is not the result of *misorientation*[5] or *dislocation*.[6] This essay is a lucid, bold, self-conscious, African-anchored effort to help salvage and raise the quality of Black people's lives. Let us turn now to the social situation confronting African females and males as the twentieth century becomes the twenty-first century.

The model is easy to describe but a challenge to embody. The model consists of a list of the personal characteristics and the public and private styles that can and should identify African-based African females and males. Implicit in the model are the cosmological, epistemological, ontological, axiological, and sociopolitical orientations that will produce, sustain, and empower present-impacting, future-shaping African females and males.

All of the aspects of the model are intertwined and essential. No aspect of the model should be considered "unimportant" or "negotiable"; every aspect is of critical importance—none can be negotiated or compromised. It is necessary for African females and males to embody and manifest—to *demonstrate*—every aspect of the model. At our best, African-based African females and males are *wholistic*. We see the connectedness of all life; and we understand that when our lives are well-integrated and circumspect—when our lives are balanced and *whole*—we have a profound positive impact upon the African community and the world community. Simultaneously, this wholistic quality marking the lives of African-based African females and males demands much of us. Indeed, to see reality wholistically and to (attempt to) live wholistically, ultimately, is a kind of exercise in extremism. Such is understandable, however, because, as was stated earlier, the oppression assaulting African females and males and the African community is most extreme—consequently, unavoidably, the corrective response required of African people is extreme.

First, African-based/African-centered African females and males are *Afrocentric*.[7] We view, analyze, and approach life from an African perspective; we are familiar with—we really *know*— African people, African history, African culture, African values. We are able to set forth and explicate the distinguishing aspects of African people and culture. For example, African-based African females and males know that various continental Africans do not "worship"—do not bow down to, do not hold as the Omnipotent-Omniscient-Omnipresent One—the Ancestors, lakes, rivers, trees, animals, mountains, and so forth. Rather, African-based African females and males know that various African people acknowledge, honor, commune with, appreciate, and respect/venerate that aspect/part of the One Invisible Almighty God-Force that resides in all of the aforementioned. Such females and males know that continental Africans, similar to other Africans and other people around the world, *worship*—bow down to, give total allegiance/deference to—only the One Invisible Almighty Creator-Sustainer.

To conclude this point, African-based African females' and males' primary and most pivotal referent/standard is African people and Africa. Our primary and most critical commitments rest with African people and are rooted in "Africa"—the concept *and* the continent. We do not seek merely to re-enact or re-live ancient African reality in our contemporary context; it would be naive and ineffective. Rather, we draw from ancient and contemporary African wisdom and teachings (and, to a lesser degree, from the constructive teachings of other peoples), then we appropriate the same for the needs and challenges of our contemporary contexts. African-based African females and males are African centered.

Second, these females and males are wholistic *truth-seekers*. African-based African females and males seek truth in every sector and sphere of life. We are *always* attempting to know the truth—about ourselves, political matters, economic matters, historical matters, religious matters, scientific/empirical matters, and so forth. This constant and consistent searching after truth, this relentless questing after truth, marks African-based African females and males as mature and maturing spiritual women and men.

We posit that only spiritual women and men dare to seek and find the truth in all areas of life. Mundane men and women often stop searching when the quest invites them to know themselves beyond safe self-delusions and comfortable illusions. Politicians often cease searching when the quest necessitates that they question/depragmaticize their ethics/morals. Historians often stop searching when the question requires understanding more than the past. Religious men and women often stop searching when the quest forces them to grow beyond the exclusivist form and dogma of their particular religions. Empirical scientists often cease searching when the quest presses into nonempirical regions of reality. Whatever our area(s) of specialization, African-based African women and men dare to grow beyond ourselves, again and again, to higher and higher and deeper and deeper levels and regions. African-based African women and men are wholistic truth-seekers; and, as such, we are spiritual women and men.

Third, these females and males are *courageous*. African-centered African females and males are willing to do all that we can to help, enhance, and further African life. We are more than mere oral militants. We risk for the African community. Sooner or later, because of our passionate commitment to Black people, African-centered African females and males find ourselves under attack by those who are anti-African consciously, semi-consciously, or unconsciously. Even so, these females and males "stand the heat." We are not weak-hearted; we stand strong and stand firm. When circumstances make it necessary, we risk our careers. Finally, before we will sell the African community out, we will first lay down our physical lives—literally—for Black people. If need be, we will die before we reach old age—we will give our lives—for the African community. You see, the love that we have for African people is immense and immeasurable. African-centered African females and males are courageous.

Fourth, these females and males are women and men of *integrity*. We are dependable and trustworthy. If we say we will take responsibility for some matter(s), we will. When we speak, our word is good. We can be trusted; we are not thieves, liars, manipulators, or "game-players." African-centered African females and males are women and men of integrity.

Fifth, these females and males manifest *excellence*. Whatever our field of constructive endeavor, African-based African females and males take it seriously. Given the talents and gifts that our Creator has given us, we work to be *our* best. If we are students, we work to master our various subjects. If we are teachers, we work to master our various subjects; and, we work to catalyze our students into desiring to learn, while learning to think critically. If we are agriculturalists, we work to grow food naturally, in whatever quantities are necessary, as quickly as is necessary—while being and remaining in harmony with the natural environment.

While African-based African females and males give appropriate attention to external measures of excellence, we understand that our true challenge is to raise ourselves up internally, intrapersonally. We understand that true excellence is attained as we hone, sharpen, refine, polish, and draw forth from ourselves the skills, talents, and Divine Self that our Creator has placed within us. African-based African females and males do not attempt to manipulate/maneuver and "get over"; we manifest excellence, so that our work/achievement speaks for itself.

Sixth, African-based African females and males are *creative creators*. We do the necessary and the new. We create and build. If a word/concept is needed that does not yet exist, we create it. We females and males have demystified the matter of word/concept creation. We understand that words/concepts are created (1) by a person being bold—bold enough to posit a helpful/empowering word/concept, (2) by undergirding that boldness with good sense and sound logic—such that the word/concept makes sense and is logical, and (3) by the created word/concept being appreciated and used confidently, consistently, and as frequently as is appropriate by its creator, and its creator's colleagues, friends, relatives, and others, until the academic and/or general community adopts it. If African people need an institution that does not yet exist, we are the females and males who build it. We do not re-create old forms that already exist and are/have always been dysfunctional. We create new, relevant, effective/functional forms.

For example, African-based African females and males do not speak of students' sophisticated efforts to create a just university environment as "protest"; rather, we refer to such efforts as "Hannibal-inspired, intentional, systematic, premeditated pressure." The wickedness that was perpetrated upon African people by European people from the 1500s into the 1800s—and into the present—is not called "a Black people's Holocaust"; it is referred to as "the MAAFA" ("The Great Disaster").[8]

Further, while racism and sexism are steadily destroying people's lives, African-based African females and males in Euro-dominated university settings do not ask naively for dysfunctional, inconsequential "Optional, Cultural/Ethnic Diversity Classes," or "Race Relations Classes," or "Gender Sensitivity Classes." Instead, we pressure university officials and force them to create functional, white racism–eradicating and male sexism–eradicating "Mandatory, White/European American Racism Classes," or "Global European Male Supremacy Classes," and "Male Sexism Classes." (Currently, men in almost every culture on Earth—including African-American culture and other African cultures—are more or less sexist, although the precise form of the sexism varies somewhat from culture to culture.) African-based African females and males do not bemoan European Americans neglecting to award Marvin Gaye a star on the Hollywood Walk of

Fame; rather, we females and males coalesce, create an "African Avenue of Fame," and award an Ankh to Brother Marvin (and any and all other deserving Africans).

African-based African females and males are more than creators; we are lucid, clear, creative creators.

Seventh, these females and males are *profound visionaries*. In short, African-based African females and males demonstrate hindsight, insight, and foresight. We know the past well. We see into and through the complexity of the present. And we anticipate, plan, and build the future.

Put another way, these females and males realize the importance of *Sankofa* ("Retrieving the Best from Our Past and Utilizing It in Our Present") for African people. We grasp the positive and the negative, the overt and the covert aspects of our community's current circumstances; and we see and map out ways to our collective future. We are committed to helping our community experience life victoriously, in all of its fullness—so that when we say *"Tumalize Duara,"* ("Let the Circle Be Unbroken," or, "Keep Our Circle United"),[9] it will be so. We are the females and males who see for ourselves and explicate for the rest of our community that the United-Completed Circle can and must be again a truth for the African community, and not only a hope. African-based African females and males are profound visionaries.

Eighth, these females and males are *flexible and tolerant contextually*. That is, as long as circumstances allow, African-based African females and males are flexible and tolerant—able to hear and appreciate ideas/perspectives that are different from and/or that complement our own. Simultaneously, because we are mission-minded and passionate about our community's wholistic health and development, when we see or discern circumstances threatening our community, we become less flexible—even rigid, and less tolerant—even unyielding. We are flexible, yet immovable; we are tolerant, yet full of conviction about our particular mission. African-based African females and males are flexible and tolerant contextually.

Ninth, these females and males are *proud and confident*. African-based African females and males strive to live without arrogance; it is never required, and our Ancestors are not pleased by it. (Even when facing and defeating the enemies of our people, arrogance is unnecessary.) Publicly and privately, African-based African females and males are proud and confident.

Tenth, these females and males possess and manifest *sophisticated consciousness*. We do not think in elementary, overly simple, dichotomous modes merely. Our thinking is advanced and wholistic, making use of complementary dialectics and victorious synthesis.

For example, African-centered females and males know when to negotiate and compromise, and we know when negotiation must be dispensed with. Further, while we wish to wear African clothing always, we are certain to wear it when it must be worn. We also know when to masquerade and wear European-style clothing—such as during a strategic interaction with a group of people who are Eurocentric. Further still, we know when to manifest *harmosis*—wearing, for instance, a long-sleeved European dress shirt and a necktie with a West African dashiki and matching or European style pants. Such attire might be worn when addressing a diverse group of African people, some of whom are not African based but curious, some of whom are moving toward African-based thought and praxis intentionally.

African-based African females' and males' consciousness enables us to see/understand and think globally while we act locally. That is, we understand the connections between the Mandelas, Daniel Ortega, Assata Shakur, Septima Clarke, and Queen Nzingah; and we understand how such global understanding necessitates that we carry ourselves and act in certain ways in our immediate locales. Further, we are not tricked or tripped up if we are asked a dichotomous, hierarchical question such as, "Whom do you prefer—Malcolm X or Martin Luther King, Jr.?" Rather, we are the females and males who respond calmly, wholistically, horizontally, "We appreciate and honor the powerful and empowering contributions of both of those African men." While more examples can be given, the point is made: African-based African females and males possess and manifest sophisticated consciousness.

Eleventh, these females and males are *caring—strong and gentle*. African-centered African females and males are not cold, coarse, condescending, cynical, harsh, aloof. We do not work for African people in the abstract—loving the community while staying away from the community. We are committed to MA'ATic principles and we care about African people. We are the females and males who love, protect, respect, affirm, support, honor, and empower each other; and we love, protect, affirm, encourage, and give a good example to African children.

Further, while African-centered African females and males interact peacefully with all peoples who interact peacefully with the African community, we will not hesitate to be violent with all peoples who are violent with the African community. We are serious; yet, we still know how to smile and laugh. African-centered African females and males are caring—strong and gentle.

Twelfth, African-based African females and males are *forever growing*. African-based African females and males understand that the nature of life is dynamic/"motionful"/swirling/unfolding; subsequently, we realize that the understanding we have today should expand as we live into tomorrow. We keep on mastering ourselves, keep on thinking, keep on reading, keep on writing, keep on teaching/sharing with others.

These females and males understand that life is not stationary, because that which is stationary atrophies and becomes lifeless. Similarly, people who are stationary atrophy and become other than productive/contributing. Therefore, since life is always pulsing and moving—since life consists of motion and growth—African-based African females and males make a conscious decision always to grow, to keep growing for as long as we walk upon the Earth. For as many breaths and as many heartbeats as the Maker and Maintainer of MA'AT allows us, until we enter the company of our Ancestors—and even then, African-based African females and males are forever growing.

Thirteenth, these females and males are *messengers and manifestations of MA'AT*. African-based African females and males announce, bring, embody, emanate, and spread MA'AT. By our exemplary way, our comportment, our behavior, our acts/actions/deeds, our being, we females and males announce and give to our community—and to the world community—personal and societal justice, equilibrium, correctness, fairness. To a community and world in extreme need, and in a time of extreme need, African-based African females and males are messengers and manifestations of MA'AT.

Here ends the model entitled "African-Based/African-Centered African Females and Males: Messengers and Manifestations of MA'AT." As we begin circling down, it is important that I reiterate a point that I hope has been implicit and explicit throughout this paper: *Both* African-based/African-centered *females and males* are messengers and manifestations of MA'AT. African females are in every way equal to, and absolutely as necessary as, African males. Such males are less than optimal when they are without such females; and such females are less than optimal without such males.

African females and African males are necessary, *equal*, compatible complements. It is imperative that All African women and men who (would) consider themselves "African based/Afrocentric/African centered" grasp—and model—this reality, in all of its fullness, with all of its ramifications. African-based African men and women do not dominate and/or manipulate each other; they appreciate and empower each other. These women and men do not compete with each other; they complement each other. With African-based African females and males there is no hierarchy; with African-based African females and males there is circularity.

As we circle down, understanding the principles that lead to wholeness and victory, we are *certain*: as African females and males are introduced to the cursory teachings set forth via this thirteen-point model, as we read and recite the teachings repeatedly, as we rehearse the teachings behaviorally, and as we are encouraged and reinforced by our mothers, fathers, guardians, each other, siblings, mates, and community, *African females and males will know ourselves, our purpose, and our mission, again and anew.*

Other African women and men will be drawn to and encouraged by our example. Our growing and coming children will be assured of good examples to follow and home lives and public lives wherein affirmation, equalizing justice, order/tranquility, and opportunity predominate and prevail. And the diverse peoples of the Earth, those of all cultures and all colors, will see a sane, humane globe being born in and through the exemplary manifestations and demonstrations of African females and males.

Then, our Ancestors will be pleased. The NTRs will be honored. And our Creator, The Amen ("The Hidden One"), the One Who Makes and Maintains MA'AT, will be satisfied.

Notes

1. The term "Africalogist" comes from Dr. Molefi Kete Asante, Chairperson, Department of African American Studies, Temple University, author of *Afrocentricity*, *The Afrocentric Idea*, and other works. An Afri-

calogist is one learned in Africalogy. Africalogy is the Afrocentric study of African people, African ideas, and other matters related to Africa. It is the study of Africa, African people, and other realities from the perspective of one *centered*, strongly rooted, *learned* in the indigenous cultural values, traditions, and history of African people. Africalogy considers/examines matters from the vantage point of African people, from the vantage point of one standing inside of African reality. Historically, generally, the study and explication of African people and Africa has been impositional, hegemonic study from the vantage point of people (a) learned only in European epistemology, cultural values, traditions, and history, and (b) often willfully ignorant of indigenous African reality. Finally, it should be understood that mature Africalogists draw heavily from past and present African values and teachings, *appropriating* and utilizing such wisdom *effectively* in *contemporary contexts*. We expect the discipline of Africalogy to continue growing, and we look forward to the emergence of increasing numbers of Africalogists.

2. "NTRlogian"—or NETERlogian—is a term that I first introduced formally at the *Journal of Black Studies* twentieth anniversary symposium, "The Making of a Discipline: Orientations and Locations in Excellence," Philadelphia, October 27–28, 1989. A NTRlogian, as I have created and define the term, is an African-based/African-centered, KMT/KEMET-referenced theologian. A NTRlogian learns of, studies, contemplates, meditates upon, and gives behavioral evidence of the existence of the NTRs—the Spirits, the Creative Forces/Active Principles/Energies/Entities—of the One Invisible Omnipresent Almighty Creator. (NTR, or NETER, is a KMTic, or KEMETic—ancient Egyptian—term).

3. See Asante's *Afrocentricity* (Trenton, NJ: Africa World Press, 1980, 1988), and his *The Afrocentric Idea* (Philadelphia: Temple University Press, 1987); also see C. T. Keto's *The Africa Centered Perspective of History* (Blackwood, NJ: K. A. Publications, 1989). Also see Asante's and Welsh-Asante's *African Culture: The Rhythms of Unity* (Westport, CT: Greenwood Press, 1985), and works by C. A. Diop, Zak Kondo, Daudi Azibo, Linda Meyers, Dona Marimba Richards, Jacob Carruthers, Asa Hilliard, Yosef Ben-Jochannan, Maulana Karenga, and others.

4. "Harmosis" is a term that I created some time ago. I am introducing it formally for the first time here. It will also appear in my dissertation—which we hope and trust will become a book—dealing with incipient, current, and future manifestations and conceptions of Afrocentricity. Harmosis means "empowering, constructive, harmonizing (African) synthesis." Because African people in contemporary times—necessarily and sometimes unavoidably—manifest synthesis in many aspects of our lives, it is imperative that our synthesis be beneficial to us, edifying for us, constructive and harmonizing for us. As we appropriate perspectives, and/or values from non-African sources, we

must be alert so that the resulting synthesis is necessarily beneficial/harmonizing. Therefore, whenever synthesis is needed and/or unavoidable, harmosis is what African people must manifest and create.

5. See the works of Dr. Joseph Baldwin, Dr. Wade Nobles, Dr. Daudi Azibo, Dr. Robert Williams, Dr. Na'im Akbar, and Dr. Bobby Wright. "Misorientation," essentially, describes a psychological state in which an African person speaks, lives, works, and apparently thinks in ways that are destructive for her/him personally and the African community collectively. An Afrocentric concept, misorientation is usually the result of conscious, subconscious, or unconscious Eurocentric or anti-African assumptions about and approaches to life.

6. "Dislocation" is an Afrocentric concept—attributable to Molefi K. Asante—similar in meaning to "misorientation." Dislocation, essentially, describes the state of an African person who is (grossly) noncentered, who lacks an African-centered, African-concerned perspective on and approach to life.

7. "African based" is a term I first heard used by Haki Madhubuti. The term "Afrocentric" comes from Molefi Asante, and the term "Africa(n) centered" can be attributed to C. T. Keto, both of whom were cited previously in this paper. The three preceding terms are closely related—though there are technical variations in their meanings. For the purposes of this paper, however, I am using the terms interchangeably.

8. See Dona Marimba Richards's *Let the Circle Be Unbroken: The Implications of African Spirituality in the Diaspora* (New York: Dona Richards, 1980).

9. Ibid.

X 1 (unknown)

Yao Bhoke Ahoto

imagine all of us
in our hells
with our fingers
twisted onto each other/
our hands tangled in prayer
our hearts banging like bells
smacking on
a thought of freedom
like butterscotch

our running feet
tangled in
our fears
swamps of bellies of nights
of young brothers/
of snakes on the bottoms
of forests we must walk through
barefoot

every Friday night
to raise the tombstones
sing the songs to send them away
on journeys
still between the death our enemies
and freedom is the only smell
blowing on the wind

hope our minds blasphemy
young boys'
futures grinding
raw spots on our ankles

knowing so little
                                        of the boys
                                        in the hood
will make it
to a simple
peace of mind

everybody gotta North
Star burning in the sky
a sprint for freedom
and X

knowing
so little
                            of the food
                            in our bellies
                            (scraps on our tables)

matters
when the North Star is their burning
when prayers
make dance
for shoes
today's dinner
tomorrow's weather
some Church picnic
sitting on Sunday
where there is more
than enuff
                                        food to eat

for once
                            let us count up our wishes
                            goodbyes to our dead
                            each and every cross
                            in our closet

let us

           speak the bitter of every
           sacrifice

make no excuses
for wanting
something
better than Amerikkka

a clean street
a great great grandparent with a name
a drum
some certainty for tomorrow
knowing the Church will stand

for what is right
for what is good
is not to be wished upon

it is to be practiced
cared for
everyday

Contributors

Faith Adiele was raised in the Pacific Northwest and majored in Southeast Asian Studies at Harvard and Radcliffe Colleges. Her journals are featured in *Ms.* magazine (January/February 1994) and Patricia Bell-Scott's *Life Notes: Personal Writings by Contemporary Black Women* (W. W. Norton, 1994). She is currently writing a memoir about her biracial (Nigerian/Scandinavian) heritage.

Yao Bhoke Ahoto (Hoke S. Glover III), a husband, father, poet, entrepreneur, currently lives in the Washington, D.C., metropolitan area. He is a graduate of Bowie State University. His work has appeared in NOMO II, the anthology *Fast Talk, Full Volume*, and *Catalyst* magazine.

Askhari, formerly known as carliss johnson, is a proud and soulful Spelman alumna, now attending Howard University graduate school, and writing for her life. She is a psychologist and freelance writer. Her work has appeared in *Catalyst, Class, Essence, Focus, Omawee*, and *Urban Profile* magazines. She has written, reported, and edited for the Afro-American newspapers, *BAMN, Artistic Pedigree*, and *The Hilltop*. Additionally, Askhari performs her poetry up and down the East Coast; poems by Askhari can be seen in *Catalyst* and *In the Tradition* and will be appearing in the upcoming anthologies *She* and *Dark Symphony*.

Adisa Sebaku Banjoko, a.k.a. the Bishop of Hip Hop, is a freelance journalist and poet from the Bay Area. His work has appeared in such publications as *The Source, The L.A. Sentinel*, and *RapPages*. A columnist for the Hip Hop magazine *4080* and author of *Contemplations of a B-Boy*, to be published soon, he is a well-respected member of the Hip Hop community. You can find him cooling out on the streets of San Francisco, Oakland, and Berkeley regularly.

Ta-Nehisi Sundiata-Paul Coates was born and raised in Baltimore, Maryland. Ta-Nehisi has been writing poetry for a little over a year and a half. He is currently pursuing a degree in History at Howard University. Ta-Nehisi plans to pursue a teaching career in African-American studies on the college level.

Lisa Clayton graduated magna cum laude from Harvard and Radcliffe in 1992. She is still at Harvard pursuing a Ph.D. in English, with a concentration in African-American literature. Her essay in *Testimony* was originally part of her senior honors creative writing project. She is from North Andover, Massachusetts.

Jelani Cobb, Jr., a twenty-four-year-old cultural critic, graduated from a hysterically Black university (Howard University) with a B.A. in English. Born and raised in New York City, Jelani has resided in the District of Columbia for six and one-half years and plans to earn a doctorate degree in History at Columbia University. His work has been featured in *Urban Profile*, *YSB*, and *One* magazines.

Michael Datcher is a graduate student at UCLA in African-American studies, researching the impact of the jazz idiom on Black literature.

Dayle B. De Lancey, a native of Philadelphia, Pennsylvania, graduated from Harvard and Radcliffe Colleges with an A.B. in History and Literature in 1992. She is currently a doctoral student in the History of American Civilization Program at Harvard University, where she is also earning Master's degrees in English and American Literature and Language and the History of Science. "Eastley Echoes," from which the piece printed in this volume is excerpted, is the pilot story in a cycle that Ms. De Lancey has been writing since her freshman year in college. (She gives special thanks to Alex Johnson for her guidance in this endeavor.)

Quinn Eli, a native of the Bronx, New York, just received his Master's degree in Creative Writing from Temple University, where he studied with David Bradley and was also Future Faculty Fellow. He has written about books for *Emerge* magazine, *Black Warrior Review*, and other publications. He is a regular contributor to the *Philadelphia Inquirer* and has recently completed a collection of short stories. He lives in Philadelphia and is pursuing a Ph.D. in English Literature at Temple.

John Frazier, Jr., is a Harvard undergraduate concentrating in Social Anthropology. He cites James Baldwin as a major influence and inspiration in his life. In addition to reading and writing, John enjoys swimming.

Cecil Gray is one of the historic, first twelve candidates for the Ph.D. in Africalogy/African-American Studies at Temple University. He specializes in Afrocentric African-based Theory and Praxis, African History and Culture, African Religion, and Racism Eradication. Ordained minister/elder with the United Methodist Church, Mr. Gray is Executive Director of the Church and World Institute at Temple University. He is also assistant to Sonia Sanchez; and he is the founder and president of the Rites of Passage Shule (ROPS), Inc. First and foremost, Mr. Gray is committed to the wholistic liberation and empowerment of all African people; thereafter, he is committed to working with other people who are sincere seekers of truth, justice, and sanity.

Tracie Hall was born in Los Angeles, California, in 1968. She attended the University of California, Santa Barbara, as an undergraduate and is currently doing graduate work at Yale University. She has also studied at the universities of Nairobi and Dar Es Salaam in Kenya and Tanzania, respectively. She has produced three original plays, "The People in My Head," "We Musn't Eat Our Mother," and "Jackal Doesn't Talk to Me When He's Busy," for which she has received several fellowships and awards. Tracie is currently at work on a volume of autobiographical poetry and on a novel.

Myronn Hardy recently graduated from the University of Michigan, earning a B.A. in English Literature. His work has appeared in several literary journals.

Yona C. Harvey is currently a student at Howard University. Originally from Cincinnati, Ohio, Harvey is majoring in English with a double minor in Art and Spanish. Harvey's poetry has been featured in *Janus* (Howard's student literary journal) and was recently awarded an honorable mention in the John C. Wright poetry contest. Harvey has also contributed a "poetic interlude" to Flatline Comics's "Flatbush Native."

Tracy E. Hopkins is a twenty-four-year-old freelance writer based in Baltimore, Maryland. She graduated from Howard University in 1992, earning her B.A. in Print Journalism. Her work has appeared in *Rolling Stone, Seventeen*, and is forthcoming in *Essence* and *YSB*. She is striving to be a content and positive individual.

Trasi Johnson is a graduate of the University of Maryland and a member of the Dark Room collective. Her work has appeared in *Callaloo, Agni, In the Tradition: An Anthology of Young Black Writers*, and *Abafazi*. She has work forthcoming in *Muleteeth*.

Jawanza Ali Keita Educated in the Quaker school system established by the Society of Friends, at Philadelphia's Friends' Central School, Jawanza Ali Keita attended the University of Maryland, College Park, on an athletic scholarship. He is currently a graduate student in Temple University's Creative Writing Program, where he also teaches composition. He has studied with Sonia Sanchez and Rachel Blau Duplessis. He is the recipient of the 1992 Shaw Guides Award for poetry. He lives in West Philadelphia.

King (J. Phillip Pringle IV) was born in St. Louis, Missouri, and then moved with his parents to Decatur, Georgia. He began writing while in high school and cites Richard Wright as his major influence. He currently resides in the (Boogie Down) Bronx, New York, and attends Lehman College.

Lichelli Lazar-Lea Originally from Trinidad, Lazar-Lea moved to England when she was two. At eighteen she moved with her family to San Francisco, where she studied illustration until she found her calling in film. A student at San Francisco State University, she is completing a feature-length screenplay, which challenges conventional images of British life with a seldom heard black perspective. As an active member of the Hip Hop community, she runs "Unsigned Hype," a showcase of Bay Area talent. She is also directing a documentary on local Hip Hop artists.

Sabrina Shange McDaniel is a twenty-five-year-old Jamaican finishing her bachelor's degree at Spelman College. As an air spirit, she has found liberation through writing and dancing. As she endeavors to fulfill her life's mission, she answers only to her family, the cause, her creator, and herself. For this reason she tries to use academic and daily life lessons as our ancestors inspired us to do, when they left the hieroglyphic message, "Know thyself."

minkah makalani, twenty-four, husband, father, nigga, poet, writer, activist, from Kansas City, Missouri, spent three years in the University of Missouri-Columbia, a year in Central State University, and four months in the Missouri State Penitentiary. He has published poems in *Obsidian II*, is working on a volume of poetry, *back alley murals & prison stick figures*, and is co-editing the anthology *Between Black Morass & Black Molasses: Viewing Black Women Through New Lenses*. He would like to say, "Peace to my niggas on lock down. No love for 1-time, C.O.'s, the american judicial system, and Ellis' mark N.B.A. superstars! This is for my brother, eric 'nobbie' mathews. Peace (that busta is gettin' his)."

Tiya Miles is from Cincinnati, Ohio, where her family still lives. She is a graduate of Harvard-Radcliffe. She is currently a student in the Women's Studies doctoral program at Emory University.

Melanie L. Mims is a graduate of Spelman College and the University of Chicago. She lives in Atlanta, Georgia, where she works as a musician and sometimes poet.

Keiko Morris is a native of New Jersey. She attended Harvard University and graduated in 1992 with a B.A. in History and Literature. She now resides in a lovely, little apartment in Brooklyn, New York, with her 25-inch color TV set and a dear friend.

Corey Olds Corey Olds's hometown is Canton, Ohio. He is an alumnus ('91) of Oberlin College and is presently pursuing a Ph.D. in eighteenth-century European intellectual history at Stanford University. His biggest and most persistent quixotism: to be an essayist à la Montaigne.

Samuel Frederick Reynolds was born November 22, 1967, with multiple birth defects and spina bifida, in Buffalo, New York, to Aaron and Marion Reynolds. He has been a magician, a Junior Olympic boxing champion, a Baptist minister, a Black nationalist/afrocentric scholar, an English professor, and a publishing/marketing professional. He is currently developing his career in creative writing and performance art/theater.

Riché Richardson, a Montgomery, Alabama, native, is a 1993 graduate of Spelman College. She majored in English and minored in Philosophy and Women's Studies. Currently, she is working on a Ph.D. in American literature and a certificate in women's studies at Duke University.

Damon Roberts graduated from Harvard in 1993 and is currently pursuing his M.F.A. in acting at Brooklyn College.

Paitra Russell is a 1992 graduate of Harvard University. She now resides in New York City where she works in magazine publishing.

Jennifer E. Smith is an editor and publisher of *Black Arts Bulletin*. Her work has appeared in *Essence, Black Books Bulletin, Fast Talk, Full Volume, WPFW Poetry Anthology*, and elsewhere. She is a student at the University of the District of Columbia and winner of the 1992 Mt. Vernon College Poetry Festival. She is the coordinator of the U.D.C. Poetry Series.

Taigi Smith is a senior at Mills College in Northern California. She is a Communications major with a minor in Sociology, and plans to pursue a career in either television or print journalism. In addition to writing, Taigi enjoys video and filmmaking. She recently completed her first documentary, on the economic state of East Oakland, and is currently working on a documentary about Bay Area Hip Hop culture.

Natasha Tarpley graduated from Harvard University in 1993 with a degree in African-American Studies. Her work has appeared in *Essence, Callaloo, Obsidian II, African American Review*, and the anthologies *In Search of Color Everywhere, Fast Talk, Full Volume*, and *City River of Voices*. As a recipient of the 1994 National Endowment for the Arts Fellowship for Poetry, as well as a 1994 Massachusetts Cultural Council Fellowship for Poetry, Natasha will be taking a year off from Georgetown Law School to work on her second book.

Touré is a Hip Hop journalist who proudly didn't graduate from Emory University, who has written for *Rolling Stone*, the *New York Times*, and the *Village Voice*, and who understands Sonia Sanchez's aphorism, "I write because that way I don't kill anyone."

Deborah Turner is working toward her Master's degree in Information and Library Studies at the University of Michigan, Ann Arbor. She is also a Head Librarian in the Residence Hall Library program there. Both she and her sister received their B.A. degrees from the University of California, Berkeley, in English and Sociology, respectively.

Omar Tyree is twenty-five years old, a journalist, author, and graduate of Howard University. To date he has published three books out of Washington, D.C.: *Flyy-Girl*, *Capital City*, and *The Battlezone*.

Sarah Van't Hul grew up in Ann Arbor, Michigan. She is a B.F.A. student in the University of Michigan's dance department. She has also studied at the Alvin Ailey Dance Center and the Martha Graham School of Dance.

Jennifer L. Vest is a woman of African, Seminole, German, Norwegian heritage, born and raised in Chicago, Illinois. She will be pursuing a Ph.D. in interdisciplinary studies (philosophy, anthropology, religion, history, Native American studies, African studies, Afro-American studies, folklore, etc.) in the fall. She has been writing since she was twelve.

Rebecca Walker is a writer and activist currently living in New York City. She is a co-founder of Third Wave, a nonprofit organization devoted to feminist and youth activism for social change, and a contributing editor to *Ms.* magazine. She currently lectures and is working on an anthology on the Third Wave of feminism to be published by Anchor/Doubleday. She is a 1993 graduate of Yale University.

Michelle White is a graduate of Temple University where she majored in Psychology. She writes, "I have discovered through my many trials and tribulations the value of perseverance and strong faith within myself. My story is dedicated to spouses and lovers who are still battling to keep their heads above water. I must also thank three important women in my life: my grandmother, who gave me love of family; my mother, who gave me breath of life; and Sonia Sanchez, a teacher who gave me inspiration and direction. Countless thanks to those who have shared their lives with me."

Godffrey Williams was born in 1973 in Seattle, Washington and is a senior at Harvard. He is at work on his first novel.

Kevin Young attended Harvard University and graduated in 1992. He held a Stegner Poetry Fellowship from Stanford University in 1992–94. His work has appeared in *Angi Review, Callaloo, Poetry*, and *Kenyon Review*. Kevin is a member of the Dark Room writer's collective in Boston. His first book, *Most Way Home* (1994) was selected for the National Poetry Series by Lucille Clifton.

Credits